D0986615

MULTICULTURAL EDUCATION SERIES

James A. Banks, Series Editor

(continued)

Latino Children Learning English

Steps in the Journey

GUADALUPE VALDÉS

SARAH CAPITELLI

LAURA ALVAREZ

Teachers College, Columbia University
New York and London

Published by Teachers College Press, 1234 Amsterdam Avenue, New York, NY 10027

Library of Congress Cataloging-in-Publication Data

Valdés, Guadalupe
    Latino children learning English : steps in the journey / Guadalupe Valdes, Sarah Capitelli, and Laura Alvarez.
        p. cm.–(Multicultural education series)
    Includes bibliographical references and index.
    ISBN 978-0-8077-5144-2 (pbk.)–ISBN 978-0-8077-5145-9 (hardcover)
1. English language–Study and teaching–Foreign speakers. 2. Education, Bilingual-Cross-cultural studies. 3. Multicultural education--Cross-cultural studies. 4. Linguistic minorities–Education–Social aspects–Cross-cultural studies. I. Capitelli, Sarah. II. Alvarez, Laura. III. Title.
    PE1128.A2V348 2011
    428.3'461–dc22

                                                                        2010030551

ISBN 978-0-8077-5144-2 (paper)
ISBN 978-0-8077-5145-9 (hardcover)

Printed on acid-free paper

Manufactured in the United States of America

18 17 16 15 14 13 12 11   8 7 6 5 4 3 2 1

*This book is dedicated to Bonnie Katz Tenenbaum,
with deep appreciation for the generous support
that made this work possible*

Contents

Series Foreword

Globalization and worldwide immigration are changing the demographic characteristics of student populations in nations around the world. In the Western nations such as The Netherlands, the United Kingdom, France, and Germany–as well as in the United States–the student population is becoming increasingly racially, ethnically, culturally, religiously, and linguistically diverse (Banks, 2009). The growing diversity of the student population worldwide is challenging the robust assimilationist ideology that dominates educational policies and practices in nations and schools from Japan to Russia (Froumin & Zakharov, 2009; Hirasawa, 2009).

The assimilationist ideology that has historically dominated schools and nations around the world has pernicious effects on school language policies, practices, and programs. Most Western nations, including the United States, have language policies that privilege mainstream languages and make language minority students ashamed of their community cultures and languages. Students comprehend the cogent message that is conveyed by dominant nation-states and societies–if you forsake your home language and culture you will experience social mobility and structural inclusion. Most White ethnic groups in the United States heeded this message and were able to attain structural inclusion into mainstream society (Brodkin, 1998; Greenbaum, 1974). However, most ethnic and linguistic groups of color remain structurally excluded when they experience high levels of cultural and linguistic assimilation (Gordon, 1964).

The assimilationist language policies in the United States evoke highly politicized and polarizing debates about bilingual education. The debates and controversies about bilingual education have generated more heat than light and resulted in the enactment of restrictive language policies in California, Arizona, and Massachusetts that have made it more difficult for teachers to create and implement effective practices that build upon the cultural and linguistic knowledge, skills, and strengths of language minority students (Gándara & Hopkins, 2010; Moll & González, 2004; Valenzuela, 1999).

This timely and incisive book is a significant contribution to the literature on the teaching and learning of students who come to school speaking a language different from the language in which formal school instruction is given. For many years during her distinguished and luminous career, Guadalupe Valdés has been concerned about the linguistic isolation of Spanish-speaking Latino students and its negative effects on their learning of English. In *Learning and Not Learning English: Latino Students in American Schools*–a book in this Multicultural Education Series–Valdés documents the detrimental effects of pullout programs and other school practices that result in linguistic minority students having limited access to English language speakers (Valdés, 2001). An important principle that underlies her earlier book as well as this one is that non-English speakers must hear and interact with English speakers in order to learn and become competent speakers and writers of English.

This creative and engaging book by Valdés and her colleagues, Sarah Capitelli and Laura Alvarez, builds upon and extends Valdés's previous research and book. The authors conceptualized and implemented an ingenious *design experiment* to provide English language learners (ELLs) "most in need of English" more access to English speakers in an after-school program. They identified a "linguistically hypersegregated" school in which Latino students had very limited access to English. Most of the adults in the children's homes and communities spoke Spanish, and a majority of the children spoke Spanish when they interacted in school. In the design experiment, *One-on-One English*, each college undergraduate or community volunteer had rich interactions in English with one child about stories.

This carefully conceptualized, well-written, and informative book will help practicing educators deal effectively with the growing ethnic, cultural, and linguistic diversity within the United States and its schools. American classrooms are experiencing the largest influx of immigrant students since the beginning of the twentieth century. About a million immigrants are making the United States their home each year (Martin & Midgley, 1999; Roberts, 2008). Between 1997 and 2006, over 9 million immigrants entered the United States (U.S. Department of Homeland Security, 2007). Only 15% came from European nations. Most came from nations in Asia, from Mexico, and from nations in Latin America, Central America, and the Caribbean (U.S. Department of Homeland Security, 2007). A large but undetermined number of undocumented immigrants also enter the United States each year. In 2007 *The New York Times* estimated that there were 12 million undocumented immigrants in the United States (Immigration Sabotage, 2007). The influence of an increasingly ethnically diverse population on U.S. schools, colleges, and universities is and will continue to be enormous.

Schools in the United States are more diverse today than they have been since the early 1900s when a multitude of immigrants entered the United States from southern, central, and eastern Europe. In the 34-year period between 1973 and 2007, the percentage of students of color in U.S. public schools increased from 22 to 55% (Dillon, 2006; National Center for Education Statistics, 2008a). If current trends continue, students of color will equal or exceed the percentage of White students in U.S. public schools within one or two decades. In the 2007–08 school year, students of color exceeded the number of White students in 11 states: Arizona, California, Florida, Georgia, Hawaii, Louisiana, Maryland, Mississippi, Nevada, New Mexico, and Texas (National Center for Education Statistics, 2008a, 2008b).

Language and religious diversity is also increasing in the U.S. student population. English language learners are the fastest growing group of U.S. students (Suárez-Orozco & Suárez-Orozco, 2001). In 2000 about 20% of the school-age population spoke a language at home other than English (U.S. Census Bureau, 2003). The Progressive Policy Institute estimated that 50 million Americans (out of 300 million) spoke a language at home other than English in 2008. Harvard professor Diana L. Eck (2001) calls the United States the "most religiously diverse nation on earth" (p. 4). Islam is the fastest growing religion in the United States as well as in several European nations such as France, the United Kingdom, and The Netherlands (Banks, 2009; Cesari, 2004). Most teachers now in the classroom and in teacher education programs are likely to have students from diverse ethnic, racial, linguistic, and religious groups in their classrooms during their careers. This is true for both inner city and suburban teachers in the United States as well as in many other Western nations (Banks, 2009).

The major purpose of the Multicultural Education Series is to provide preservice educators, practicing educators, graduate students, scholars, and policy makers with an interrelated and comprehensive set of books that summarizes and analyzes important research, theory, and practice related to the education of ethnic, racial, cultural, and linguistic groups in the United States and the education of mainstream students about diversity. The dimensions of multicultural education, developed by Banks (2004) and described in the *Handbook of Research on Multicultural Education* (Banks & Banks, 2004), provide the conceptual framework for the development of the publications in the series. They are: *content integration, the knowledge construction process, prejudice reduction, an equity pedagogy,* and *an empowering school culture and social structure.*

The books in the series provide research, theoretical, and practical knowledge about the behaviors and learning characteristics of students of color, language-minority students, and low-income students. They also provide knowledge about ways to improve academic achievement and race relations in educational settings. Multicultural education is consequently as important for middle-class White suburban students as it is for students of color who live in the inner city. Multicultural education fosters the public good and the overarching goals of the commonwealth.

This readable and informative book will help teachers, other educational practitioners, and teacher educators acquire more sophisticated and nuanced understandings of ways to help language-minority students experience sustained, productive, and effective interactions with English speakers that will facilitate their acquisition of English speaking and writing skills. This book also enriches theory and research about second language teaching and learning. The authors describe theoretically rich and practical principles derived from their research. They report the results of their design experiment with caveats and a description of external factors that may have influenced their findings with intellectual integrity that exemplifies the best scholarly tradition in education and the social sciences.

This skillfully crafted and adept book deserves careful reading and reflection by classroom teachers, teacher trainers, researchers, and policy makers in these turbulent and highly politicized times in which the debate over second language teaching and learning is often bereft of the kind of careful, insightful, and practical theory and research described in this illuminating and engaging book.

–*James A. Banks*

REFERENCES

Banks, J. A. (2004). Multicultural education: Historical development, dimensions, and practice. In J. A. Banks & C. A. M. Banks (Eds.), *Handbook of research on multicultural education* (2nd ed., pp. 3–29). San Francisco: Jossey-Bass.

Banks, J. A. (Ed.). (2009). *The Routledge international companion to multicultural education*. New York: Routledge.

Banks, J. A., & Banks, C. A. M. (Eds.). (2004). *Handbook of research on multicultural education* (2nd ed.). San Francisco: Jossey-Bass.

Brodkin, K. (1998). *How the Jews became White folks and what that says about race in America*. New Brunswick, NJ: Rutgers University Press.

Cesari, J. (2004). *When Islam and democracy meet: Muslims in Europe and the United States*. New York: Pelgrave Macmillan.

Dillon, S. (2006, August 27). In schools across U.S., the melting pot overflows. *The New York Times*, pp. A7, A16.

Eck, D. L. (2001). *A new religious America: How a "Christian country" has become the world's most religiously diverse nation*. New York: HarperSanFrancisco.

Froumin, I. D., & Zakharov, A. (2009). Educational policies for ethnic and cultural groups in Russia. In J. A. Banks, (Ed.), *The Routledge international companion to multicultural education* (pp. 486–497). New York: Routledge.

Gándara, P. C., & Hopkins, M. (Eds.). (2010). *Forbidden language: English learners and restrictive language policies*. New York: Teachers College Press.

Gordon, M. (1964). *Assimilation in American life.* New York: Oxford University Press.

Greenbaum, W. (1974). America in search of a new ideal: An essay on the rise of pluralism. *Harvard Educational Review, 44,* 411–440.

Hirasawa, Y. (2009). Multicultural education in Japan. In J. A. Banks (Ed.), *The Routledge international companion to multicultural education* (pp. 159–169). New York: Routledge.

Immigration sabotage [Editorial]. (2007, June 4). *New York Times,* p. A22.

Martin, P., & Midgley, E. (1999). Immigration to the United States. *Population Bulletin* (Washington, DC), *54*(2), 1–44.

Moll, L. C., & González, N. (2004). Engaging life: A funds-of-knowledge approach to multicultural education. In J. A. Banks & C. A. M. Banks (Eds.), *Handbook of research on multicultural education* (2nd ed., pp. 699–715). San Francisco: Jossey-Bass.

National Center for Education Statistics. (2008a). *The condition of education 2008.* Washington, DC: U.S. Department of Education. Retrieved August 26, 2009, from http://nces.ed.gov/pubsearch/pubsinfo.asp?pubid=2008031

National Center for Education Statistics. (2008b). Public elementary/secondary school universe survey, 2007-2008. *Common Core of Data.* Retrieved January, 20, 2010, from http://nces.ed.gov/ccd

National Center for Education Statistics. (2008c). State nonfiscal survey of public elementary/secondary education, 2007–2008. *Common Core of Data.* Retrieved January, 20, 2010, from http://nces.ed.gov/ccd/stNfis.asp

Progressive Policy Institute (2008). *50 million Americans speak languages other than English at home.* Retrieved September 2, 2008 from http://www.ppionline.org/ppi_ci.cfm?knlgAreaID=108&subsecID=900003&contentID=254619

Roberts, S. (2008, August 14). A generation away, minorities may become the majority in U.S. *The New York Times,* pp. A1, A18.

Suárez-Orozco, C., & Suárez-Orozco, M.M.(2001). *Children of immigration.* Cambridge: Harvard University Press.

U.S. Census Bureau. (2003, October). *Language use and English-speaking ability: 2000.* Retrieved September 2, 2008, from http://www.census.gov/prod/2003pubs/c2kbr-29.pdf

U.S. Census Bureau. (2008, August 14). *Statistical abstract of the United States.* Retrieved August 20, 2008, from http://www.census.gov/prod/2006pubs/07statab/pop.pdf

U.S. Department of Homeland Security. (2007). *Yearbook of immigration statistics, 2006.* Washington, DC: Office of Immigration Statistics. Retrieved August 11, 2009, from http://www.dhs.gov/files/statistics/publications/yearbook.shtm

Valdés, G. (2001). *Learning and not learning English: Latino students in American schools.* New York: Teachers College Press.

Valenzuela, A. (1999). *Subtractive schooling: U.S.-Mexican youth and the politics of caring.* Albany: State University of New York Press.

Acknowledgments

As is the case with most books, the work and the thinking that led to the writing of this book began many years before it was written. There are, therefore, many people from different stages of the project to whom we owe a debt of thanks for the role that they played in its conceptualization, funding, planning, implementation, and analysis as well as for the assistance they offered us in preparing this book for publication.

We are indebted first of all to our collaborator Savitha Moorthy. Savitha's commitment and dedication to the education of English language learners were instrumental in the beginning stages of *One-on-One English*. She played an important role in the early conceptualization of the design experiment, in the drafting of funding proposals, and in the teaching of the first course directed at undergraduate volunteers. Working with a committed young professional was a special gift for all of us, and we know that had she been involved in the writing of these materials, we would have profited much from her advice and wise counsel.

Our greatest debt is to the children who were part of the program. We particularly appreciate their eagerness, their patience with our demands, and their joyful enthusiasm. They were truly a joy to spend time with, and we all took great pleasure in watching them grow and develop. We are also profoundly grateful to the families of the children in the program. Their patience with the ever-changing programmatic logistics was just a small indication of their commitment to their children's education and development of English. It was a true pleasure to celebrate their children's accomplishments with them at the end of every school year.

We are also indebted to the educators who supported our work over many years. Maria de la Vega, Marco Chavez, and Jeremy Hilinski welcomed us into the school with open arms. They made time for us in their incredibly busy days to discuss the students who were participating in the program, to hear about our challenges, and to celebrate our small triumphs. We thank them for believing in our work and for making certain that *One-on-One English* had a true "home" at a very special school.

We owe a very special thanks to Allison Briceño, Tami Becker, Luis Poza, and Corie Geballe. These teachers served as our project liaisons at the school and worked closely with us in identifying students, finding us classrooms to do our work, communicating with other teachers, and communicating with parents. They all spent considerable time after-school after long days of teaching helping the project staff run the program. Our work would have been impossible without their deep commitment to the children that they teach.

We also deeply appreciative of the countless ways that Maria Gutierrez, Fatima Fuentes, Xiomara Nickings, and Jocelyn Guansing supported the program. Whether it involved helping us locate children after school, contacting parents, storing our materials, or helping us find spaces to assess students, they were always willing to lend a hand. Their willingness to support the program is a testament to their commitment to the education of the students at the school where we spent many years. Without their support, our program would not have functioned successfully.

We would especially like to thank the Silicon Valley Community Foundation for its generous support of out project. We were particularly fortunate in having had a strong champion for the project in our project officer, Manuel Santamaria. His understanding of the challenges that newly arrived immigrant children face in schools and his tireless commitment to the education of Latinos were an inspiration. We are grateful for his presence in our lives and for his guidance in moving our work forward.

We would also like to thank the staff at the Haas Center for Public Service at Stanford University for their commitment and contributions to the project during its first three years. Our undergraduate volunteers benefited tremendously from having their own space to meet and discuss the project and their students. We are particularly grateful for Suzanne Abel, Len Ortolano, and Jackie Schmidt-Posner's efforts on behalf of our work. As we began to incorporate community volunteers into our efforts, the commitment of the First United Church of Palo Alto was greatly appreciated. We are especially indebted to Archer Summers, Rebecca Smith, Chuck Hebel, and Ted Dolton for their efforts in bringing attention and ultimately volunteers to the program. A special thanks goes to Ashley McCullough for her work with and coordination of the community volunteers during the last year of the project.

This program depended heavily on the commitment and passion of volunteers. Nowhere was this made more obvious than in the work of the project's volunteer coordinators. Corie Geballe, Miguel Ortega, Christine Dehnert, Lauren Horton, and Ada Ocampo were instrumental in the work of this project. They left no stone unturned in their efforts and wore various hats while volunteering for the program. They recruited volunteers, communicated with them regularly, organized materials, contributed to and assisted in the trainings, participated in and contributed to program staff meetings, and worked with children. We are extremely grateful for their commitment to the project and to the young English language learners they worked with.

One-on-One English relied heavily on the presence of people who were not working with students to document the project. We owe a special thanks to Morghan Young and Martha Castellon for stepping in and assisting in the documentation of the project.

Over five years, our project collected very large amounts of data that needed organizing, uploading, compressing, and transcribing. This task was monumental, and we were lucky to have the help of some wonderful undergraduate and graduate students. Doris Madrigal, Miguel Ortega, Allison Briceño, Christine Dehnert, Ada Ocampo, and Frankie Preciado all worked tirelessly with the project's data. We owe them all special thanks.

Given that much of our data included many hours of videotaped interactions of children and volunteers, data storage, data management and data backup were a serious challenge. We are deeply grateful to Chris Wesselman for helping us to make decisions about data storage, for his efforts in setting up servers that could be accessed remotely, and for his willingness to work with us on multiple details over the course of the project.

We owe a special thanks to Jim Banks for including this volume in the Series on Multicultural Education and for his strong support and wise counsel throughout its preparation. We are grateful also to Brian Ellerbeck and other members of the Teachers College Press editorial staff for their critical engagement with every aspect of this book.

Finally, we are grateful to Nat Corey-Moran for raising the questions that led to this project and to our colleagues and friends who have, over the many years in which we have been involved in the project, listened patiently to our descriptions, expressed enthusiasm, and encouraged us to keep going. We especially want to thank Lily Wong Fillmore, Kenji Hakuta, Deborah Stipek, Connie Juel, and Sharon Greenberg. A very special thanks is also due to our spouses Bernard Gifford, Peter Ross, and Nathan Pellegrin.

Introduction

Lino is 5 years old. He is a curious, talkative little boy who loves planes and big trucks and other vehicles that make noise. At school he sometimes skips when he is supposed to walk, fidgets in his seat, and often engages in games of pushing and shoving with other little boys as he stands in line on his way to lunch or recess. Like other little boys his age, he is interested in the world around him and eager to touch and handle new things. As a new kindergartner, everything in his school offers a new adventure, and he is eager to share his comments and reactions to new books, new pictures, and new games. He loves the climbing structure in the play yard and talks excitedly about how high he climbed during the last recess.

Marisol is also 5, but unlike Lino, she is quiet and appears shy to school personnel. Her large brown eyes take everything in as she sits in her seat watching her classmates and her teacher's every move. Very little escapes her notice, but she says little. When she speaks, she does so in a low voice. Most of the time, she talks only when spoken to by the teacher or one of her classmates. Like Lino, she eagerly looks at colorful books and enjoys playing in the doll corner with stuffed animals. Her favorite possession is her rolling pink *Beauty and the Beast* backpack with its rhinestone decorations and large silver wheels.

Although they are different, both Lino and Marisol are fluent and competent speakers of Spanish. Like all other normal children who arrive in kindergarten, they acquired their first language in the course of interacting with their parents and their families. As kindergartners, they can talk quite skillfully about a number of topics. They can participate actively in conversation, take turns appropriately, complain about their siblings, tell stories, quarrel with their cousins, persuade their friends to do something, tell jokes, and attempt to amuse others. As Clark (2003) points out, they sound "quite adultlike much of the time" (p. 16). Their comprehension, moreover, far exceeds their production. They are able to understand varieties of Spanish other than their own, as well as more formal styles of speaking that are typical of school settings.

Like children all over the world who acquire their first language in their families and in their communities, Lino and Marisol have acquired the abil-

1

ity to communicate orally with members of their families and communities. They know when to talk and how to talk to whom. They have learned the sound system (*phonology*) of their language, the ways in which words are structured, and the ways in which *morphemes* (building blocks of words) combine with other morphemes to convey different meanings (e.g., plurality, possession). They have also learned which sequences of words and constructions (*syntax*) are permissible in their language. Additionally, they have acquired the vocabulary they need to refer to things that surround them, that matter to the people with whom they communicate regularly, and that are part of their particular experiences in the world. In Marisol's case, she has also acquired vocabulary that is typically expected in school settings, including names of colors, labels for farm animals, domestic animals, and vehicles.

Had Lino and Marisol remained in Mexico, their families' country of origin, they would have arrived in their kindergarten classrooms with oral, age-appropriate Spanish—that is, with the background assumed by teachers to form a sound basis for their acquisition of literacy in their first language. For a number of reasons, however, Lino and Marisol did not remain in Mexico. They are in the United States because their family members moved from their original place of residence to this country. They are among the increasing numbers of international migrants around the world, who move across national boundaries and form a part of the globalization process. Bendixsen and Guchteneire (2004), for example, place the total number of migrants at 175 million, or 3% of the world population. They point out that, as a result of such dramatic increases, "both host countries and countries of origin must deal with issues such as brain drain, migrants' rights, minority integration, religion, citizenship, xenophobia, human trafficking and national security" (p. 1). Moreover, in the case of the children of migrants—whether foreign or native born—host countries must grapple with the challenges of providing them with a quality education in spite of both linguistic and cultural challenges.

THE CHALLENGE OF ACQUIRING ENGLISH

In the United States, children who arrive in school without speaking or understanding English, the language spoken by the majority society, face two simultaneous challenges: They must acquire English itself, and they must learn *through* English; that is, they must acquire the knowledge and the skills that are considered essential in this country for becoming productive members of society. Like their English-speaking peers, they must learn to read very early in their academic lives. They must develop the ability to draw meaning from texts and the ability to continue to learn about a variety of subjects through reading over the course of their school years. Indeed, it is not hard to argue that children's academic futures everywhere will depend primarily on their success in becoming proficient readers.

At the same time that they are acquiring literacy, however, English language learners (ELLs) must also acquire numeracy skills. They must understand mathematical concepts, operations, and relations; acquire skill in carrying out mathematical procedures; formulate, represent, and solve mathematical problems; and develop a capacity for logical thought, reflection, explanation, and justification (National Research Council, 2001). To be educated, children must also learn about the world that surrounds them. They must acquire knowledge about animals and plants, continents and oceans, and about the history of the country and the world in which live.

For all young children, becoming educated in the ways expected by the society in which they live involves numerous years of school attendance, progress in acquiring a defined body of knowledge and skills, and, ideally, drawing from the school's curriculum and instructional activities to develop their individual gifts and talents. As might be expected, for those children who begin school with little or no knowledge of the language in which instruction is offered, the challenge of becoming educated is enormous and, in too many cases, unattainable.

In theory, when children do not speak the societal language, educational institutions in nation states have three choices: (1) to educate in the societal language; (2) to educate in the children's first language; or (3) not to educate at all. Clearly, in the United States, the third option—that is, to exclude children who do not speak English from educational services—is not acceptable. No matter what the legal status of their parents might be, the Supreme Court decision *Plyer v. Doe* (1982) clearly established that the denial of an elementary education to such children cannot be justified. However, the remaining two choices outlined above also bring with them a number of challenges. Choice two, educating children in non-English languages (e.g., Spanish, Chinese, Hmong), is both expensive and complicated. Investments must be made in preparing teachers, developing curricula, writing materials, developing assessments, and the like, and in countering negative views about the use of non-English languages in education.

Unfortunately, the first option, educating children in English is also problematic. Allowing children to attend schools where they do not understand or speak the language of instruction does not mean that they will receive an education. Children cannot learn through a language that they do not understand. As established by the *Lau v. Nichols* Supreme Court Decision (1974), children who do not speak or understand English must receive an education that is both meaningful and comprehensible. It is not just a question of teaching English but rather a question of providing large numbers of students with access to the curriculum at the same time that they are learning English. Key sources of federal law (Title VI of the Civil Rights Act of 1964; *Lau v. Nichols,* 1974; the Equal Educational Opportunities Act of 1974; *Castañeda v. Pickard,* 1981) prohibit discrimination against students on the basis of language and require that districts take affirmative steps to overcome language barriers. *Castañeda v. Pickard* (1981), in particular, makes clear that districts have a dual obligation to teach English and to provide access to academic content instruction. Programs designed for English language learners, in theory, must ensure that students either "keep up" with age-appropriate academic content while they are learning English; or, if they are instructed exclusively in English as a second language for a period of time, that they are given the means to "catch up" with the academic content covered by their same-age peers. It is especially important that in either case, English language learners do not incur irreparable deficits in subject matter learning.

In California, for example, there are five different types of instructional services available for elementary school children who are English learners:

1. *English Language Development* (ELD) is the term used to refer to English language instruction that is appropriate for the student's identified level of language proficiency. ELD should be consistently implemented and designed to promote second language acquisition of listening, speaking, reading, and writing.

2. *ELD and Specially Designed Academic Instruction in English* (SDAIE) is an instructional service that requires that English language learner (ELL) students receive ELD and, at a minimum, two academic subjects required for grade promotion or graduation taught in English through Specially Designed Academic Instruction in English. SDAIE is an approach to instruction that focuses on increasing the comprehensibility of the academic courses normally provided to fluent English-proficient and English-only students in the district. Students receiving ELD and SDAIE do not receive instruction in their first or primary language.

3. *ELD and SDAIE with Primary Language Support* is a service that provides ELD and SDAIE as described above, with Primary Language Support, that is, first language (L1) support, in at least two academic subject areas. L1 may be used to clarify meaning and facilitate student comprehension of academic subject matter taught mainly through English and may also include oral language development in the student's primary language.

4. *ELD and Academic Subjects Through the Primary Language (L1)* is an instructional service that provides at least two academic subjects through the primary language (L1). In kindergarten through

Grade 6, primary language instruction is provided in language arts (including reading and writing) and in mathematics or social science. In Grades 7 through 12, primary language instruction is provided at a minimum in two academic subjects that are required for grade promotion or graduation. In theory, the curriculum provided in L1 must be equivalent to that provided to both fluent English speakers and English-only speakers. Students receiving primary language instruction may also be receiving SDAIE.

5. *Other Instructional Settings* is a label given to services that are not included in the descriptions provided under the four previous categories.

6. *No English Learner Services* is a category to be reported to the state by schools and school districts when no services are provided for ELLs.

Because of the difficulties surrounding the teaching of subject matter content to children who do not understand English, there have been many acrimonious debates around the country about the ways that instruction can be made meaningful to children at different ages and at different stages of English language development. For example, the debate about *bilingual education* (instruction in primary language while children are acquiring English) is one manifestation of the continued controversy about the role of children's first language in learning (Goldenberg, 2008). Discussions about ways in which English language content instruction can be made comprehensible to ELLs by teachers as well as disagreements about the types of direct English language instruction that are appropriate for children are other manifestations of this country's challenges in providing education to all children. Unfortunately as Horwitz et al. (2009) argue:

> Over the years, researchers and commentators of all sorts have devoted considerable attention to strategies and approaches for educating English Language Learners (ELLs), but little research has and actually been done on how school districts have succeeded or failed with these students. Much of the work to date has been oriented around the investigation of various models of how ELLs might be immersed in English or transitioned to it. Unfortunately, these efforts have been subjected to considerable philosophical and political contretemps that ultimately shed little light on what worked and didn't work with this growing population of students. (p. iii)

From the point of view of children, the issues are much more straightforward. In order to succeed in school, they must be able to understand their teachers' directions and explanations, and they must be able to display their understanding or knowledge of what they have been taught in a language that the teacher can comprehend. In order to learn to read in English, moreover, they need to quickly develop at least a rudimentary oral communicative ability similar to the age-appropriate Spanish language facility that they have developed in their first language.

It is important to emphasize that educating English language learners is challenging not because these young learners are limited in their ability to learn. The children of immigrants who arrive or are born in this country are normal, competent youngsters who simply happen to be native speakers of languages other than English. But there are so many children, and school systems all over the country are overwhelmed. It is difficult enough to educate disadvantaged children who are native English speakers; it is much more difficult to educate children who do not share a common language with their teachers. As a result, reasoned discussions about the best or ideal instructional approaches for educating children who do not speak English have frequently given way to angry debates and real-world conditions in schools and school districts where increasing numbers of ELLs are entering school, where there are few trained teachers who can work with these children in their primary languages, and where there are legislative limits on the length of time that non-English languages can be used in instruction. Moreover, because of the No Child Left Behind Act (NCLB) (about which we will say more in Chapter 1) schools are being held accountable for the performance of non-English-background children on standardized tests of mathematics and language arts as well as for the English language development of these children.

THE CHALLENGE OF LINGUISTIC ISOLATION

Linguistic hypersegregation is yet another challenge currently facing children of immigrants in American schools. Across the country, 70% of young English language learners are being educated in 10% of all elementary schools. In these hypersegregated schools, ELLs make up more than 50% of the total school population (Consentino de Cohen & Clewell, 2007). In California, as a result of residential segregation the percentage of Spanish-speaking ELLs in elementary schools is often higher. In 403 elementary schools, for example, 86% of the children enrolled are Latinos and English language learners (Gifford & Valdés, 2006). In such schools, typical of those described in the case of *Eliezer Williams et al. v. State of California* (2004), children are often taught by marginally qualified teachers, in inadequate classrooms, and with limited access to texts and materials. Not surprisingly, these schools are routinely identified as in need of program improvement.

What is not as obvious is that in such hypersegregated settings, Latino ELLs have very limited access to English. Most hear only Spanish in their homes and communities, and, because most student-to-student interactions take place in Spanish, they often use more Spanish than English at school. In the school environment, children hear English primarily from their teachers on a 1:20 or a 1:30 ratio. They speak English only when called upon to recite in class and occasionally when they have the opportunity of interacting on a one-on-one basis with their teachers. They may also occasionally speak English to other monolingual English-speaking school personnel in casual hallway or lunchroom encounters.

Currently, educational stakes are high for both mainstream, English-speaking children and for the schools in which they are educated. They are particularly high, moreover, for underresourced, majority-minority schools in which English language learners are isolated from peers who are native speakers of English and who might provide them with access and exposure to English in their classrooms. In this book we will talk about one such under-resourced school and describe the challenges to both teachers and children as they struggled to find the best solutions to educating newly arrived children. We describe one attempt to influence the journey that children undertake in acquiring English in such contexts and to lessen the challenges faced by Lino and Marisol and their other newly arrived classmates as they began to read in English.

In the pages that follow, we examine a language development program that took place at Golden Hills Elementary, a school setting in which young English language learners were linguistically isolated. English language learners went to school every day in classrooms full of other children who also knew little or no English. They were surrounded in their communities by parents and other family members who primarily spoke Spanish. *One-on-One English*, an after-school intervention program that we describe here, had as its purpose the altering of the linguistic equation (i.e., a few fluent English speakers to many English learners) by training volunteers (both college undergraduates and community members) to provide elementary-age ELLs with one-on-one access to English. Seen against the enormity of the problem of educating children who do not speak English, this book describes a very small attempt to make a difference in the lives of young English language learners. It does not provide simple formulas for closing the achievement gap, and it does not offer quick fixes for teachers who must teach reading and math to children who cannot understand the language of instruction. Our effort is small. We hope, however, that this book, because it describes an intervention that focuses on the acquisition of English, which is often described as the "greatest barrier" to educating immigrant children, can provide practitioners, teacher educators, and researchers with some insights about the process of second language (L2) acquisition and with a deeper understanding of the challenges faced by schools in creating a context in which English can be acquired. What we hope the book will do is to provide information about the small steps that children take in their journey to learning English when they have frequent one-on-one contact with English and that this information can assist teachers, principals, other school administrators, and policy makers in designing instruction for this group of very vulnerable youngsters.

HOW *ONE-ON-ONE ENGLISH* STARTED

As is the case with many interventions, *One-on-One English* was established in response to a particular set of circumstances and conditions that included (1) a national context in which volunteer participation was seen as a solution to many educational and social problems, (2) a university context with a strong service learning tradition within which students were eager to work with English language learners, and (3) the very high need of young ELLs enrolled in hypersegregated, linguistically isolated schools[1] in a nearby local school district.

For me (Valdés), *One-on-One English* began in my office one afternoon some years ago when Nat, a volunteer coordinator for a campus organization that used a phonics-based program to teach reading to monolingual Spanish-speaking kindergartners and first graders, marched into my office and vented his frustration about the work that they were doing. "They don't know the words, and they don't remember the words we teach them from one time to another," he said heatedly. "I'm just not sure that we are doing them any good. We are certainly not teaching them to read."

I listened to Nat carefully. I knew him to be a thoughtful, very dedicated student, who had acquired Spanish over many years and who had spent summers in southern Mexico working with indigenous children. On campus, he was tireless in organizing other students to make a difference, to protest instances of injustice, and to work in nearby poor communities with immigrant workers and their families. It mattered to Nat that he and his fellow volunteers actually help the students with whom they worked several times a week.

Because he had taken several classes with me, Nat knew my work in L2 acquisition and my interest in underachieving children of immigrant origin. He requested that I look at the materials that he and his fellow volunteers were using to teach reading and that I provide him and his group of volunteers with suggestions for adapting the material to make the tutoring enterprise more successful. For Nat, the problem was that children in the program did not appear to be making progress and, what was worse, in Nat's eyes, they appeared to be losing interest in reading. When his volunteers read books in English to the children, they could not understand the stories, and when they followed the program manual and taught them phonics, children repeated and imitated sounds, but they did not know what they were saying. They could not recognize the meaning of the words they had "decoded."

The problem that Nat shared with me did not have simple solutions. The schools in which the young volunteers were working were deeply committed to children's success. Teachers cared about the children that they taught, and administrators were working hard to educate children who were new to the community and to the country. They were also caught in a moment in time in which frustration at the limited effects of existing instructional programs in reading had led the entire country and the state of California to the increasing use of phonics-based textbooks. The volunteers focused on phonics because they were supporting what was current practice in the schools in which they volunteered. Both the schools and the volunteer program clearly recognized the difficulty of teaching Spanish monolingual children to read in English, a language that they neither spoke nor understood. They simply hoped that one-on-one work with volunteers might help the young English language learners grow more skilled in sounding out words, a step that they believed would help them become strong and competent readers. It was an important and valuable effort.

It is important for us to emphasize that sounding out words and using phonics in teaching reading was not itself the problem. Indeed, had these young English language learners remained in Mexico, they might have been exposed to schools in which the *método onomatopéico* (a phonics, syllable-level approach) was in use. If so, they would have been introduced to initial reading by being made to copy and pronounce sequences of consonants and five simple Spanish vowel sounds such as:

ma-me-mi-mo-mu
sa-se-si-so-su
na-ne-ni-no-nu
ba-be-bi-bo-bu
cha-che-chi-cho-chu

After they had "mastered" the recognition of such sequences, the children might then proceed to "reading" meaningful sentences with words made up of these same combinations of vowels and consonant sounds presented in familiar syllable format such as:

mi-ma-ma-me-mi-ma-mu-cho

Or possibly presented more conventionally as:

Mi mamá me mima mucho.
My mother spoils me a lot.

Using this particular approach to reading instruction in Spanish, children would be guided to draw on their knowledge of oral Spanish (phonology, morphology, syntax, and vocabulary) to make sense of such sequences of sounds and morphemes and to interpret the meaning of these sentences. Connecting sound to meaning, however, is not altogether without challenges for children. In this example, understanding the meaning of the sequence *mi-ma-ma-me-mi-ma-mu-cho* upon hearing it, depends on a child's having acquired an internalized linguistic system which allows her to recognize the possessive adjective *mi*, the noun *mamá*, the direct object pronoun *me*, the verb *mimar* conjugated in the present tense, and the adverb *mucho*. Without such internalized knowledge, children might be able to call out long sequences of syllables, but they would make little progress in learning how to read, that is, in learning how to draw meaning from textual representations of language.

Phonics programs in English present problems for ELL children for precisely this reason. In order to make meaningful connections between sounds and meanings, children need to recognize what the words and the sentences that they sound out actually mean. Otherwise, they may simply learn how to produce particular sounds in response to particular symbols with no understanding whatsoever of the words they have produced. The situation is quite different for native English speakers. Children who have already acquired English because they have heard this language all of their lives can immediately assign meanings to familiar words that they sound out (e.g., *rat, bake, cake, pail*), but this is not the case for ELLs. Children who know very little English, for example, might be able to sound out the word *weed*, and even recognize that it rhymes with *seed*, but this does not mean that they understand what these words mean. They have simply learned that, in English, two *ee*'s together make a particular sound.

THE DEVELOPMENT OF ONE-ON-ONE ENGLISH

There were no simple answers to the issues that Nat raised in my office that afternoon, but the conversation that I had with him ultimately led to a new direction in my research, to the recruitment of a team of talented graduate students (Moorthy, Capitelli, and Alvarez) to work with me, and finally to a multiyear project that came to be known as *One-on-One English*, a program that we hoped might help support children who were at both zero English and zero reading by providing them with increased access to English in one-on-one interactions with ordinary speakers of English.

One-on-One English, then, was conceptualized as a design experiment that focused on developing the abilities of volunteers to provide access to English to ELLs enrolled in kindergarten, first, and second grades in schools in which there are few opportunities for these children to interact frequently with fluent English speakers. The project had as its primary purpose developing a model volunteer-preparation program that would enable college students and community volunteers to assist elementary school students in developing both receptive and productive oral English language proficiencies in linguistically isolated schools largely populated by other monolingual Spanish-speaking students.[2] Informed by second language acquisition research, the project sought to generate knowledge about

- The kinds of input that can be provided to children by ordinary speakers of English
- The degree of English language growth that results from exposure to increased input
- The most effective methods for preparing ordinary speakers of English to provide rich language input to young children who have little proficiency in English

This book reports on the results of that effort. It documents the activities of *One-on-One English*, an effort that sought to implement an intervention in an authentic context (an after-school program) in order to accomplish a useful and practical educational goal: supporting the acquisition of English in K–3 ELL students. The principal purpose of the study was to explore to what degree the English language acquisition of K–3 children enrolled in hypersegregated schools might be accelerated if they were exposed regularly to one-on-one interactions in English. Drawing from L2 acquisition theory and primarily on work conducted by Wong Fillmore (1976, 1982, 1985a, 1985b, 1991), we hoped to provide ELLs with rich exposure to English through exchanges with volunteers that centered around colorful children's books. In setting up our program, we were centrally concerned both about the ELLs and their unique needs and also the undergraduate volunteers. We clearly saw the challenges faced by young volunteers who eagerly sought to "help" ELLs, even though they knew very little about immigrant children, about schools, and about the process of L2 acquisition. We thus aimed to implement a program that would train volunteers to offer ELLs the opportunity of developing their English by exploring books and stories over a period of time in the context of a growing mentoring relationship.

Over the course of a 5-year period, we selected a group of children identified as most in need of English-language intervention. We collected baseline data on the children and paired them with undergraduate and with community volunteers. We provided ongoing training for volunteers, and we videotaped segments of every interaction between children and their English buddies. We carefully sought to identify the characteristics of successful and unsuccessful interactions, children's responses to volunteers, characteristics of children's developing English, and growth in volunteers' abilities to provide children with a wide range of affordances for acquiring English. We adapted ways of assessing children's language growth; we changed and modified specific recommended activities to be used in interactions; and we continued to explore the best ways of preparing inexperienced volunteers to work with young children. We tentatively revised our understanding of theories of children's second language development, and we explored different ways of documenting evidence of children's growing language proficiencies from daily field notes, video transcriptions, and annotations.

This book, then, contributes to the existing literature on non-English-background youngsters by offering a glimpse of the ways in which English language proficiencies develop in newly arrived K–3 immigrant students over a 2- to 3-year period. It raises questions about existing expectations of rapid English growth present in schools and implicit in state language assessment instruments such as the California English Language Development Test (CELDT). It also offers insights about ways in which children begin to see themselves as English "speakers" over time and as capable of interacting with unknown adults who are speakers of English. Finally, the book also contributes to the fields of education and applied linguistics and to their broader understanding of second language acquisition in the context of design experiments.

OVERVIEW OF THE BOOK

The book begins with an overview of the second language acquisition field and its relationship to the field of second language pedagogy. Although the project and the book were a collaborative endeavor (with Valdés as lead author), we note the responsibilities of different authors as we offer an overview of the book's contents. In Chapter 1, (sole-authored by Valdés), we provide a brief history of the field of second language acquisition. We outline important controversies in the field and describe the current division between researchers who view second language acquisition as a cognitive and individual process and those who see it as a social and interactive process. We then discuss the relationship between second language acquisition theory and second language pedagogy and recall Hatch's (1978) warning that SLA findings can only be applied to pedagogy with extreme caution. In this chapter we also summarize the limited information we currently have about the acquisition of second languages in children, the need for longitudinal studies, and the need for more specific information about conventional methods used in language teaching with children. We end the chapter with a discussion of assessment instruments and the implication of assessment policies in the placement and instruction of children who are acquiring English.

Drawing from the many questions about English-language development in children that were outlined in the chapter on second language acquisition, in Chapter 2 (written collaboratively) we describe the design experiment and intervention study that we refer to as *One-on-One English*. We begin by describing the setting of the study and the community in which we carried out our work, as well the policy context in California at the time. We then proceed to a discussion of design research in general and provide details about the characteristics of design studies emphasizing the iterative cycles of testing and refinement that are involved in such work. We devote the remainder of the chapter to a detailed description of the design and implementation of *One-on-One English*. We discuss the study's local instructional theory, our interpretive framework, the preimplementation process, and the various phases of the design experiment itself. We provide details about the key elements of the implementation, including student selection, assessment instruments, material selection, volunteer training, and quality control. We also describe our analytical process and our ongoing modifications to both our practice and our theory.

In Chapter 3 (also written collaboratively) we describe the types of interactions in which young English language learners and adult volunteers engaged as they participated in *One-on-One English*. We provide a picture of the types of talk that went on between English-speaking volunteers and ELL children who were often absolute beginners in their acquisition of English. Our goal is to offer examples of children's participation in different kinds of interactions and to identify the affordances that were available to them in their acquisition of English. We also describe the challenges that the volunteers encountered in interacting with young learners. By so doing we hope to provide a foundation for Chapter 4, which includes an analysis of the changing interactional proficiencies of the children who participated in *One-on-One English*.

In Chapter 4 (also written collaboratively) we present an analysis of children's participation in one-on-one interactions with volunteers. We describe their initial uncertainties and confusion, and their growing ability to comprehend rapid conversational speech that contained flaws, redundancies, fillers, self-corrections, and abandoned and incomplete utterances. We also document the changes in their productive language and the range of communicative behaviors that they displayed over time. We emphasize the impact of individual differences in children and volunteers and the varying opportunities for hearing and using English that were available to different children. For all nine of the focal children whom we chose for extensive analysis, we were successful in documenting change, but there was much variation in the kinds of change that were manifested by different children.

In Chapter 5 (written collaboratively, with Alvarez as lead author) we present the results of an analysis of children's linguistic growth on yearly pre- and postassessments, focusing on an oral retelling of a familiar picture book. We describe the changes that occurred over 2 or 3 years in the language children used to retell stories. In doing so, we look at multiple dimensions of language, including syntax, morphology, vocabulary, and features of the narrative genre. Finally, we examine the issue of grammatical accuracy, which is often a key criteria in standardized language proficiency assessments used with English language learners.

In Chapter 6 (with Valdés as lead author) we reflect on what we learned over 5 years about the acquisition of English by young ELLs and the different kinds of affordances made available to children through their interactions with ordinary speakers of English in *One-on-One English*. We then consider the implications of this research for the education of English language learners. We offer a preliminary framework to understand the different kinds of language children need to acquire in order to function successfully in classrooms and emphasize the importance of conversational language, which is often minimized in comparison to "academic language." We also raise concerns about current educational approaches that intend to support the English language development of ELLs. Finally, we suggest key principles that might guide a more comprehensive or integrated approach to the education of English language learners.

In sum, in this book we provide evidence that interrogates the commonly held view of young children as rapid and effortless learners of new languages. We describe interactions between volunteer "English buddies" and ELL children and highlight ways in which children begin to comprehend and produce English. We depict successful language-rich interactive sessions and offer examples of the types of materials and activities that can be used with young ELL children to engage them in interactions in a new language. We also discuss the challenges of training volunteers to create a context in which children are engaged in meaningful one-on-one exchanges with fluent speakers of ordinary English and point out the dilemmas faced in documenting language growth. We conclude by examining and problematizing a number of practices that are increasingly being used in the teaching of English to young immigrant children in an attempt to accelerate the second language acquisition process.

CHAPTER 1

Realistic Expectations

English Language Learners and the Acquisition of "Academic" English

As we pointed out in the introduction, educating children in a language that they neither speak nor understand is an enormous challenge. The dimensions of the challenge have become most clearly obvious under the No Child Left Behind Act of 2001 (NCLB) because of its role in the movement for accountability in public education. The main federal law affecting K–12 education, NCLB has led to an increased focus on the achievement gap between language-minority children and majority children (e.g., Capps et al., 2005; Fry, 2007; Hakimzadeh & Cohn, 2007; Short & Fitzsimmons, 2007). In the case of ELLs, there are many questions about the role of language in school performance and about appropriate interventions for developing the types of English-language proficiency that children need in order to succeed in school. These questions include: How long does it take to learn a second language? What is the role of instruction in the language acquisition process? What kinds of instruction are successful in the acquisition of which aspects of language? Are there ways to accelerate the acquisition of English? The hope is that answers to these questions will allow practitioners to develop and document a set of practices that are based on a clear understanding of the process of second language acquisition and that can be implemented widely across the country.

Unfortunately, language is extraordinarily complex. There are no easy or quickly generalizable answers to the above questions, and there is little agreement about a number of fundamental issues in the fields of both second language acquisition and second language pedagogy. There is also little agreement about the assessment of English language proficiency and about the aspects of language that can be measured in assessing children's growth in the acquisition of a second language. What is evident is that if we are to make progress in educating children who do not speak English in this country, educators, researchers, and policy makers need to be provided with

15

information that will help them understand the complexities of the process of second language acquisition, the many unanswered questions surrounding the ultimate attainment of second languages, and the conditions that are essential in order for acquisition to take place.

In this chapter, then, I present an overview of the field of second language acquisition and make a deliberate attempt to capture the dilemmas and the debates currently taking place in this field. I also provide information about existing and continuing disagreements on various types of second language instruction that have engaged the second language teaching profession as well as a brief overview of research that has been conducted on the effectiveness of various approaches. I call attention to the fact that evidence on second language acquisition in children in both tutored and naturalistic environments is limited and emphasize the need for an increasing number of longitudinal studies with both children and adults that will allow us to understand the process of second language acquisition over time. In the final section of the chapter, I discuss key issues surrounding the development of English by immigrant children and the challenges of assessing both language development and content knowledge in ELLs on high-stakes, standardized assessments. I also touch on the debate surrounding the acquisition of what is referred to as "academic English" or "academic language" and on the ways that various different definitions have influenced conceptualizations about both instruction and assessment. I conclude with a brief discussion of the ways in which our qualitative, small-scale study of language development in K–3 children might contribute to our deeper understanding of the acquisition of English in children and of the social and cultural nature of this process. As Baker (2007) and Durán (2008) suggest, such work is needed if we are to better map curriculum goals and students' growth in the acquisition of a second language and if we are to accumulate evidence of growth that is sensitive to students' backgrounds and to the unique contexts in which children learn.

THE FIELD OF SECOND LANGUAGE ACQUISITION

The field of second language acquisition (SLA) studies the learning or acquisition of a language other than a native language, which is referred to as a *second language* or by the shorthand term *L2*. A first or native language (*L1*), is used with a child by parents or other interlocutors in infancy and/or in very early childhood for primary socialization; an L2 is not. Still a relatively young field of inquiry, SLA has employed theories and methodologies drawn from the disciplines of linguistics, psycholinguistics, social psychology, neurolinguistics, and sociolinguistics in order to understand the process of second language acquisition in instructional and noninstructional (naturalistic) settings. As Bardovi-Harlig and Dörnyei (2006) point out, SLA itself is an umbrella term that covers a range of research approaches and perspectives. It is, moreover, a field in which there are many debates and disagreements about the theoretical foundations underlying the field, about the methodologies used to study the process of second language acquisition/ learning, and also about the goals and ultimate outcomes of the process itself.

From the perspective of educational researchers and practitioners who are concerned about the practices that can support children's acquisition of English in order to succeed in school, the field of SLA offers limited clear guidance. Policy makers want to mandate the implementation of effective practices for accelerating children's acquisition of English and teachers want to understand how best to teach English language learners. Faculty members working in the area of teacher preparation often look to SLA research hoping that it might provide future teachers with knowledge about ELLs and about the process of second language acquisition. It is sometimes the case that they present SLA findings in their classes in order to support particular views about appropriate pedagogies and learning goals that they believe will work effectively for new teachers in their classrooms. Ellis (2005c), however, suggests that, given controversies in the field, it might be unwise to attempt to formulate a set of general principles of instructed language acquisition and suggests that Hatch's (1978) warning, "apply with caution," is as pertinent today as it was some 30 years ago. He concludes that:

> If SLA is to offer teachers guidance there is a need to bite the bullet and provide advice, so long as this advice does not masquerade as prescriptions or proscriptions (and there is always a danger that advice will be so construed) and so long as it is tentative, in the form of what Stenhouse (1975) called "provisional specifications." (Ellis, 2005c, p. 210)

In the case of immigrant-background children who acquire the societal language in school contexts and who must use this language in order to learn academic content (mathematics, social studies, language arts, science), the question of what needs to be acquired by children and what needs to be taught by teachers is possibly much more complex and more urgent. Certainly, immigrant children who need to learn English in order to be educated in that language must acquire the linguistic system. But, as Van Patten (2003) argues, second language acquisition is a slow and time-consuming process. What this means is that young learners, if they are to achieve in school, will need to use English while they are still learning it—before they have had time to acquire the full linguistic system. If they are to understand instruction, to learn how to read and write, and to display what they have learned about academic content, they must use an "interlanguage," that is, a learner's variety of English that is not yet grammatically accurate or consistently fluent. In American schools, ELLs cannot be made to wait to use the language until they speak and write like native speakers. They must learn through and with flawed English, and teachers must become skilled at supporting their subject matter learning during the time that they are acquiring English and using "defective" language for many classroom assignments and activities. They must keep in mind, moreover, that nativelike ultimate attainment is characteristic of only a small number of L2 learners of all ages and of all languages.

SLA: The Development of the Field

A number of recent works have attempted to offer a brief history of the field of second language acquisition including Block (2003), Johnson (2004) and Sharwood Smith (1994). While not identical, all three works divide the development of the field into periods and stages, including the behaviorist period, the creative construction period (focusing on the role of the learner and encompassing the studies of interlanguages), and a current period that has focused more on producing basic research in the disciplines of linguistics, psychology, and cognitive science than on informing the practice of language teaching.

The groundwork for the field of SLA was first established during and after the Second World War, at a time when there was an increasing interest by the defense community in the use of foreign languages in counterintelligence. Drawing from structural linguistics and behaviorism, early work on the learning of second or foreign languages focused on the influence of the first language on the *target language* (TL)–the language to be acquired–and developed a set of classroom practices known as audio-lingualism that were widely adopted by language teachers. Language was seen as a set of first language habits that would directly interfere with the establishment of a new set of habits to be acquired in the process of learning a second language. Much attention, therefore, was given to the development of *contrastive analysis* (CA) in which researchers contrasted learners' native languages with the particular target language that learners hoped to acquire. By carrying out such analyses, they hoped to anticipate the L2 structures that would be most likely to cause difficulties for learners and to develop language teaching curricula that would attend to those aspects of a target language in which the structures of the learners' L1 and the L2 were most different.

The second period of the field of SLA according to Sharwood Smith (1994) is one in which the learner was seen as an autonomous creator of linguistic systems. This period rejected the perspectives of contrastive analysis, noting that learners did not exhibit predicted difficulties nor did the similarities between their L1 and the target language result in positive transfer. By the 1960s and 1970s, moreover, theories of language had shifted, and psychology had moved from behaviorism to the information-processing model of cognition. Conscious of the limits of contrastive analysis and convinced that similar errors in particular grammatical structures could be found in learners speaking very different native languages, a number of researchers carried out work in what is known as *error analysis*, that is, the systematic study of learners' errors in order to describe the *interlanguages*–the intermediate stages in learners' development (Corder, 1967, 1981; Selinker, 1972) or approximative systems (Nemser, 1971) exhibited by L2 learners. Block (2003) maintains that, given changing views of language, errors came to be seen not as undesirable habits, but as evidence of a developing competence at a particular stage of development, which is systematic and coherent. Error analysis had many implications for language teaching. Corder (1981), for example, argued that learners have a built-in syllabus and that, therefore, they will only learn those structures according to an internally programmed order. He thus conjectured that the direct teaching of structures in an order dictated by, for example, traditional views of language instruction would be unsuccessful at altering the systematicity of the developing system.

As pointed out by Johnson (2004), the field of SLA was strongly influenced by the work of Chomsky (1965, 1980, 1981) on first language acquisition and by his views on grammatical competence, that is, of a native speaker's implicit (unconscious) knowledge of the formal properties of his or her L1 grammar. For Chomsky, *grammatical competence* is the implicit knowledge of syntax that all native speakers acquire as the result of a genetically programmed *universal grammar* (UG) as well as a result of input (i.e., the available language data of variable quality that normally surrounds children). Given the poverty of the stimulus (the often questionable systematic exposure to well-formed, audible language) and at the same time the striking uniformity of the grammars of native speakers, Chomsky posited that children are able to acquire an L1 only because they are born with an innate language mechanism that is independent of other cognitive mechanisms. The innate system only needs to be triggered by the language of the environment but does not depend on the social aspect of language use.

Chomsky's theory of first language acquisition has influenced the field of SLA, and researchers have strongly debated whether L2 learners have or do not have access to UG. Unfortunately results of studies that have attempted to answer that question have not resolved the issue. There are researchers (e.g., Bley-Vroman, 1989) who argue that L1 and L2 acquisition processes are fundamentally different and that adult L2 learners do not have access to UG, thus accounting for their less-than-perfect ultimate attainment. Other researchers (e.g., Flynn, 1987) believe that L2 learners do indeed have full access to UG, while others (White, 1989) believe that UG is available to learners only through the language that they have already acquired. As Johnson (2004) points out, unresolved though the issue of UG access in L2 learners may be, the impact of Chomsky's theories have been profound on the field of L2 acquisition.

According to Block (2003), the second stage of the field of SLA drew directly from work on L1 acquisition and led to a series of morpheme acquisition studies exemplified by the work of Dulay and Burt (1973, 1974) who argued that L1 interference errors were much less frequent than natural developmental errors across learners of English from various language backgrounds. According to these researchers, children learning English produced errors similar to those of native English speakers acquiring the same morphemes. These early morpheme studies, although now questioned seriously from methodological and other perspectives, nevertheless raised important questions about the primary role of L1 transfer in the process of L2 acquisition. Block (2003) places Krashen's work (whom he credits with developing the first wide-ranging theory of SLA) within this particular period of the development of the field and points out that Krashen drew directly on the morpheme studies in his five interrelated hypotheses.

Krashen's work had extensive influence on language teachers and particularly on bilingual education teachers in this country. Summarizing briefly, Krashen (1985) proposed that there was a natural order for morpheme acquisition that was fixed and predictable and independent of the order that rules might be taught in a formal context. He further argued that acquisition (a subconscious and incidental process) was different from learning (a conscious and intentional process). The first process, he maintained, led to tacit or implicit learning and the second to explicit linguistic knowledge. For Krashen, according to his input hypothesis, language is acquired from comprehensible input, language that is at the developmental level of the learner or just slightly beyond it. Moreover, according to his affective filter hypothesis, learners, because of motivation, anxiety, or stress, can put up an affective filter that blocks the internalization of comprehensible input surrounding them and thus the acquisition of an L2. Finally, the monitor hypothesis predicted that in order for learners to monitor the accuracy of their production, they require sufficient time to use their explicitly learned rules to correct and rephrase their utterances.

Criticisms of Krashen's position have been many and have focused on the fact that his hypotheses cannot be subjected to empirical testing (McLaughlin, 1987), on aspects of his theory such as the noninterface position between acquisition and learning, the exact definition of comprehensible input, and its failure to distinguish between child and adult second language learners. Johnson (2004) points out that Krashen did not distinguish between the understanding of a message and simple exposure to comprehensible input. She further argues that while input became far more important in Krashen's theory than it was in L1 acquisition theory, Krashen confused the social and the cognitive and failed to distinguish between one-way and two-way interaction.

It is important to stress, however, that, in spite of the criticism that his hypotheses generated, Krashen's influence on the field of second language acquisition was extensive. It drew attention to the importance of input, to the possibly limited role of grammar instruction in second language teaching, and to the difference between implicit and explicit learning. Moreover, as Block (2003) maintains, Krashen's theories drew on the three epistemological databases of SLA: the experiential, the observational, and the empirical. Krashen was a learner of languages, a former ESL teacher, and a language researcher, and his perspectives were those of the original applied linguists who worked in the early period of second language learning and acquisition. In spite of the fact that some have been dismissive of his work, in part because of the broad acceptance of his theories by language teachers, it is important to recall that, as Lightbown (1984) concluded, Krashen brought attention to the complexity of SLA and drew from the fields of linguistics, psychology, and sociolinguistics at a time when no one else had proposed a broad encompassing theory of L2 learning. Importantly for those of us concerned about English language learners and the pedagogies and practices that might impede or enhance their acquisition of the target language, Krashen–especially in his work with Terrell (Krashen & Terrell, 1983)–sought to contribute both to basic theories of SLA as well as to the application of these theories to the teaching of language in classrooms. In many ways, moreover, his ideas have directly influenced ongoing examinations of a number of key issues including the nature of input, the distinction between explicit and implicit learning, and the role of instruction in second language acquisition. Gass and Mackey (2007) for example, emphasize that the current SLA approach known as the interaction hypothesis (Gass, 1997) subsumes Krashen's (1982, 1985) input hypothesis adding to it the dimensions of interaction and output (Swain, 1993, 1995, 2000, 2005).

Recent Research and SLA Theory

The third period of SLA has been characterized by Sharwood Smith (1994) as one in which there has been much less interest in the application of SLA theory to second language teaching but an increasing interest in basic research including the contributions of SLA theory to other theoretical disciplines. As Doughty and Long (2003) in their introduction to the *Handbook on Second Language Acquisition* point out, "A good deal of what might be termed 'basic research' goes on in SLA without regard for its potential applications or social utility" (p. 6). SLA researchers, for example, have engaged in testing very different theories of acquisition, including nativism, functionalism, emergentism, and connectionism; and they have sought to contribute to cognitive psychology by studying implicit and explicit learning, incidental and intentional learning, automaticity, attention, memory, and individual differences. They have also contributed to the understanding of topics in linguistics by studying variation, language processing, crosslinguistic influences, fossilization, and the relationship of second language acquisition processes to the processes of pidginization and creolization. Finally, SLA researchers have sought to contribute to knowledge in neuroscience by focusing on how and where the brain stores linguistic knowledge, which areas are involved in the L2 acquisition process, how maturation affects L2 acquisition and the differences in ultimate attainment between children and adults.

Two relatively recent handbooks of SLA (Doughty & Long, 2003; Ritchie & Bhatia, 1996) both include the following topics: universal grammar and second language acquisition; maturational constraints, universal grammar, and SLA; crosslinguistic influence (language transfer); information processing in L2 acquisition (implicit and explicit learning, incidental and intentional learning, attention, memory automaticity, variation, stabilization, and fossilization) and the role of the environment in SLA (including the social context as well as input and interaction).

According to Zuengler and Miller (2006), in the last 15 years the field of SLA has been divided into two parallel worlds, the positions of which have been characterized as incommensurable. One group of researchers (cognitivists) see the acquisition of an L2 as an individual cognitive process that takes place in the mind of the individual learner, while another group of researchers (sociointeractionists) see language acquisition primarily as a social process that takes place in interactions between learners and speakers of the target language. The cognitive view has been dominant in the field, and work in this tradition is often referred to as "mainstream SLA." Researchers working within this tradition take the position that SLA's area of interest is the internal mental processes of what they term second language acquisition, which exclusively involves the development of the internal linguistic system of learners. According to Larsen-Freeman (2007), who provides a concise view of the two existing views of SLA, cognitivist SLA researchers view language as a mental construct and learning as change in a mental state. They are interested in "the aggregation of and increasing complexity and control of linguistic structures by learners," and they measure progress by "where along the route toward target language proficiency the learner is as indicated by the learner's linguistic performance" (p. 780). Representative of this perspective are what Johnson (2004) categorizes as information-process approaches to SLA, such as Krashen's (1985) input hypothesis; Swain's comprehensible output theory (1985, 1993, 1995), Gass and Selinker's (2001) model of SLA acquisition, Van

Patten's (1996) input-processing model, and Long's (1983, 1996) interaction hypothesis. According to Block, the input-interaction-output model (Gass, 1997), which subsumes the views of Krashen, Swain, and Long, is "the most tangible result of over thirty years of increasingly more intensive research into how individuals learn second languages" (Block, 2003, p. 30).

Socially oriented theorists by comparison, argue that the cognitivist orientation views learners from a deficit perspective and focuses on learners' limitations and their failure to become identical to native speakers. These researchers criticize mainstream SLA for taking the position that what is to be acquired is "a stable a-priori system that is used only for the transfer of information from one person's mind to the other" (Mori, 2007, p. 850). Lafford characterizes this same perspective as "decontextualized minds learning grammatical rules" (Lafford, 2007, p. 742). Critics of mainstream SLA point out that views about approximative systems, interlanguages, and nonnative-like ultimate attainment rests on the acceptance of a single native-speaker norm as the goal and the measure of the acquisition of a language other than the first.

The socially oriented position considers that SLA, rather than focusing exclusively on the developing linguistic systems of learners, should be concerned with understanding how speakers of one language become *users* (speakers, writers, readers) of a second language. Such perspectives include: Vygotskian sociocultural theory (Frawley & Lantolf, 1985; Lantolf, 2000, 2006; Lantolf & Appel, 1994; Lantolf & Frawley, 1983; Lantolf & Thorne, 2006); language socialization perspectives (Duff, 1995, 2002; Harklau, 1994; Ochs, 1988, 1991; Schiefflin & Ochs, 1986; Watson-Gegeo, 2004); notions of learning communities and communities of practice (Lave & Wenger, 1991; Toohey, 1999); Bakhtinian perspectives on dialogism (Toohey, 2000); ecological perspectives on language acquisition (Kramsch, 2002; van Lier, 2002, 2004); and critical theory (Canagarajah, 1993, 1999, 2005; Norton, 1995, 1997, 2000; Pennycook, 1990, 1999, 2001). For these researchers, the goal of second language learners is not to become like native speakers of the language but to use the language to function competently in a variety of contexts for a range of purposes. Moreover, since it is estimated that only 5% of L2 learners achieve nativelike competence (Han & Odlin, 2006), and yet most of these learners go on to use the language in their everyday lives for a number of purposes both inside and outside of L2-speaking countries, it seems unwise to perpetually brand individuals who use a less-than-perfect second language in their everyday lives as mere learners. Cook (2002) argues for the term *L2 users*, rather than *L2 learners*, for individuals who "exploit whatever linguistic resources they have for real-life purposes" (p. 2).

The fundamental difference between cognitivist and social views of second language acquisition has to do with their contrasting views about exactly what it is that has to be acquired in the process of learning a language other than the first. Cognitively oriented researchers are focused on understanding how speakers of one language internalize the linguistic system of another language. They want to know, for example, how learners develop an implicit grammar of a second language, how they process input (the language that they hear and read), what the developing linguistic system looks like at different stages, what kinds of errors learners make with different structures at different points of acquisition, and whether direct instruction on grammatical structures can change the pace of acquisition of those structures. Socially oriented researchers, by comparison, are concerned with the ways that second language learners learn "how to mean," that is, with the ways in which learners, by interacting with speakers of the L2, are able to develop and use evolving/imperfect linguistic, sociolinguistic, textual, and pragmatic systems to carry out numerous communicative actions. Zuengler and Miller (2006) conclude, moreover, that the debate between the two perspectives involve conflicting ontologies (basic questions about the nature of reality) and reflect an irreconcilable debate on the role of positivism and relativism in theory construction. They are not optimistic about the possibility of integrating the social and the cognitive. For Larsen-Freeman (2002), however, there is hope. She proposes chaos/complexity theory (C/CT) as a possible perspective "that is large enough to accommodate two competing points of view" (p. 33). She believes that C/CT supports a social view of language but does not exclude the individual psychological perspective of the cognitivist SLA perspectives.

As is the case for many areas of inquiry, the field of SLA has undergone a number of shifting emphases over the many years that it has been in existence. Klein (1998), however, argues that there is no one SLA theory in sight because the field wants "to discover the principles according to which people who have already mastered one language acquire another" (p. 529), and many acquisitional phenomena (e.g., vocabulary learning, pronunciation, syntax, and interactive behavior) must be accounted for. From Klein's perspective, SLA has, at best, "reliably and generally explained some few specific phenomena, for example certain selected syntactical or morphological constructions, and even these explanations are arguable" (p. 329).

For teachers, what this review of the second language acquisition field (SLA) is intended to suggest is that language acquisition is complicated and that researchers focused on understanding the process disagree not only about what is to be acquired but also about how the process takes place. Unfortunately, there is also little agreement within the language teaching profession about what to teach and how. As Kelly (1976) indicated, in the 25 centuries during which educators have been concerned about the teaching of second languages, "theories have been put forward about every aspect of language teaching, the matter of the course, the methods of transmission, and the media of teaching" (p. 2). In the section that follows I offer a brief overview of current concerns in the field and conclude with a summary of shifting perspectives over a longer period.

SLA and Second Language Pedagogy

As I pointed out above, the field of SLA has been primarily concerned, not with practice, but with the development of theories that can contribute to the understanding of the human language faculty. As a result, there is much disagreement about whether and to what degree there should be a relationship between SLA and language pedagogy, and there continues to be a concern about the perceived lack of relevance of SLA to classroom teaching (Crookes, 1997). Lightbown, in two articles published 15 years apart (1985, 2000), maintains that while SLA theories might still be one component of teachers' knowledge base, they cannot be the principal source of information that can guide them in their everyday practices and pedagogies. She recalls suggesting in 1985 that "the proper role for SLA research in teacher education was to help in setting realistic expectations for what language teachers and learners could accomplish in a second or foreign language classroom. SLA research on order of acquisition, crosslinguistic transfer effects, and age factors could potentially explain why some things were so difficult, in spite of effort and good will on the part of both teachers and learners" (Lightbown, 2000, p. 431).

In spite of concerns by major figures in the SLA field about the relationship between second language pedagogy and SLA, second language and foreign language teachers, and in many states content teachers, are currently required to take courses in the field of second language acquisition. Not surprisingly, as Van Patten (2003) comments, teachers approach these courses asking for answers to concrete teaching questions. They want to know, for example, how best to teach grammar, how vocabulary is to be presented, how errors are to be corrected, and how to deal with *long-term ELLs* (students who have not been officially redesignated as fluent English speakers by state mandated criteria after many years of residence and study in this country). Some teachers come to these courses with clear ideas about teaching and learning languages and often assume that there are known facts about the process of acquisition. Lightbown (2000), for example, comments that over the years teachers in her classes have had strong opinions about what "everybody knew" about learning languages. In the 1950s and 1960s, "everybody knew" that second languages were learned through reading and translating literary texts. In the late 1960s "everybody knew" that they were learned through imitation, repetition, drill, and overlearned dialogues. By the 1970s, the period of communicative language teaching (CLT), prospective teachers and everybody else "knew" that exposure to comprehensible input and group interaction was essential. There was little interest in focusing on language forms. Lightbown points out that some of these changes were indeed informed to some degree by SLA research, but she points out that these changes were due to factors other than research findings and included specific movements in language pedagogy itself (e.g., views about learners' needs, trends such as the British national-functional syllabus movement, and the rejection of structure-based approaches).

The questions asked by second or foreign language teachers who focus only on the teaching of the L2 language in classrooms are in many ways different from those asked by bilingual teachers and content teachers who must teach both content and English in their classes. Their questions, moreover, often reflect current concerns that directly affect both teachers and learners in the present policy context. For example, the impact of the NCLB legislation and the focus on both subject matter and L2 testing for ELLs strongly has had a clear impact on what "everybody knows" must be "taught" in order for ELLs to achieve in school. Faculty members working with teachers of ELLs in content classrooms, for example, might expect answers to questions such as the following:

1. What are the best ways of making instruction in specific discipline areas comprehensible to beginning ELLs?
2. What are the best ways of teaching vocabulary to ELLs?
3. What are the best ways of teaching the language of specific disciplines to ELLs?

On the other hand, teachers who are also concerned about students' ability to do well on state-mandated tests of English language development (CELDT, ACCESS, ELDA, LAB-R) and about the interaction between subject matter tests and the development of children's English language proficiency might expect answers to questions such as the following:

1. What is the role of instruction in developing children's second language?
2. What kinds of instruction are successful in the acquisition of which aspects of language?
3. What evidence is there that systematic and explicit ELD instruction for learners–especially young children–makes a difference?
4. Do learners have a built-in syllabus and can it be altered by instruction?
5. What is the best way to deal with students' interlanguages (their imperfect and developing learner varieties)?

6. Should teachers be concerned about fossilization?[1]
7. Can accuracy be accelerated by instruction?
8. What is the impact of corrective feedback on the development of accuracy in the L2?[2]
9. What is the role of "practice" in L2 acquisition?
10. What is the impact of "junky" data (the flawed language of peers) on language learners?[3]
11. What is the role of input and exposure to the target language in language acquisition?
12. How long does the process of L2 acquisition take? Is there a point at which L2 acquisition can be said to be complete?

Finally, both groups might want specific suggestions about specific methods to be used in "teaching" language.

Approaches to Language Teaching in the Classroom

In a detailed and extensive literature review prepared for the New Zealand Ministry of Education (Aukland Regional Office), Ellis (2005b) presents a number of perspectives on several of the above questions. He begins by discussing the three approaches to language teaching that he identifies as representative of classroom instruction: the oral situational approach, the notional functional approach, and the task-based approach. He identifies the learning theories that underlie each of these pedagogies and argues that both the oral situational and the notional function approaches are undergirded by skill-learning theory and built around a present-practice-produce (PPP), accuracy-oriented methodology. From his perspective, task-based approaches that have interactional authenticity, by comparison, give primacy to fluency over accuracy without denying that learners have to attend to language form.

Ellis (2005b) then reviews classroom-based research on language teaching and learning and makes a distinction between two main theoretical perspectives that have informed instruction: the computational model (associated with concepts such as input processing, input, intake, interlanguage development, and the learner's built-in syllabus) and the sociocultural theory of mind perspective (associated with social interaction, collaboration, zone of proximal development, and scaffolding). He divides curriculum into two broad types of curriculum—direct and indirect intervention—and reviews research related to both types of intervention. Drawing from the work of Norris and Ortega (2000) in terms of the direct teaching of grammar, Ellis (2005) concludes that "learners can benefit from instruction on specific grammatical features if their goal is to perform well on discrete-point tests like the TOEFL" (p. 10). He points out there is little or no evidence, however, that grammar instruction results in the development of learner's ability to use these features spontaneously in oral communication. He concludes, more-over, that grammar instruction cannot circumvent the learners' natural route of acquisition. Contrary to what is now the position of ELD development programs in some parts of the country where "systematic and explicit" in-struction in English is being advocated for elementary school children, Ellis's review of the research literature leads him to the conclusion that the results of explicit teaching are evident only when learners' knowledge was exam-ined through "experimentally elicited responses rather than in communica-tive use" (p. 14), and that explicit approaches researchers reported on were implemented in narrow and restricted ways. He thus argues that "caution needs to be exercised in concluding that explicit instruction is more effective than implicit" (p. 14).

A close reading of Norris and Ortega (2000) makes evident the difficulty of using the terms *explicit* and *implicit* instruction casually. In their synthesis of the effectiveness of L2 instruction, Norris and Ortega reviewed findings from 77 experimental and quasi-experimental studies published between 1980 and 1998 which they categorized as instruction (1) involving focus-on-form or focus-on-forms, (2) using explicit or implicit approaches, and (3) mea-suring responses through metalinguistic judgments, selected responses, con-strained constructed responses, or free constructed responses. Studies were characterized as *focusing on form* (FonF) if there was an integration of form and meaning, if learning was unobtrusive and documented students' mental processes, if forms were selected by taking into account learners' needs, and if interlanguage constraints were considered. Studies were categorized as *fo-cused on forms* (FonFS) when none of the above strategies could be identified and learner attention was somehow focused on particular structures. Instruc-tional treatments were considered *explicit* if rule explanation was a part of the instruction or "if learners were asked to attend to particular form and to try to arrive at a metalinguistic generalization on their own" (p. 437). Norris and Ortega report that in all the studies reviewed, learner proficiency levels were either noted minimally or noted inconsistently. Only one of the 77 stud-ies was conducted with elementary school learners, 10 were conducted with junior high school students, 5 with high school learners and 51 studies were conducted at the college level. A total of 11 studies were conducted with adults outside of a college context. Instructional treatments ranged from a low of under 1 hour to a maximum of 7 hours.

In reporting their conclusions about what appeared to be superior results of explicit instruction that focused on forms, the authors remind their read-ers that

> measurement of change induced by instruction is typically carried out on instruments that seem to favor more explicit memory-based performance. Thus, in the current domain, over 90% of the dependent variables required

the application of L2 rules in highly focused and discrete ways, while only around 10% of the dependent variables required relatively free productive use of the L2. . . . Thus, it is likely that effect sizes observed within any given study may be directly associated with the type of response required from learners on outcome measures, and associated interpretations of study findings should be tempered by the realization that a different test type would likely have produced different results. (p. 483, pp. 486–487)

Ellis (2005) presents a much more abbreviated summary of indirect interventions. He characterizes them as having been conducted both from the perspective of the information-processing or computational model of L2 acquisition and from the sociocultural perspective. Work on tasked-based approaches to implicit instruction within the computational model of L2 learning has examined issues such as off- or online planning (Crookes, 1989; Wendel, 1997). Research within the sociointeractional model, by comparison, has examined scaffolding, collaborative dialogue, and task engagement. In both cases, Ellis maintains that work on implicit, task-based pedagogies conducted as part of both models of L2 acquisition has tended to focus more on language use rather than on the acquisition of the linguistic system.

Shifting Perspectives in the Language Teaching Profession

According to Kelly (1976), the language teaching profession can be said to have had its beginning 25 centuries ago. The profession has been rooted in traditions associated with the teaching of Latin and other classical languages structured around translation and the methodologies of grammar. Over time, the modern-language teaching (as opposed to the classical-language teaching) profession has engaged in a continuing search of pedagogies and practices appropriate for developing students' ability to comprehend and/or to produce a language other than the first. Ideas from the study of logic, grammar, rhetoric, philosophy, and later from linguistics and psychology, have deeply influenced the teaching of languages. Comparing the linear development of sciences with the cyclical development found in art, Kelly argues that all teachers, including language teachers, "unwittingly rediscover old techniques":

Whereas artists are willing to seek inspiration from the past, teachers, being cursed with the assumption that their discoveries are necessarily an improvement on what went on before, are reluctant to learn from history. Thus it is that they unwittingly rediscover old techniques by widely different methods of research. (p. 396)

This same discovery and rediscovery of ideas informing language teaching in the United States is well captured in the recent retrospective summaries of articles published since 1916 in the *Modern Language Journal*, a journal specializing in language learning and teaching. According to Mitchell and Vidal (2001), articles published over this 94-year period make evident that language instruction has been influenced by a set of dichotomous views (e.g., the importance of fluency versus accuracy, the need to teach integrated skills versus separate skills) as well as by various theoretical positions (e.g., contrastive analysis, behaviorism, structural linguistics, and generative linguistics). Among the major mainstream methods listed by Mitchell and Vidal are (1) the Grammar Translation Method, used in the teaching of Greek and Latin, (2) the Direct Method, which taught language by the direct association of words with actions and objects, (3) the Reading Method, which argued for reading as the principal skill to be acquired by college foreign language learners, and (4) the Audiolingual Method, which derived from the Army Specialized Training Program (ASTP) and involved memorization and pattern drill. This program was implemented during World War II to meet the nation's need for military personnel who could "identify, decode, translate, and interpret strategic messages" (Mitchell & Vidal, 2001, p. 29). The Audiolingual Method first appeared in the late 1940s and became dominant in the 1960s and 1970s. Focusing primarily on oral language, its theory of language learning was behaviorist. Stimulus, response, and reinforcement were important. The syllabus was organized around key phonological, morphological, and syntactic elements. Contrastive analysis was used for selection of elements, and grammar was taught inductively. Dialogues and drills were used extensively as students responded to stimuli, memorized, repeated, and imitated. Teachers were seen as models of language, conducting drills, teaching dialogues, and directing choral responses. The Audiolingual Method was abandoned largely as a result of shifting views about language based on the work of Chomsky (1957, 1959), which argued that language is not merely a process of habit formation, but rather a process of creative construction.

Since the 1970s, members of the second language teaching profession have moved to the implementation of what have been called "communicative teaching methods." These varied methods view language as communication and consider the goal of language study as the acquisition of functional competence in actual communicative interactions using both the written and the oral mode. Moreover, they assume that activities involving communication and meaningful tasks will promote learning. Syllabi for communicative courses vary, but generally include lessons on structures and functions and task-based activities. Instructors expect students to play the role of negotiators, contributors, and actors, while instructors are expected to facilitate the communication process, act as participants in communication, and serve as analysts of the communicative needs of students. The dilemma for these educators is how to design teaching programs that can result in both functional competence in face-to-face communication as well as in the accurate use of the written language in both receptive and productive modes.

In sum, there have been profound changes in the thinking of researchers and practitioners involved in second language teaching over time. However, in spite of strong efforts by professional associations to change the focus and emphasis of language teaching, the day-to-day practice of classroom instruction draws primarily from "traditions of practice." The audiolingual and contrastive analysis theories identified as central to students' second language learning are still present in language teaching materials used currently. The materials continue to present the same set of linguistic items.[4]

New theories about the stages and order of acquisition of structures in a second language conducted by SLA researchers (e.g., that the order of acquisition of particular structures may not be amenable to direct instruction) have had little impact in most classrooms.

Many ESL teachers and programs continue to focus primarily on the teaching of grammatical structures using grammar-based syllabi. As long as the focus is accuracy, and as long as teachers continue to believe that the direct teaching of grammatical rules can increase accuracy, grammatical syllabi and grammatical approaches will continue to dominate the practice of language teaching. Other teachers describe themselves as "eclectic" and report combining grammar and translation with communicative language teaching. Given the very different theories of language and language learning that underlie these two methods, it is highly possible that teachers are not fully aware of the contradictory positions of the two approaches. Conversely, it may be the case that ESL teachers and regular teachers engaged in English language development (ELD) are less concerned about the incompatibility of underlying theories than they are about students' passing the types of language proficiency assessments that are required of them.

KEY LIMITATIONS OF EXISTING RESEARCH ON SLA

For those concerned about the acquisition of a societal language by children and about understanding developmental sequences and progressions that can inform instruction, there are two key limitations in existing research in SLA that must be attended to by all researchers. The first limitation is the result of a very small number of existing longitudinal studies of language learners in both instructed and naturalistic settings. The second limitation is that surprisingly few studies have been carried out on the process of SLA in children in comparison to the large numbers of studies conducted on adult learners.

Longitudinal Studies of Second Language Acquisition

It is important to emphasize that SLA, from both the cognitivist and sociointeractional perspectives, has had very little to say about a process of L2 acquisition as it takes place through and over time. Reviewing the longitudinal SLA research literature and concluding that discussions about longitudinal research are rare, Ortega and Iberri-Shea (2005) argue that time is central in SLA and that many questions in second language acquisition are "questions of time and timing" (p. 37). SLA researchers, therefore, must be necessarily concerned about questions that focus on "at what age" and "for how long." Time, moreover, is central in policy and instructional decisions about early or late exit from programs, about optional instructional time devoted to language development in classrooms, about articulation between levels (e.g., high school and college), and more recently about the earliest time in the L2 acquisition process that children can be required to take large-scale assessments on subject matter knowledge in their second language.

Ortega and Iberri-Shea note that there has been a tendency for SLA researchers to implicitly posit longitudinal claims for cross-sectional studies carried out from a variety of perspectives. As was the case in the review of experimental and quasi-experimental studies discussed above (Norris & Ortega, 2000), the majority of the 38 longitudinal studies examined by Ortega and Iberri-Shea (2005) focused on the college-level population of L2 learners. Different epistemological perspectives were represented by the selected studies, including descriptive-quantitative examinations of linguistic features as well as qualitative interpretive studies of sociointeractional dimensions of language use. Four categories were used for grouping studies included in the review: (1) descriptive-quantitative longitudinal studies of L2 development, (2) longitudinal research on L2 program outcomes, (3) longitudinal investigations of L2 instructional effectiveness, and (4) recent qualitative longitudinal SLA research. Ortega and Iberri-Shea conclude their discussion with suggestions for future directions and raise important questions about the optimal length of observation in longitudinal studies, the choice between biological time and institutional time as units of analysis, the challenges of multiwave data collection, the need to use statistical analyses specifically available for use with longitudinal data, and the importance of thick descriptions in ethnographic longitudinal studies. The authors conclude by advocating for "the diversity and accumulation of recent and future longitudinal research" that they hope "will help chart the development of advanced L2 capacities and help us understand the appropriate timing, duration, and content of optimal educational practices for L2 learning across educational settings and multilingual contexts" (p. 43).

Focus on Children in the Study of Second Language Acquisition

Contrary to what might be expected given the large number of children around the world who must acquire a second language in order to obtain access to education, the field of second language acquisition has primarily focused on adults. Philp, Oliver, and Mackey (2008) consider the lack of focus especially noteworthy because research carried out with children inform many of today's leading approaches to the study of SLA. It is important to point out, however, that the study of second language acquisition in children has been complicated by questions about categorizations and definitions–particularly views about simultaneous versus sequential or successive bilingualism. For most researchers, children who are raised from infancy with two languages are referred to as child bilinguals and are considered to have acquired two first languages simultaneously. McLaughlin (1978), for example, includes in this category children who have been regularly exposed to two languages before the age of three. De Houwer (1995) and Deuchar and Quay (2000), however, consider that children engage in the process of bilingual acquisition only when they are exposed to two languages within the first month of birth. De Houwer considers children exposed to two languages after the first month of birth and up to the age of 2 as involved in a different process, which she refers to as "bilingual second language acquisition." Most researchers currently distinguish child SLA from bilingual acquisition, setting the lower boundary between the ages of 2 and 4. Schwartz (2003) for example, points out that in bilingual acquisition contexts, the grammars of two languages are being worked out simultaneously or sequentially, while in L2 acquisition context, the child acquires a new language after acquiring an almost complete grammar of a first language.

Interpreting existing research on child SLA has presented some challenges. Bialystok (2001) argues that this is the case because there are problems in defining a point at which a child has "almost" completely acquired the L1 grammar and when the acquisition of L2 can be said to begin, as well as which children can or should be included in the category of child bilingual. Paradis (2007), for example, argues, that the term *child bilingual* has unfortunately been used as synonymous with "child L2 learner" and further points out:

> Second language (L2) acquisition in children has been seldom studied as a subfield with its own issues and questions separate from adult L2 acquisition on the one hand, or bilingualism and educational outcomes on the other. Consequently, we know little about second language acquisition (SLA) issues, such as individual differences, as they pertain to child as opposed to adult learners, and we know less about the developing oral language proficiency of L2 children than we know about their literacy development. (p. 387)

In the introduction to a recent volume–intriguingly titled *Second Language Acquisition and the Younger Learner: Childs Play?*–Philp and colleagues (2008) remind readers of the current problematic views about children's L2 acquisition as "child's play" and point out that much more work is needed in the area of child SLA, including the different periods of child SLA, the uniqueness of the child learner, ultimate attainment in children, and the processes and mechanisms of L2 acquisition in children. They strongly argue for longitudinal studies, for richly detailed descriptions of "the many and various factors which interact to impact a given child's L2 development" (p. 13), and for close attention to the study of pedagogy and child L2 learning.

Philp et al. (2008) also call attention to the fact that since the 1960s much interest in child SLA has focused on whether or not there is a critical or sensitive period for second language acquisition and whether or not there are age-related effects that, as Hyltenstam and Abrahamsson (2003) state, offer an advantage to children in terms of both rate of acquisition and ultimate attainment of a second language. As opposed to what is generally believed by the public about the natural superiority of children as L2 learners, there are many disagreements among researchers about age and L2 acquisition. Most researchers agree that–in general–children are more successful language learners than adults, but there is much debate about the explanation for these effects and about the degree to which most child learners attain nativelike proficiency in all subcomponents of language. Bialystok & Hakuta (1994), in reviewing existing research, conclude that older learners are faster in terms of rate of acquisition of morphology and syntax, and younger learners are better in terms of final level of attainment of accent-free, nativelike proficiency. They also point out, however, that explanations for differences in attainment (including social and experiential factors as well as biological explanations such as the critical period hypothesis or the sensitive period hypothesis) are limited in explanatory power. Hyltenstam and Abrahamsson (2003) report that research has found "non-native features in the ultimate attainment of even some very young starters" (p. 545). They conclude their extensive review of the literature on maturational constraints in SLA by stating that "both adults, in rare cases, and children, in most cases, seem to reach nativelike proficiency in a second language" (p. 578). However, they also note that "much of the data discussed in the literature on maturational constraints and specifically on the CPH has not been analyzed in sufficient detail to make possible any claims about whether the subjects are nativelike in all respects" (p. 571). They suggest, therefore, that rather than nativelike, many of the learners–including young children–described in existing studies should be referred to as "near-native." Because maturation has a strong influence on L2 acquisition, they view nativelike proficiency as unattainable and suggest that what is remarkable is that learners–both adults and children–can compensate for subtle differences between even near-native and nativelike proficiency in their everyday use of language that are seen as highly problematic by linguists in their research laboratories.

SLA work focusing on children can generally be grouped into several categories: (1) research that has primarily focused on the acquisition of the linguistic system (Hakuta, 1976; Philp & Duchesne, 2008; Unsworth, 2005); (2) research concentrating on the acquisition of linguistic and participatory competence (Achiba, 2003; Toohey, 2000; Wong Fillmore, 1976); and (3) an extensive body of work that has investigated the relationship between second language acquisition and school achievement (August & Hakuta, 1997; and more recently by Genesse, Lindholm-Leary, Saunders, & Christian, 2006).

While the purpose of some research focusing on the acquisition of the linguistic system has been to compare the L2 acquisition processes of adults and children including, for example, responses to feedback, negotiation of meaning in task-based interactions (e.g., Leeman, 2003; Oliver, 1998, 2000; Unsworth, 2005), other research has studied children on their own terms. As compared to research on adult SLA, which all too often takes place in intact language-as-a-subject classrooms, about which few details are given by researchers, and in laboratory settings, most studies of child SLA have tended to provide information about the context and the circumstances surrounding the acquisition experience. The collection edited by Philp et al. (2008) brings together good examples of current research on child SLA informed by broader SLA perspectives and includes work on the effect of age on two Russian sisters acquiring L2 German morphology (Dimroth, 2008); the impact of social goals and participation in the L2 development of a 6-year-old in a first-grade classroom (Philp & Duchesne, 2008); language-learning affordances in a Swedish immersion classroom (Cekaite, 2008); the negotiation of meaning and reading comprehension (Van den Branden, 2008); the acquisition of the pronouns *his* and *her* (White, 2008); and learning how to explain and describe in an L2 within a family context (Mitchell & Lee, 2008).

Given the dearth of research on second language acquisition in children in both instructed and in naturalistic settings, it is extraordinarily difficult for program designers and instructors to find ways of building meaningfully on research that has been conducted on second language teaching and learning in general. If they do so, it is imperative that they take into account the fact that existing knowledge on instructed second language acquisition is drawn from work done primarily on adult learners. We know little at this time about the direct teaching of language to children and about the ways that such teaching can accelerate young learners' performance on standardized measures of both content area knowledge *and* progress in acquiring English. In the section that follows, I discuss the challenges related to the assessment of English language learners in the current policy context and in the light of our limited knowledge about second language acquisition in children.

SECOND LANGUAGE ACQUISITION, ASSESSMENT, AND IMMIGRANT CHILDREN IN SCHOOLS

As compared to the basic research perspective of SLA research, work on the study of second language acquisition as it relates to school achievement for minority children is being carried out under much more pressing real-world circumstances and in a political context in which popular debates often inform policy decisions about the appropriate education for such children. As U.S. citizens have become increasingly concerned about "new" arrivals and about the ways that they can be integrated into American society, much attention has been given both by the public and by educators to the ways that educational institutions can successfully prepare large numbers of immigrant children to contribute to America's continued progress. Language itself has taken on a central role in discussions surrounding the education of immigrant students as heated debates take place in the national media about the number of both authorized and unauthorized immigrants in this country, about the security of our borders, and about the challenge of assimilating groups of individuals who appear not be learning English (Huntington, 2004). In many parts of the country, concern about the deep changes in American society coupled with misconceptions about the supposed effortlessness of L2 acquisition by children has led to educational policies that are based on the assumption that a second language can be acquired by young children in a single year. These misconceptions are supported by recollections of successful adults of immigrant origin and the supposed relative ease with which they acquired English in a single year, a single summer, or even a few weeks.

To date, research focusing on the challenges of educating L2 learners in English language classrooms in the United States has focused on a number of different issues and questions having to do with the learning of English in school settings, the relationship between L1 and L2 proficiencies combined with a variety of other factors (e.g., age, length of residence, parent education, SES, previous education in an L1, language of instruction), and educational achievement measured and defined in a variety of ways. The work of August and Hakuta (1997) and Genesse et al. (2006) synthesize the research literature on the education of K–12 English language learners that was published primarily in the last 20 years.

Since the passage of NCLB, educators in every state in the country have given increasing attention to English language learners. In a National Council of La Raza's (NCLR) Issue Brief, Lazarin (2006) explains that the No Child Left Behind Act holds schools accountable for improving academic achievement among all groups, including ELL students, and makes certain that information is gathered and reported on their academic outcomes. ELLs can no longer be excluded from state accountability systems, and current law includes requirements to close the achievement gap specifically for English language learners. As might be expected, much controversy has surrounded the implementation of NCLB requirements, and there have been efforts to change or modify them significantly. Lazarin provides an overview of the manner in which local, state, and federal decision makers have implemented these provisions and presents policy recommendations informing the future of the law as it relates to English language learners. Summarizing briefly, Lazarin outlines the promise of closing the achievement gap and bringing all students to 100% proficiency in core academic subjects by the year 2014. As a result, states have been asked to set yearly benchmarks for all students as well as for certain subgroups including ELLs. As summarized by Abedi (2007), within the context of NCLB, ELLs are defined as students who are between the ages of 3 and 21, who are enrolled or preparing to enroll in an elementary or secondary school, who were not born in the United States or whose native language is not English, who are Native Americas, Alaskan natives or native residents of outlying areas, or from environments where a language other than English has had a significant impact on students levels of English proficiency, who are migratory and from environments where English is not the dominant language, and/or who have difficulties in speaking, reading, and writing the English language to the degree that these limitations may deny students opportunities to achieve in school or to participate fully in society. English language learners are one of the several disadvantaged populations on which NCLB specifically focuses. States are required to identify and implement educational programs and curricula for language instruction that are based on scientifically based research on teaching limited English proficient children and to help limited English proficient children meet the same challenging state academic achievement standards as all other children are expected to meet (NCLB, 2001). By the year 2007–08, states were required to administer reading/language arts and math assessments on an annual basis that were aligned to state academic content standards. Additionally, the tests designed to measure children's performance were required to be valid, reliable, and of adequate technical quality.

Valid and reliable assessment, therefore, is a critical component of accountability and of the continuous improvement processes in schools and districts. Moreover, the assessment of ELLs used in schools today must address both content area knowledge and progress in learning English. Unfortunately as a number of recent discussions of assessment and ELLs have made clear (Abedi, 2004, 2007, 2008; Durán, 2008; Kopriva, 2008; Lazarin, 2006; Parker, Louie, & O'Dwyer, 2009; Solorzano, 2008), there are many questions about the validity and reliability of currently used instruments and measurement procedures used across the country and much unease about types of testing accommodations (e.g., extra time, small group administration, use of dictionaries) that are currently being provided for ELL students in recognition of the fact that tests currently being used were not developed for use with this population of students and may therefore be invalid and inappropriate for assessing ELL's academic competence (Durán, 2008; Lazarin, 2006; Rivera, Stansfield, Scialdone, & Sharkey, 2000; Solorzano, 2008). Additionally, the unnecessary linguistic complexity of test items has also raised a number of questions. Work conducted by Haladyna and Downing (2004) and by Solano-Flores and Trumbull (2003) revealed that this unnecessary complexity leads ELL students to misinterpret and misunderstand test questions and is an additional source of measurement error.

English language proficiency (ELP) assessments used in the classification of English language learners have also been found to be problematic. Abedi (2008), for example, examines the impact of existing assessments on the ways in which the various definitions of English language proficiency have been used in creating ELL classifications. Differentiating between pre- and post-NCLB assessments, he notes that pre-NCLB language proficiency assessments exhibited discrepancies in theoretical bases and differed in their approaches to defining language proficiency, types of tasks to be included in specific item content, and grade-level ranges and specific time limits. He claims, moreover, that they may not have measured the types of language proficiency needed to be successful in mainstream classrooms. Citing Del Vecchio and Guerrero (1995), Abedi also comments on the wide disparities in these ELP assessments with respect to purpose, administration, items, test design, theoretical foundation, and validity. From Abedi's (2004, 2008), Kopriva's (2008), Lazarin's (2006), and Solorzano's (2008) perspectives, there are also problems with post-NCLB language proficiency assessments. Abedi underscores the fact that while, in theory, these assessments are supposed to be aligned with ELP content standards, the term ELP has not been defined in the literature. The various state consortia that developed new ELP instruments used or created different ELP standards as well as different standard-setting approaches which may have introduced inconsistencies of various types in the definition of the proficiency levels in the different modalities (listening, speaking, reading, and writing). Abedi (2007) is particularly concerned about dimensionality issues, that is, the degree to which the overall composite of the four subscales is used by some states while other states use a weighted composite proficiency score, using subscores in the different modalities and giving more weight, for example, to reading and writing than to speaking and listening. He argues that researchers must ask whether the four domains should be considered as four separate subscales/dimensions or whether they should be considered as a single latent trait that encompasses all four domains. He argues that if an overall proficiency test score is based on the total test of all four modalities, there should be evidence that the four modalities are highly correlated. Abedi further maintains that the issue of dimensionality needs to be addressed before deciding whether to use subscale or total scores.

Like Abedi (2008), a number of researchers including Solorzano (2008) and Durán (2008), currently focusing on NCLB and the resulting classification of English language learners at the state level, point out the challenges involved in classifying ELLs for the purposes of reporting adequate yearly progress (AYP). They mention problems of definition as well as differences in identification and redesignation procedures across the states. Abedi (2008), in particular, raises questions about the use of standardized achievement tests in conjunction with scores from language proficiency tests to reclassify ELL students in 76% of the states that were surveyed. Noting the lack of appropriateness of many standardized achievement tests for assessing the content knowledge of the students, Abedi is particularly concerned about the various cutoff scores that have been set by different states, ranging from the 33rd percentile to the 40th percentile with some states using reading/language arts and/or math. From his own research on the validity of the ELL classification based on data from several randomized field studies, Abedi concludes that "standardized achievement tests may not be a valid criterion for assessing ELL students for classification purposes as a single criterion or even when combined with other criteria" (p. 24).

In sum, a cursory examination of the efforts carried out to date by individual states and state consortia to assess English language proficiency and to measure ELL students' subject matter knowledge suggests that our current understanding of the best methods for assessing L2 acquisition and growth continues to be limited. We have much to learn not only about assessing language growth and development uniformly but also about the ways in which language limitations interact with the measurement of content area knowledge in standardized assessments.

THE CONCEPT OF ACADEMIC LANGUAGE

It is important to emphasize that in all materials I reviewed that discuss current, post-NCLB assessment practices including both ELP and content-based assessments, a strong concern was expressed about the concept of academic language, and much attention was given to discussing, defining, and examining the characteristics of the language needed by students to succeed in school. Francis and Rivera (2007), for example, indicate that this concern has its roots in the interpretation of NCLB that requires a fair assessment and evaluation of the degree to which children develop oral language and reading and writing skills in English. Abedi (2007) cites the goals of NCLB Title

III as committed to ensuring that limited English proficient students develop high levels of "*academic competence* in English, and meet the same challenging state *academic* achievement standards that all children are expected to meet" (p. 126, emphasis added). Both Francis and Rivera (2007) and Durán (2008) note that under Title III states are required to conceptually align their English development standards and ELP assessments with subject matter standards in reading, mathematics, and science. This is interpreted as requiring them to expand their ELD standards and ELP assessment blueprints so that they include "academic language" relevant to subject matter learning in these three areas. In theory, this goal will require schools to attend to the academic language learning needs of EL students as well as to their attainment of subject matter knowledge.

Unfortunately, however, as Francis and Rivera (2007) emphasize, there is not an agreed-upon definition of academic language. They cite the work of Cummins (1981), Solomon and Rhodes (1995), Scarcella (2003), and Bailey and Butler (2007) and call attention to different definitions of and perspectives on *academic language,* including the fact that it is contrasted with conversational language, that it is thought to be context reduced, that it is a register of language used in professional books, and that it is characterized by linguistic features that are associated with academic disciplines.

From the perspective of a second language acquisition field, the current tendency to contrast *academic language* with *conversational language* adds one more set of dichotomies (e.g., learning versus acquisition, context-reduced versus context-embedded language) that Snow (1987) has characterized as capturing a single underlying opposition. While to some degree useful, dichotomous views of language often simplify complex realities that matter in important ways to both students and their teachers. The concept of academic language has penetrated into educational thinking because of its links to assessment without a very deep or broad agreement about its meaning and without an understanding of children's progress over time in the acquisition of various ways of speaking in a second language. Unfortunately, we know very little about the acquisition of linguistic repertoires (various ways of speaking or using language for different purposes) by either adults or children. The term *academic language* and its assumed opposites, *oral, conversational,* or *ordinary* language are being used by well-meaning practitioners, researchers, and test developers with a variety of meanings.[5] More important, however, the use of these terms often incorporates views about the characteristics of the language to be attained by second language learners at various stages of development based on very little empirical evidence. Advanced proficiency, for example, is often assumed to be characterized by accurate or nativelike features in spite of a body of research evidence that has raised many doubts about nativelike ultimate attainment in all second language learners (Cook, 2002; Firth & Wagner, 2007; Han & Odlin, 2006).

SCHOOLS, IMMIGRANT CHILDREN, AND SECOND LANGUAGE ACQUISITION

In this book, we are concerned with contributing to the understanding of the progress made by children in acquiring a second language in a linguistically isolated school in which they had very few opportunities to interact with fluent English speakers other than in a many-to-one ratio. In carrying out an intervention in which children regularly worked one-on-one with ordinary speakers of English, we hoped to increase our knowledge about the ways that a second language is used in interaction while it is being acquired and about changes in the participatory/interactional competence of children in an L2 as they engaged in various activities with trusted adults over time. We wanted to understand how youngsters moved or did not move from limited to fuller participation in interactions, how they interpreted cues about ways of speaking and behaving with members of the broader English-speaking society, and whether and to what degree they appropriated the utterances of their interlocutors. While not our main goal, we also expected to provide some evidence of the ways in which children's linguistic system changed over time.

In reviewing the literature on both second language acquisition and second language pedagogy, I have suggested that we have limited knowledge about second language acquisition in children and that we have very modest evidence about the role of instruction in the second language acquisition process for children. As states move forward to draft NCLB-influenced policies and practices that support ELL children's second language development and subject matter knowledge, we believe that it is essential for policy makers, researchers, and practitioners to have realistic expectations about the kinds of attainment that are possible for children under different kinds of circumstances. If we are to assess the development of English language proficiency and provide support for such development, it is imperative that we do not penalize children for not making the kinds of progress that may only be the product of the imagination of monolingual policy makers or well-meaning, standards-setting panels and not supported by research on children's L2 development in real-life settings. Academic language—especially if it is defined as nativelike oral and written production—may not be attainable under the best of circumstances as quickly or as completely as might be desired by those who hope to accelerate the acquisition of English in immigrant-origin children.

In the chapter that follows, we describe details of the design experiment that we refer to as *One-on-One English.* We describe the school and setting in which the intervention took place and provide information about the design experiment itself including our local intervention theory, our interpretive framework, and the ways in which our everyday activities led us to modify and rethink both our practice and our theoretical assumptions.

CHAPTER 2

One-on-One English

A Design Experiment

THE SETTING

Golden Hills is a pleasant, well-maintained elementary school that is part of a small school district serving approximately 5,000 students, 69% of whom were classified as English language learners in 2003–04 when the study began. The school shares a campus with an upper elementary and middle school, and during the years of the study (2003–2008), it went from a K–3 to a K–5 configuration. At the time that the study began, the percentage of English language learners at Golden Hills had increased from 84% in 2001–02 to 93% in 2003–04, reflecting the growing immigrant population in the community. In 2003–04, 87% of students were Spanish-speaking ELLs; the very few ELLs from other language backgrounds spoke Tongan (4%), Hindi (1%), or Samoan (1%) as their primary language. At Golden Hills, ELLs made little progress in acquiring English. A very small number of students were redesignated as fluent English speakers according to state criteria. During the entire period of the study, redesignation rates ranged from a high of five students in 2006–07 to a low of zero in 2004–05.

Given that nearly all of Golden Hills students are English language learners, the school provides two different instructional programs, both of which are designed for ELL students: (1) Structured English Immersion (SEI) in which academic instruction takes place in English using SDAIE strategies intended to make it comprehensible to children learning English; and (2) a Spanish bilingual program in which students receive ELD, some academic subjects through the primary language, and some subjects through English.

In 1998 California voters approved Proposition 227, a voter initiative requiring that English language learners be placed in English-medium classes. Blaming low achievement among ELLs on "experimental language programs" (California Secretary of State, 1998), Proposition 227 intended to eliminate bilingual education. However, the law did allow parents to sign annual waivers if they wanted their child to receive primary language instruction. In 2003–04 approximately one fourth of Golden Hills students were enrolled in the bilingual program and three fourths were in the SEI program. By 2007–08 the bilingual program had grown, now serving 45% of Golden Hills students.

According to Proposition 227, schools were to place ELLs in SEI classrooms for "a temporary transition period not normally to exceed one year." After this period, students were to be exited into mainstream classes, in which they would be taught along with native English speakers. The expectation underlying the proposition was that students would acquire sufficient English to succeed in mainstream classes after one year, based on an assumption that children acquire second languages quickly and with ease. Despite the expectations outlined in Proposition 227, most English language learners remain in SEI classes for much longer than one year. In reality, only 2.5% of ELLs in California are redesignated as "Fluent English Proficient" after one year, and Parrish, Perez, Merickel, and Linquanti (2006) estimate that 75% of ELLs in the state are still not redesignated after 5 years. At Golden Hills, all students are enrolled in SEI or bilingual classes through fifth grade, and the school does not offer any "mainstream" classes.

During the 5 years of *One-on-One English*, Golden Hills was typical of the underresourced public schools described in the case of *Williams v. California* (2004), a case brought against the state of California on behalf of students across the state (California Department of Education, 2008). This case argued that the state of California did not give millions of students—mainly low-income students, immigrant students, and students of color—the basic tools of a decent education. In particular, the *Williams* case pointed out that many teachers lack sufficient training, and classrooms often do not have enough textbooks and instructional materials for students. Many of these underresourced schools, including Golden Hills, are in "Program Improvement" status for failing to meet targets for adequate yearly progress (AYP) under No Child Left Behind. Golden Hills was first designated as a Program Improvement school in 2003–04 when only 4% of third graders scored proficient in English Language Arts on the California Standards Test. By 2007–08, the school was in its fourth year of Program Improvement, having achieved its targets for improvement only once, during the 2006–07 school year.

In addition to establishing accountability measures such as AYP, through the Reading First program, NCLB also required schools to spend federal money to purchase reading programs "based on scientifically based reading research" (U.S. Department of Education, 2002) As Cummins (2007) explains, the criteria used by Reading First to evaluate programs emphasized sequential, systematic, and explicit instruction in phonics rules.[1] The move toward mandating systematic phonics instruction at a federal level paralleled an earlier and highly politicized shift in reading instruction toward phonics that took place in California in the 1990s (Lemann, 1997).[2] At the time of our study, California districts could choose between two state-adopted reading/language arts curricula, one of which, *Open Court Reading*, was used at Golden Hills. According to California's Reading First plan, teachers were required to spend one hour in kindergarten and 2.5 hours in first through third grade teaching the adopted curriculum.[3]

In addition to the reading/language arts block, the state also mandated a separate English Language Development (ELD) period, which during the study was 30 minutes and is now 60 minutes (Thompson, 2009). During ELD, Golden Hills students within a given grade level were grouped in leveled classes with students at similar English proficiency levels. As Thompson points out, the policies and curricula regarding ELD parallel the movement toward explicit and systematic instruction in reading. Both reading/language arts and ELD instruction is to be "explicit, sequential, linguistically logical, and systematic" (California State Board of Education, 2007, p. 292, 298). However, this ELD policy has been mandated statewide without a clear research backing and despite many unanswered questions regarding the effectiveness of explicit language instruction with elementary-school-aged English language learners (Thompson, 2009).

GOLDEN HILLS ELEMENTARY AND *ONE-ON-ONE ENGLISH*

As we pointed out in the introduction to this volume, *One-on-One English* was designed as an after-school intervention program in which volunteers (both university undergraduates and community members) provided elementary-age English language learners with individual access to English. The program took place 4 days a week for a total period of 5 years, and it involved a group of committed individuals including the project leader, three doctoral students, five undergraduates who served as volunteer coordinators, four teachers who served as project liaisons, and a large number of college-age and community volunteers. It also involved two supportive school principals, a sympathetic district administrator who encouraged our efforts, the staff of a campus service learning center, and the generous support of a community foundation. In retrospect, it was an enormous undertaking that took time, energy, and enthusiasm, and that, from time to time, seemed extraordinarily challenging.

During any one of the 5 years that the project was in operation, visitors to Golden Hills Elementary who wanted to see how One-one-One English worked could have gone into one of the several classrooms in which child and volunteer dyads were engaged with books, games, puzzles, and other materials. One impression they would come away with as they observed might be that each room was noisy and lively. They would hear laughter, shrieks of excitement, singing, and occasional games of Simon Says. The children, all between 5 and 8 years old, would display a variety of attitudes and behaviors. Some children would be serious and others playful; some would be eager to look at new books, and others would be ready to draw, wander outside, or engage the volunteer in other activities. Most, however, would be enjoying the experience of having the undivided attention of an English-speaking adult who appeared interested, caring, and eager to support and applaud the most minimal utterance made in English.

The volunteers would be trying hard to keep children interested in the colorful books they had selected to use with their young buddies. They would exaggerate, repeat, and pantomime. Some would walk outside with their child and talk about playground equipment, arriving school buses, and the activities of other youngsters preparing to go home. Some would use books that they themselves had purchased, crayons, drawing paper, and other materials that they hoped would engage their young and often quite tired English language learners.

Project staff would be easy to identify. Several would be circulating among the dyads aiming video cameras with long microphones at each pair. They would be capturing the interaction, especially the language and the demeanor of the children. From time to time, they would stop to offer just-in-time support to a struggling volunteer. They would make sure that things ran smoothly, that every child was paired with an adult, that interactions involved as much language as possible, and that, when the activities ended, children were delivered to the after-school program or to waiting parents who had come to pick them up.

If they stayed a little bit longer, visitors might also see that at the end of 45 minutes, volunteers would gather their materials and walk to the school parking lot for a ride back to the university campus or to their homes in the neighboring community. Project staff would help tidy up the classroom, lock up if necessary, and chat momentarily with other project staff about things that they had noticed and needed to attend to. If one of the visitors was a fellow graduate student or another researcher, project staff might share the fact that, before the day ended, they would all send brief observation summaries to each other about the day's events and carefully describe what they had noticed about children and their volunteers.

What would not be evident to the casual visitor is that *One-on-One English* was structured as a *design experiment*, that is, as a formative, exploratory study (Barab & Squire, 2004; Brown, 1992; Reinking & Bradley, 2008; Van den Akker, Gravemeijer, McKenney, & Nieveen, 2006), with the following objectives:

1. Implement a particular educational intervention involving one-on-one interactions between ordinary English speakers and young ELLs
2. Study and document the intervention over time
3. Refine and redesign procedures and key aspects of the intervention over the life of the project, documenting the effect of each change
4. Carry out an extensive study of the entire project and its effects at the end of the implementation period that would examine both the initial hypotheses about the impact of one-on-one interactions on children's English language development as well as the effectiveness of various pedagogies and practices

DESIGN RESEARCH

Because of the importance of design research to our work, we begin the description of our intervention with an explanation of what design experiments are and how they work so that readers can understand and follow our discussion of the various phases of *One-on-One English,* our account of the different modifications that we made to our procedures over time, and the procedures that we followed in simultaneously implementing and analyzing our practice.

The term *design research,* according to Van den Akker et al. (2006b), is commonly used for a family of research approaches that are specifically interventionist, iterative, process oriented, and both utility and theory oriented. Barab and Squire (2004) define *education design research* as "a series of approaches with the intent of producing new theories, artifacts, and practices that account for and potentially impact teaching and learning in naturalistic settings" (p. 2). Design research (also known as *formative research, formative evaluation,* and *engineering research*) does not focus on isolated variables, nor does it strive to arrive at context-free generalizations. Its goals are quite different from those of experimental or quasi-experimental research (Brown, 1992). Rather, as Walker (2006) points out, design research begins with a researcher's analysis of a learning problem or a problem of practice that leads to specific ideas about appropriate interventions. Such studies are not designed to test theories, although theory does guide the design of interventions and their particular features. The point of design research, however, is to create interventions that allow researchers to study how students respond to particular features of the intervention using a range of indicators, including ethnographic observations, videoanalysis, artifact gathering, and the like,

FIGURE 2.1. Predictive and Design Research Approaches in Educational Technology Research (Reeves, 2006)

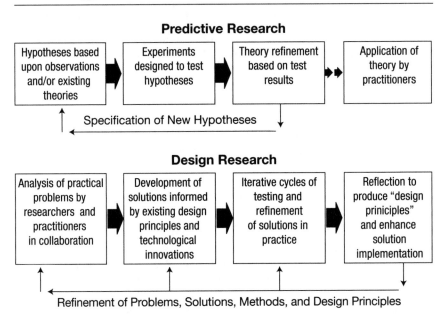

that are specific to the context and to the goals of the intervention. Design studies, moreover, typically develop their own indicators of learning because traditional tests are too imprecise to test for the kinds of learning that researchers envision.

Figure 2.1 contrasts design research (in the lower half of the graphic) with experiments designed to tests hypotheses (in the upper half of the graphic). Design research involves the development of solutions based on informed conjectures about a possible learning process and about various means that might support that learning process. It also involves an implementation that consists of iterative cycles of testing and refinement of the solutions being implemented. Such iterative cycles are informed by an ongoing analytical process that feeds back into the design of the intervention.

For Gravenmeijer and Cobb (2006), design research involves three phases: Phase 1–preparing for the experiment; Phase 2–the design experiment itself; and Phase 3–retrospective analysis. The three phases as described by Gravenjeijer and Cobb (2006) are presented in Figure 2.2. A key step in Phase 1 of design research is the development of an implementation or local instructional theory. Local implementation or instructional theories draw from a variety of sources including available research literature, but often

FIGURE 2.2. The Three Phases of Design Experiments

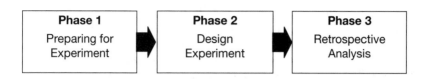

involve tinkering with and adapting practices, materials, and instructional approaches in order to reach the desired learning outcomes. It is important to point out that in design studies the goal is not to demonstrate that the researchers' initial local instructional theories worked, but rather to develop a clear understanding of how the initial instructional theory worked, or did not work, and how modifications of the local instructional theory and practices impacted student learning.

Phase 2 of design research involves "a cyclic process of (re)designing and testing instructional activities and other aspects of the design" (Gravenmeijer & Cobb, 2006, p. 24). The point is to examine student progress in order to improve the local learning theory by conjecturing about the effects of various modifications on this progress and by implementing appropriate modifications. A key aspect of the examination of the design features as they are implemented is the use of an interpretive framework that can help make sense of the complexity of the events present in day-to-day practices. This framework is used to systematically interpret key elements of the intervention environment as well as student progress.

Phase 3 involves a retrospective analysis of the design experiment that examines all of the data gathered during the entire period of the implementation of the intervention. The goal of the analysis is to further develop the local instructional theory, to examine and scrutinize initial key assumptions, and to place the intervention in a broader context by discussing the particular events examined in the intervention as exemplars of other similar events and cases. Design research aims, not for models suitable for replicability in the standard understanding of that term, but for descriptions that can inform the adaptation of interventions to other contexts and settings.

According to Barab and Squire (2004), design research endeavors to provide evidence of what was accomplished in the design study's implementation to meet local needs and to document demonstrable changes in the specific context of the study. Additionally, however, "design research *requires more than simply showing a particular design works but demands that the researcher* (move beyond a particular design exemplar to) *generate evidence-based claims about learning that address contemporary theoretical issues and further the theoretical knowledge of the field*" (pp. 5–6, italics in original).

One-on-One English as a Design Experiment

As we pointed out in the introduction, in the case of *One-on-One English*, the "learning problem" or the "problem of practice to be solved" involved providing access to English to K–3 Latino students enrolled in an elementary school where 93% of the students were classified as English language learners. Specifically, our research was aimed at increasing our understanding of the process of L2 acquisition in young children when they had frequent and regular access to English. Drawing from L2 acquisition theory, primarily on work conducted by Wong Fillmore (Wong Fillmore, 1976, 1982, 1985a, 1985b, 1991), the project sought to generate knowledge in the following areas:

- Whether and to what degree children in grades K–3 enrolled in linguistically hypersegregated school settings could grow in their English language proficiency when given regular one-on-one access to English by "ordinary speakers" of the language
- Whether ordinary speakers of English could be prepared to provide "rich language input" to young children who have little proficiency in English.

Design and Redesign Over a 5-Year Period

In the sections that follow, we describe the principal elements of the experiment as it unfolded over a 5-year period. The challenge, as Barab and Squire (2004) point out, is "to characterize the complexity, fragility, messiness, and eventual solidity of the design and doing so in a way that will be valuable to others" (p. 4). We thus offer some details of the implementation and include some particulars about the challenges faced in organizing and running a volunteer program designed to support elementary school children in their English language development. We do so in order to convey a more realistic sense of work of the type we conducted that, as opposed to neatly controlled experimental research, was constantly responding to a wide variety of pressures. As Wells (1985) notes, in presenting long-term research there is always a tension between including the "muddle and misadventure" (p. 1)–which were only a part of the total experience–and offering a traditional style of presentation suggesting that everything went smoothly and according to plan. In the case of design experiments, it is our position that conveying something of the day-to-day experience is essential.

Figure 2.3 presents the three phases of the design approach used in *One-on-One English*. In this figure, we have included some details about (1) the development of solutions and (2) the iterative cycles of the testing and re-

FIGURE 2.3. The *One-on-One English* Design Experiment

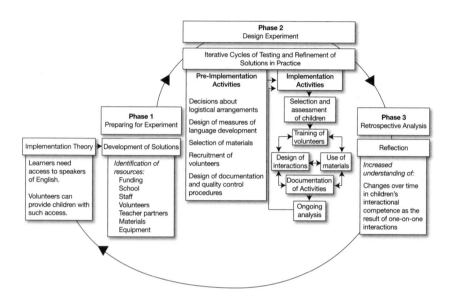

finement of our solution. It is important to stress that during each year of the project, the various implementation activities listed were adapted and redesigned frequently as a result of our documentation and ongoing analysis of activities. Additionally, the outcome of each year's cumulative analysis directly informed the modification of the project's design that was implemented the following year. The full retrospective analysis was carried out at the end of a 5-year period.

The Study's Implementation Theory

Our implementation theory involved two elements. The first element drew directly from existing hypotheses in the second language acquisition field and from the work of Wong Fillmore (1991) who emphasized that in order to acquire English two conditions were necessary:

- Learners must have available to them speakers of English who know the language well enough to provide both access to English and help for learning it.
- The social setting must bring learners and English speakers into frequent enough contact to make language learning possible.

The second element involved an informed conjecture about the activity of "volunteer assistance" as a means of supporting the second language acquisition process in children. Specifically, we conjectured that by bringing together volunteers and children regularly and frequently, access to English for young learners could be provided if they engaged in the kinds of interactions that could make language learning possible. Volunteer assistance itself was seen as entailing actions that could be construed broadly as "teaching," including instructing, explaining, guiding, testing, questioning, assisting children in making connections, expanding, and scaffolding. These activities, except for the teacher-to-learner ratio, were considered to be similar to those carried out in school classrooms. However, in the case of one-on-one activities, volunteer assistance was viewed as instantiating particular identities for both participants engaged in the one-on-one activity. For the adult, these identities included "more knowledgeable other" and "caring adult," and, for the children, possible identities might include "child," "less knowledgeable other," "novice," and "non-English speaker."

Following Ochs (2002), we viewed action, stance, identity, and activity as interdependent, and activities as entailing particular actions. In the case of volunteer-child sessions in our cultural setting, then, we saw children as expected to display certain kinds of stances and acts, including listening attentively, following volunteers' directives, responding to questions, engaging in activities structured or planned by tutors, engaging with materials selected for joint attention, and cooperating in the interaction as designed by the person in the role of more knowledgeable other. What children engaged in such interactions could not do—if they were to be seen as active participants in the activity—was to refuse to cooperate by not engaging in the activities planned by the tutor and by not responding to questions, suggestions, or requests for joint attention.

From our perspective, actions, stances, identities, and activities that are part of volunteer assistance activities are seen as similar in important ways to those present in one-on-one interactions between children and parents who are engaged in "teaching" or socializing their own offspring. According to Scollon (2002), in engaging in interactions with their young children, parents construct them as (1) socially competent actors who have intentions and social graces and (2) language learners who can learn both language labels as well as their meaning. In *One-on-One English*, we hoped to create activity settings, defined by Gallimore and Tharp (1988) as "contexts in which collaborative interaction, intersubjectivity, and assisted performance occur" (p. 72), that would engage K–3 Latino children in interactions with competent speakers of English. We expected that these interactions—while not identical to those that take place between parents and their young children—would be reminiscent of them. We specifically envisioned interactions with supporting adults committed to these children's acquisition of English and to giving them access to an Anglophone middle-class range of materials, behaviors, topics, and world knowledge considered appropriate for children. This is an important element because, in comparison to other interactions found in classrooms including group work or dyadic pairings between peers in which learners may have little investment in their peers' growth and development, the identities afforded or entailed by "volunteer assistance" include the clear role of supporting adult. Our position, then, was that one-on-one interactions could provide L2 Latino children with access to "caring" adults focused on playing the role of more knowledgeable others who could both monitor a child's current skills and support or scaffold the child's extension of knowledge. According to Gallimore and Tharp (1988), assistance by such adults includes modeling, contingency management, feedback, questioning, and cognitive structuring. We conjectured, then, that in middle-class undergraduate and minority-ELL child interactions, L2 learners would have the opportunity of participating as novices in joint activities with competent members of the English-speaking community, that is, with adult knowledgeable "ordinary speakers of English" who had committed their time to playing the role of more capable others.

The Study's Interpretive Framework

The interpretative framework used to examine the evidence of change (i.e., growth and development in the acquisition of English by K–3 children) was one in which the focus was on *participatory competence* rather then on the acquisition of the linguistic system. We sought to examine the ways in which children would begin to function as members of an English-speaking community by engaging in interactions with English-speaking volunteers. In designing our work, we sought to enrich the field's existing understanding of L2 acquisition by young children and to advance credible assertions about the ways in which young children function in one-on-one interactions with limited language, how they grow in their ability to participate in such interactions, and, to a lesser degree, what kinds of growing participatory competence are reflected by changes in the linguistic system. Additionally, as applied researchers who have a commitment to improving practice, we also hoped that our work would inform both policies and practices about direct oral language instruction programs currently being implemented in elementary school classrooms (Saunders, Foorman, & Carson, 2006). The study's interpretive framework directly informed the design of our quality control procedures, the documentation of volunteer and child interactions, and our ongoing analysis.

PREIMPLEMENTATION ACTIVITIES

As shown in Figure 2.3 above, the preimplementation phase of the program included several key elements: (1) making decisions about initial logistical arrangements; (2) designing measures of language development that would allow us to obtain baseline information about changes in children's language over time; (3) collecting materials around which volunteers and children would interact; (4) designing a procedure for recruiting volunteers; and (5) designing quality control, documentation, and ongoing analytical procedures.

Initial Logistical Arrangements

We were fortunate in obtaining permission to work at Golden Hills Elementary and to work with a principal who was a former bilingual education teacher and deeply committed to the education of English language learners. After initial conversations in which we explained our objectives, the principal and school district personnel agreed to allow us to work at Golden Hills and to implement the program. The school agreed to identify children in need of additional English support, to make quiet space available for assessing children's language as needed, to assist us in contacting parents in order to obtain their informed consent, and to provide classroom space where volunteers and children could meet and interact comfortably. Together with the principal, we determined that an after-school implementation was best suited for the project because it did not require children to be pulled out during the school day. Except for minor logistical details, including the improvement of our procedures designed to guide teacher nomination of students and the selection of a liaison teacher to work directly with the project, there were not many changes made in our arrangements with the school during the 5-year project period.

The selection of children for participation in the program was based on teacher recommendation. Program staff gave teachers guidelines for recommending students (which were modified and improved over time). These guidelines suggested that teachers use students' most recent CELDT scores and information on how long the student had been in the country to help guide their recommendations. The guidelines also described the purposes of the program and described what the program did and did not do. Because there were a limited number of volunteers, there were a limited number of students that could participate in the program.

During the first year, teachers at Golden Hills Elementary recommended ELLs at the beginning and early intermediate levels of English language development to participate in the project. Language assessments were administered (audiotaped and videotaped) for every ELL recommended to the program. These assessments helped document the English language competence demonstrated by the participating children so that we could study their language development and growth in English over time. They also allowed us to select children whom we identified as needing particular help in English. We did not select children suggested by teachers who were in the high intermediate range of English language development or those who were identified as needing special attention for behavioral or special education challenges.

In subsequent years we enlisted the assistance of teacher liaisons (one each year). We relied heavily on them to communicate with other teachers about the program and to make clear to their colleagues the language characteristics of the students for whom the program was designed. During the 5-year period of the project we focused on serving children enrolled in kindergarten through second grade who were newly arrived in the country and who had little access to English in their family. In several cases we worked with children in third grade who were identified as in particular need of English language enrichment.

The Design of a Measure of Language Development

One of the key tasks undertaken in the preimplementation phase of the project involved the design of a procedure for measuring or assessing children's language. These assessments were seen as essential in helping us document the changes in the English competencies of participating children and in allowing us to select children whom we identified as needing particular help in acquiring English.

In designing a measure of English language development for the children involved in *One-on-One English*, we were mindful of the challenges surrounding the assessment of language proficiency in general and of the need to obtain a sample of children's language behavior that would allow us to reach conclusions about their initial receptive and productive proficiencies in English as well as about these same proficiencies at the end of the intervention period. We elected to develop our own elicitation procedure, rather than using available language assessment instruments, because we sought to describe the characteristics of the language children produced at a particular point in time (Time 1) and to compare it with the language they produced after having been involved in the intervention (Time 2). We decided to develop a procedure that was diagnostic, that required a qualitative interpretation involving transcription and analysis of linguistic characteristics, and deliberately did not result in the calculation of general mean scores of L2 proficiency. Influenced also by the work of Bachman and Palmer (1996),[5] we were particularly concerned with developing a procedure that was authentic (i.e., that corresponded to the language used by children in schools and classrooms) and interactive (i.e., that called upon children's language knowledge, topical knowledge, metacognitive abilities, and affective schemata). Additionally, we wanted to ensure a close relationship between what Bachman and Palmer have referred to as "non-test language use" (i.e., the language used by children in school) as well as the language expected by the California English Language Development Test (CELDT)[6] and the language required of children by our assessment procedure.

Given the focus of the intervention program–the development of receptive and productive oral English proficiencies as a first step in preparing to read in English–we identified three aspects of English language acquisition that we viewed as central to children's ability both to interact with English-speaking individuals in schools and classrooms and to engage in and enjoy interactive book reading in English. These aspects are interpersonal interactive language, high-frequency school vocabulary, and story comprehension.

In order to assess these three different aspects, we developed an informal elicitation procedure that sought to determine the degree to which children would show growth in the following abilities:

- Comprehend personal information questions (*What's your name? How old are you?*)
- Produce responses to personal information questions
- Demonstrate comprehension of common, high-frequency vocabulary by pointing to illustrations
- Produce common, high-frequency vocabulary to identify objects in illustrations
- Comprehend a story narrated with the aid of colorful book illustrations
- Produce a narrative of the same story using book illustrations

The elicitation procedure was initially divided into three separate segments or phases as illustrated in Figure 2.4. The key difference between the procedures of the first and subsequent years was that different materials were used for Segment 2 (the assessment of vocabulary knowledge) and for Segment 3 (the assessment of story comprehension and production). After Year 3, the assessment of vocabulary knowledge was abandoned. More details about the assessment procedure and the modifications made to the basic procedure are included in Chapter 5.

The procedures were designed for use as pre- and postassessments for each child at the beginning and the end of each academic year. They were administered by project personnel following a general script that included

FIGURE 2.4. Elicitation Procedure, Year 1

		Materials Used (First Year)
Segment 1	Personal information questions	List of personal questions to be asked
Segment 2	Vocabulary knowledge	Illustrations from children's magazine showing common objects
Segment 3	Story comprehension and production	Three children's stories (*The Three Bears, The Three Little Pigs, Little Red Riding Hood*) from which the child chose a story

questions and tasks but allowed individual examiners to adapt their language to the child's level of comprehension. Since at the time of the administration of the initial assessments, children were not acquainted with project personnel, an effort was made to set them at ease before beginning the assessment by explaining in Spanish that we were interested in finding out how much English they already knew. As was previously mentioned, language assessments were administered (audiotaped and videotaped) for every ELL recommended to the program.

Selection of Materials

As we pointed out in the introduction to this book, *One-on-One English* was established in response to an immediate need for a campus volunteer program that could address the needs of young English language learners as they began to read in English, a language that they neither spoke nor understood. *One-on-One English*, then, was initially conceptualized as providing a possible bridge to scripted reading programs, like *Open Court*, for those children who were monolingual Spanish-speaking and who did not have enough vocabulary in English to begin effective phonics instruction. Because of this early preoccupation, in the beginning the program brought together a collection of colorful and well-illustrated texts that had been successfully used by an early literacy program with families and young children in surrounding counties. The collection of texts was seen as a vehicle around which volunteers could interact in meaningful ways with ELL students in order to develop their English, their background knowledge, and their interest in reading. By focusing on preparing children to read to (or to explore books), we hoped that volunteers would engage in activities with ELL students in which children would have access to rich language and in which reading would come to be seen as purposeful activity in which sharing excitement over stories and characters is essential.

Recruitment of Volunteers

During the first three years of the program, we established an ongoing collaboration with the campus service learning center and with members of their staff, who had much experience in recruiting undergraduate volunteers. *One-on-One English* was featured along with other campus programs and publicized as an activity that welcomed volunteers interested in English language learners. The center provided working space for volunteer coordinators, for training sessions, and for a few members of the program staff. It was an important collaboration, and we learned much about the challenges of managing campus volunteer programs.

Over the life of the program we continued to work with undergraduate volunteers; however, during the last 2 years of the program, we also worked to recruit volunteers from the community. We established a working relationship with a local church and were joined by volunteers from this organization during the last two years of the project. We also created a Web site that was used in introducing potential community volunteers to *One-on-One English*. The Web site included videotapes of volunteers and children working together as well as a presentation of the goals and purposes of the program. It also included a link to another program Web site that contained a volunteer manual entitled *Activity and Interaction Guide,* which we used routinely in our training. This site contained many video examples of what we considered to be "good practice," as well as multiple strategies for working well with young ELL children.

IMPLEMENTATION ACTIVITIES

Implementation activities included selecting and assessing children, training volunteers, designing the structure of one-on-one sessions, using materials to maximize the use of language in one-on-one sessions, documenting all activities, and carrying out ongoing analyses. As noted in Figure 2.3 above, these activities were modified and refined frequently as a result of our ongoing analysis. We discuss several elements of the implementation activities here and include details about other elements in the chapters that follow.

Training of Volunteers

The first year of the project we undertook the teaching of a service learning course directed at undergraduates. Entitled Critical Perspectives in Tutoring and Teaching ELLs, the course explored a variety of topics: the English language needs of immigrant children and their parents, disadvantaged children and school achievement, language and inequality in schools, second language acquisition, the process of learning to read for second language learners, the role of the volunteer in the acquisition of language and literacy, developing rapport and trust with English buddies and their families, and the process of becoming self-aware of any internalized deficit ideologies that might impact on interactions with ELLs. The students were required to complete four field assignments that took them into schools to engage in interactions with ELLs in classroom settings.

While the teaching of the course was a good idea, we soon determined that we would not be able to attract the number of volunteers that we needed to run the program if we imposed a course requirement for all volunteers. We therefore moved to developing and implementing training procedures for volunteers that would take place during the entire academic year. At the start of each quarter, participating volunteers attended a training meeting before they began working with an ELL. During this training, they were introduced to the program, its goals and objectives, and the activities that they could carry out while working with their students. Footage from video recordings made of child-volunteer interactions during previous years was edited to provide examples of "successful" interactions between volunteers and ELLs and to demonstrate techniques that volunteers could use to scaffold rich language input.

Biweekly meetings were held during each quarter that supported volunteers on an ongoing basis. During these meetings, volunteers debriefed about their experiences working with their English buddy; watched and discussed segments of video that depicted their and others' interactions with ELLs; and received additional training around the topics that project personnel, from their observations of the interactions on site, considered necessary.

In addition to centering their interactions on books, volunteers were guided in experimenting with the use of a variety of games and puzzles and other materials. During the training, project personnel explained to volunteers how these materials could be used for the purposes of providing language input. Project staff designed handouts aimed at explaining the "dos and don'ts" of using particular materials with ELLs, selected video of "successful interactions" that highlighted using particular materials with ELLs, and explained through demonstrations the problems with using particular games with the students.

Project staff encountered a number of challenges in the training and supporting of volunteers. Our trainings for and support of the volunteers focused on explaining the importance of rich input for young ELLs and showing the volunteers what rich input looked and sounded like. Program staff showed video examples of peers and program staff working with students, created role playing activities for volunteers to "practice" providing rich input, asked strong volunteers to share their activities and strategies with the whole group, and provided countless pointers and the dos and don'ts of what the rich language and interactions should look like. Despite the many ways we tried to show what rich input looks like, we found that many volunteers had a difficult time imagining and ultimately executing interactions that provided young ELLs with access to rich input or encouraged them to produce and practice their developing English.

A volunteer training manual designed to guide activities and interactions was compiled and distributed and later made available online to all volunteers. Additionally, project staff focused on close supervision of interactions at the school in order to provide just-in-time interventions and support to volunteers on site. The experience of developing the online *Activity and Interaction Guide* illustrated the value of developing training materials that "showed" volunteers effective ways of working with children. The use of videotapes at training meetings made clear that volunteers needed to see—rather than read about—the most effective ways of supporting students' English language development. Moreover, the illustration of procedures and materials using videotapes had to be supported with texts that guided volunteers in identifying exemplary practices. We will say more about the challenge of monitoring and identifying successful child-volunteer interactions in the several chapters that follow.

Use of Materials

During the first year of the program, we were fortunate in securing a donation of many of the books and materials used by the local early literacy program, many of which had a multicultural orientation. However, within a very short time it became clear that not all beautifully illustrated books with ethnic themes lent themselves to the use of rich language during volunteer-child interactions. After the first year's implementation, books that appeared to work best were identified as ones that allowed volunteers to provide children with extensive language input because they told a story, had illustrations that supported interactions between children and volunteers, allowed the story to be inferred from the pictures, and connected to the prior knowledge of ELL children.

During the next 4 years of the project, we continued to explore the use of various types of materials that could support good interactions between

FIGURE 2.5. Materials Used in the Project Over a Five-Year Period

Year 1 2003–04	Year 2 2004–05	Years 3, 4, and 5 2005–06, 06–07, 07–08
Materials		
Books	Books Puzzles Vocabulary cards Lotto games Wordless books Rhyming games Big books Sequencing cards	Books Vocabulary cards Lotto games Wordless books Puppets Vocabulary mats Sequencing cards Book sequencing cards
Rationale		
One-on-one meaningful interactions around books	More materials would provide volunteers and students more choice during the 45-minute session	Add materials that would support interpersonal language, vocabulary, and development of narrative skills; remove materials that did not support rich language from the volunteer or students

volunteers and their English language buddies and experimented with the use of a variety of games and puzzles and other activities representing a wide variety of genres: lotto games, including animal lotto and around the house lotto; concentration, card games, including Old Maid; floor puzzles; and four-scene sequencing cards.

Figure 2.5 presents an overview of the materials used in the project, of the modifications and changes made to the types of materials we provided for volunteers, and a brief comment of our the reasons for including and excluding particular materials.

Quality Control, Documentation, and Ongoing Analytical Procedures

Quality control and documentation procedures were established that were designed to allow us both to monitor child-volunteer interactions and to create a record for subsequent analysis. Project staff (Valdés, Moorthy, Capitelli, Alvarez, and volunteer coordinators) used handheld video cameras with external shotgun microphones to record interactions between volunteers and children. Staff rotated between the various classrooms used for the program and videotaped different pairs at various points during the 45-minute period. On a day-to-day basis, project personnel sought to identify practices that were successful in providing ELLs with quality exposure to English and troubleshoot problems that volunteers encountered in engaging their learners. In order to maintain quality, they often offered tips about how best to talk to and interact in English with the children and modeled ways of using the various materials available for project use.

Each summer of the period that the project was in operation, project personnel worked to carry out an appraisal of the following dimensions of the program:

1. The degree to which language growth and development could be identified in participating ELLs in one-on-one interactions
2. The degree to which "successful" volunteer and ELL buddy interactions could be identified
3. The effectiveness of our methods for preparing ordinary speakers of English to provide English language input
4. The effectiveness of the materials used in the project

The data examined by the team consisted of audio- and videotapes of pre- and postassessments; videotapes of everyday interactions among volunteers and ELLs; field notes written by project staff of their observations after all site visits; and taped interviews with participating volunteers. Our analytical procedures were developed to inform us about both the theoretical aspects of the project (i.e., children's language development and characteristics of language interactions that led to language growth) as well as about the modifications that needed to be made in the training of volunteers, selection of materials, and other project details. Our yearly summer analysis of the project included the transcription of selected pre- and postassessments of the children and the development and use of a coding scheme designed to describe and categorize a number of the aspects of the interactions between volunteers and ELLs. At different points in the project, transcripts were subjected to various analyses to identify key characteristics of language growth and development including increased use of English utterances, increasing the mean length of utterance (MLU), increased use of appropriate elliptical responses in interaction, increased use of full sentences (both flawed and nativelike), and a growing ability to narrate stories modeled by the adult volunteer.

A large amount of project staff attention was given to the analysis of the videotaped interactions between children and volunteers. We struggled to identify (and to code videotapes for) what we could agree were "successful" interactions between children and adults. We worked to recognize key characteristics that resulted in children's remaining engaged in interactions as well as activities that resulted in children's shutting down, becoming distracted, and so on. We noted, for example, that activities that attempted to "teach" language directly led to children becoming easily bored or distracted and that the use of questions designed to engage children with a topic (e.g., Have you ever seen a swimming pool? What is the best thing you have done at a beach?) only led to silence from children when they were not familiar with the topic, could not understand the question, or did not have the language to respond to the question. Our views of successful and unsuccessful interactions evolved over time and were modified by our tracking of a group of children that we invited to continue in the project so that we could follow their progress from one year to another. At the end of each summer, our perspectives on successful interactions, including our views on the types of materials that supported such interactions, directly impacted the procedures that we used in volunteer training the following academic year.

RETROSPECTIVE ANALYSIS

At the end of the fifth year of implementation, we began the full retrospective analysis of what was learned over the course of the previous 5 years. This analysis focused on the following data:

- Children's interactions with their volunteers in all sessions for which we had videotaped records
- Recordings of the language produced by children in pre- and postassessments in which they were involved

For this detailed analysis, we selected a group of nine focal students who had each been in the program for a period of 2 or 3 years. It is important for us to stress that when we designed the project, our focus was on working with the "neediest" children. What this meant in practice, is that during the first two years of the project, we worked exclusively with youngsters in the school who were identified by their teachers as newly arrived and/or as having little access to English outside of school from brothers, sisters, or other relatives in the area. Moreover, because of the large number of children who fit these categories, we did not continue to work with students for a second year if they had already received our services for an entire academic year. During the latter 3 years of the project, however, it became apparent to us that we needed to gather data on children over time so that we might obtain a more extensive view of the ways that the children grew in their ability to participate in interactions with ordinary adult speakers of English. We therefore decided to allow a number of children to continue in the program so that we could examine changes in their English over time.

Of the children who participated in the program beyond a single year, we selected nine youngsters for whom we had the most extensive data. These were youngsters who attended faithfully and whose families remained in the area. Figure 2.6 includes a list of these children, the grade of each child at the time of entry into the program, their total participation time, and the dates of their participation.

It is important for us to point out that we have limited information about the children's access to English outside of school. What we do know is that, because children were residing in the United States in a context in which English is the societal language, their contact with English went much beyond what took place in our program and in the school setting. Although children were residents of a predominantly Spanish-speaking immigrant community in which most individuals were living in what the U.S. census refers to as linguistically isolated households,[7] several were part of large extended families including aunts, uncles, and cousins who had been in this country for many years and who probably used English to some degree in their everyday lives. We do not claim, therefore, that growth in children's interactive proficiencies were exclusively or even primarily the result of their participation in the program. What we do claim is that their involvement in *One-on-One English* allowed us to observe them carefully and to document the ways in which they could function as participants in conversational exchanges with English-speaking adults, as well as the manner in which both subtle and more obvious changes in their interactional proficiencies became manifest over time.

Analysis of Interactions and Conversations with Young English Language Learners

The retrospective analysis of the conversational interactions, exchanges, moves, and communicative acts that were carried out by both adult volunteers and children in their face-to-face encounters was based on the videotaped data of *One-on-One English* sessions in which nine focal children took part. The examination of these sessions (344 videotaped interactions) allowed us to identify the principal types of interactions in which volunteers and young English language learners participated.

Videotaped sessions available for each child varied from a small number (24) for Lino and a large number (54) for Selena. Each video session

FIGURE 2.6. Focal Children for Retrospective Analysis

Child	Grade at Entry	Time in Program	Years in Program
Marisol	Second grade	2 years	2004–2005 2005–2006
Graciela	Second grade	2 years	2004–2005 2005–2006
Selena	Second grade	2 years	2004–2005 2005–2006
Adriana	First grade	2 years	2004–2005 2005–2006
Lino	Kindergarten	2 years	2005–2006 2006–2007
Fabiola	Kindergarten	2.5 years	2005–2006 2006–2007 2007–2008
Aracely	Kindergarten	2.5 years	2005–2006 2006–2007 2007–2008
Elsa	Kindergarten	3 years	2005–2006 2006–2007 2007–2008
Ernesto	Kindergarten	3 years	2005–2006 2006–2007 2007–2008

(ranging in length from 45 seconds to a full 45-minute session) was viewed as many times as necessary to produce a close description for each one of the interactions, noting the name of the volunteer working with the child, the focus of the interaction (e.g., book, game), the specific materials used in the interaction, details of the interaction (e.g., volunteer narrates pointing to pictures in book, child is silent), child's demeanor (e.g., child looks away, plays with her belt), participation (child looks at the book, turns pages, points to objects spontaneously), description of speech acts produced by child at each turn (complies with request for display of information, produces non-verbal response), particularly notable details of language use (stutters, self-corrects), and evidence of change over time (can narrate by himself). Segments of the videotapes for each child were transcribed in order to capture particular details of his or her growing participatory competence. Segments of entire videotapes selected for transcription include examples of children's

English language production, evidence of particular interactional competencies, or other details thought to illustrate children's developing participatory or linguistic competence.

In describing how children used English as they engaged in various types of one-on-one interactions in English, we drew from the perspectives of Atkinson, Nishino, Churchill, and Okada (2007) on alignment and interaction to examine how youngsters "come into coordinated interaction with the language being learned in tandem with a full array of sociocognitive affordances" (p. 172) including a socially defined situation (after-school tutoring session), adult volunteers, literacy tools (e.g., books, games, puzzles), and embodied tools (e.g., physical orientation, gestures, eye gaze). We were interested in understanding children's achieved communicative acts (Ninio, Snow, Pan, & Rollins, 1994), that is, the actions that young ELLs carried out by means of speech (e.g., responding, disagreeing, narrating) and that were accomplished interpersonally between themselves and the individuals with whom they were engaged in interaction. Our goal was to understand the talk produced in interactions with *One-on-One English* volunteers as well as in the ways in which space was made by these interactions for young ELLs to become "effective communicators and sense makers" (Cook-Gumperz & Kyrantzis, 2001, pp. 591–592) in an English-speaking world. In our analysis, we drew also from conceptualizations of joint attention (Tomasello, 2003), interactional routines (Shieffelin & Ochs, 1986), affordances (Greeno, 1994), involvement (Tannen, 1989), contextualization cues (Gumperz, 1982), the relationship between language and context (Goodwin & Duranti, 1992), and the construction of context (Goodwin & Goodwin, 1992).

In attempting to describe change over time in the interactional competencies of young English language learners, we faced a number of analytical challenges similar to those faced by researchers examining the development of pragmatic competence in children who are acquiring a first language. Like Wells (1981, 1985), Ninio and Snow (1996), and Ninio el al. (1994), we worked to develop a descriptive system that would allow us to talk about what children could do and not do with language in various types of interactions with volunteers. We took into account critiques of other researchers' classification systems (e.g., Ninio et al., 1994) but still endeavored to find a way to convey to practitioners the degree to which young ELLs are able to communicate meanings in English beyond their formal grammatical or lexical competencies.

Our analysis was framed by the following perspectives about language and communication:

- Communication is collaborative and constructed as individuals engage in interaction.
- Communicative effects are achieved interpersonally in conversations

Our categorization of different types of conversational exchanges, conversational moves, and communicative acts in conversational sequences borrowed terms, concepts, and interpretive principles from the work of Sinclair and Coulthard (1975), Coulthard (1992), Edmondson (1981), and Wells (1981, 1985). However, our assignment of utterances to particular communicative acts involved judgments about what was dominant to us as analysts and as members of the project staff who had examined such interactions over a 5-year period. We took the position that (1) conversational exchanges have a particular topic or theme that can be recognized; (2) units of expression do not stand in a one-on-one relationship with communicative acts; (3) in interaction, adults and children exchange both ideational and interpersonal meanings; and (4) the system must be derived from the data itself.

Analysis of the Language Produced by Children in Language Assessments

In Chapter 5, we describe changes in the language children produced during pre- and postassessments conducted each fall and spring. We specifically analyze children's language production in the story retelling segment of this assessment. For this analysis, we focused on six of the nine focal children for whom we had three or more (up to six) retellings produced over a 2–3-year period. All audio recordings of these six children's retellings were transcribed for analysis. These transcripts included examiner prompting and interruption, so that we could describe the increasing role that children took in constructing the narratives over time.

Clahsen (1985) and Cook (1999) caution SLA teachers and researchers against measuring second language development against a native speaker standard, an approach which would simply cast our focal students as deficient native English speakers. Instead, we sought to describe children's developing linguistic competence as L2 users on their own terms and analyzed children's language production in terms of multiple dimensions of language. To describe their developing competence with the narrative genre, we examined children's use of features that have been emphasized in discussions of children's narrative development (e.g., Berman & Slobin, 1994; Goodell & Sachs, 1992; Peterson & McCabe, 1991): narrative structure, use of temporal markers and conjunctions as cohesive devices, and use of reported speech. To examine children's changing use of English syntax, we examined changes over time in turn type and length (e.g., word-length turns, sentence-length turns, multisentence turns), use of English and Spanish, and sentence structure. To describe children's morphological development we focused on verbs, counting their use of different morphological markings for tense and person. We also note children's growth in English vocabulary by counting the number of different lexical items they used over time. Finally, we discuss changes in children's grammatical accuracy, as this aspect of language proficiency is often emphasized in the language proficiency assessments used with English language learners in schools.

REFLECTIONS ON *ONE-ON-ONE ENGLISH*

The design research carried out as part of *One-on-One English* allowed us to explore solutions to the challenge of providing access to English to students who are being schooled in hypersegregated settings where the majority of children are English language learners. In this chapter, we have described the various phases of our work including the identification of resources, pre-implementation and implementation activities, ongoing analysis, and modifications of activities and methodologies used in our retrospective analysis. We have emphasized that during the entire 5 years of operation, activities and procedures went through iterative cycles of revision. In the chapters that follow we will focus on both what we learned about the language development of the children during the period of implementation as well as a number of other aspects of our working situation that we had not recognized in the original formulation of our design. Chapter 3, in particular, describes the types of interactions the children and their volunteers engaged in and the types of affordances available to them—some of which we had not entirely anticipated.

CHAPTER 3

Interactions and Affordances

Fabiola sat at a table next to Sarah, a member of the *One-on-One English* project team. It was Fabiola's first time in the *One-on-One English* program, and she looked interested but still a bit tentative as Sarah talked about the brown bear on the cover of the book that was on the table in front of them. Sarah told Fabiola that the bear was big and brown and made lots of noises. She pantomimed to show bear's claws as she growled. Fabiola was definitely interested. Her eyes stayed on the book as Sarah turned the pages describing a red bird, a yellow duck, and a blue horse. When Sarah asked her to point to various pictures (*Can you point to the brown bear?* and *Can you show me the blue horse?*), Fabiola immediately did so. In the context of the interaction, Fabiola either understood Sarah's questions as a request for display of information or—because she was already 5 years old and had engaged in many similar interactions in her first language at home and school—she simply recognized that they were engaged in a turn-taking endeavor in which filling her turn might involve such displays. Fabiola was clearly at the beginning of the very long journey of becoming a competent user of English in a school setting. Sarah, on the other hand, in her role as *One-on-One English* staff, was engaged in working with Fabiola and modeling a *story-talk[1] activity* for a new volunteer in the program, a young undergraduate who had no experience working with children but who had committed to working with Fabiola twice a week after school during a 45-minute period.

This chapter describes the types of interactions that young English language learners and adult volunteers engaged in as they participated in *One-on-One English*. It is our purpose to provide a picture of the types of talk that went on between ordinary speakers of English and children who were often absolute beginning learners of English. We offer examples of children's participation in different kinds of interactions and identify the different types of affordances that were available to them in various types of verbal exchanges as well as different challenges they encountered in interacting with adult volunteers who were often uncertain about how to talk to beginning English language learners.

TALKING AND INTERACTING

On any given afternoon when *One-on-One English* was in operation, adult volunteers arrived at Golden Hills Elementary and went to the classrooms that were being used for the program. There they would meet the child assigned to them, engage in ritual greetings, and sit down to work with the books and other materials that the volunteer had selected for that afternoon.[2] During the next 45 minutes some volunteers would engage their young "English buddies" by interacting with them around colorful books and by telling stories using pictures. They would point to various illustrations, talk and gesture about the animals or objects found on the page, and by exaggerating, repeating, and combining both pantomime and talk, they would support the child's comprehension of the story. Many of these volunteers used books that had repeated patterns such as *Five Little Monkeys, The Gingerbread Boy,* and *The Little Red Hen.* They encouraged the child to join in the refrain, to participate in the unfolding action of the story, and to begin using formulaic sequences in English. Volunteers were quite creative in using a combination of strategies to maintain the child's attention and to ensure that he or she would comprehend or attempt to comprehend what the volunteer intended to communicate about the books or objects that were the focus of their interaction. These volunteers generally talked a great deal and intuitively understood that their English buddies did not speak enough English to fill their turns at talk. In interacting with beginners in particular, this group of volunteers saw their job as modeling language including routine greetings, questions and answers, narrating stories, and pointing out the world around them to their young friends. For example, when they asked questions, (e.g., *What do you think this book is going to be about?*), they immediately modeled logical responses and expanded on their answers (*I think the book is going to be about this bunny right here, with the big teeth and the long floppy ears*). It was not unusual to see these volunteer dyads crawling on the floor to make meaning evident to their buddies, or making flying motions pretending to be birds.

Other volunteer-child interactions were much more school-like. In these interactions, volunteers took on a role that resembled a traditional tutor or classroom teacher who elicits information from students and follows up by accepting, rejecting, and evaluating children's responses. These interactions generally consisted of a series of questions and answers: The volunteer would ask a question (e.g., *What color is this?*) to which the child was expected to respond. Most of the time the questions were quite simple and were limited to types of information that they believed the child should know, such as numbers or colors. Typically, volunteers who engaged in such interactions chose books and materials that allowed children to count, to respond to questions about colors, and to label animals and parts of the body. While many of these interactions were not particularly language-rich, they were reassuring to volunteers.

At different points in the 45-minute session, most child-volunteer dyads would engage in playing games. Our collection of materials included word and animal lotto-type games, cards containing pictures to be sequenced, memory pictures games, puzzles, and stick puppets, and volunteers were encouraged to vary their routines to make the time enjoyable. Walking into the room, a visitor might see one dyad on the floor making a puzzle, another playing Simon Says, and yet another engaged in sequencing a series of pictures. If all went well, the activity would involve a great deal of language, but if it did not go well or the volunteer was not very skilled, the activity of making a puzzle or sequencing pictures would be carried out primarily in silence or by using a very limited set of repeated formulas (e.g., *Let's look for the edges. Is this an edge?*).

For both volunteers and ELL children in the *One-on-One English* program, the process of getting acquainted and developing a comfortable interactive procedure was complex. Volunteers—particularly those who had not had much contact with young children—found the challenge of engaging in talk with kindergartners and first and second graders who did not speak or understand English a very difficult task. Some volunteers were more receptive to the conceptualization of their roles, behaviors, and language that we presented in initial and ongoing volunteer training sessions than were others. Volunteers who were receptive to our initial perspective saw themselves as responsible for engaging ELLs in interactions centering around books in ways that offered children a "steady stream of talk" anchored in the here and now that was made "comprehensible" by including repetitions, gestures, exaggerations, and other modifications that provided children with scaffolds for both understanding and participating. This group of volunteers understood that ideal interactions most resembled caregiver talk with very young children that included establishing joint attention and creating a context in which communicative intentions could be understood (Tomasello, 2003). Even for these volunteers, however, getting started was a challenge. Five- and 6-year-old children are not young babies or toddlers, and volunteers were uncertain about how to establish good relationships with them using a suggested interactional procedure that seemed inappropriate for the age group in question. This position is easily understandable because, as Wells (1981) made clear, in order for successful communication to take place speakers must attend to what he calls the "orientation" of the interaction in order to adjust the purpose, topic, and content of their talk to the particular context of the exchange.

With respect to topic, orientation influences both what information is included and how it is organised. One of the most important decisions a speaker has
to make concerns the amount of information relevant to his topic that he can
assume to be already shared with his intended hearer. To underestimate what
his hearer already knows will lead him to appear to be "talking down," which
may cause his hearer to feel insulted; on the other hand, to overestimate is to
risk failing to communicate effectively altogether. (p. 52)

As might be expected, for young ELLs, participating in regular interactional exchanges with adult English language speakers (even young undergraduates) was a new experience. They had not had much contact with what
we termed "ordinary speakers of English." Even though during program
time volunteers and ELL dyads met in one or two classrooms where children
could see other schoolmates engaged in similar buddy relationships, meeting
a strange adult volunteer—especially one that they could not understand—was
clearly a bit disorienting. Young children were often shy and apprehensive.

TYPES OF INTERACTIONS

In the sections that follow, we present examples of different participatory
behaviors in order to bring attention to the ways in which children began to
function as participants in dyadic pedagogical interactions which—because
of the particular characteristics of the activity of "tutoring" and the identities
taken on by those engaged in such after-school activities—were similar in
some respects to those found in other school activities (Sinclair & Coulthard,
1975; Tharp & Gallimore, 1988). We attend to the nonlinear, nonuniform
aspects of the process and to the ways that different children responded to
various types of affordances available to them in one-on-one interactions.
We suggest that the structure of the sequences of talk that took place between
young English language learners and adults in our program and the elements
present in the interactive process were instrumental in the changes that took
place over time in children's interactional and participatory competence.

Our retrospective analysis identified three principal types of *interactions*
in which volunteers and young English learners participated. These include:

1. *Engaging and telling interactions.* These were interactions in which
   volunteers engaged youngsters in activities using extensive
   amounts of learner-directed language targeted at child L2
   learners. This talk was used to focus the child's attention on
   a topic of joint interest, to provide information, to narrate, to
   describe, to expand children's background knowledge, and to
   model language.

FIGURE 3.1. Types of Interactions and Exchanges

Interactions	Exchanges
Engaging and telling	Storybook Content book Vocabulary book
Eliciting and evaluating	Laminated school and community scenes Sequence cards (cards depicting a narrative sequence Games
Game playing	Sequence cards Word and animal lotto Puzzles Puppet role-play Memory picture games

2. *Eliciting and evaluating interactions.* These interactions primarily followed the Initiation-Response-Evaluation (IRE) sequences identified by other researchers (e.g., Mehan, 1979). These types of interactions were made up exclusively of a long series of questions and responses. Volunteers elicited replies from children and followed up by accepting, rejecting, and/or evaluating children's responses. Occasionally, volunteers provided additional information about the topic or object of joint interest.
3. *Game-playing interactions.* These interactions included several types of activities in which volunteers engaged in establishing rules for participation, deciding on specific activities to be carried out, and agreeing on game outcomes. They also included the playing of the game itself as well as the use of organizational language needed to move the game forward (e.g., *It's my turn*).

These three types of interactions incorporated what we have called *exchanges*. We classified exchanges based primarily on the types of materials that were used in those interactional sessions, which included storytelling activities, content-book activities, vocabulary activities (including both books and laminated scenes), and games (including word lotto, animal lotto, memory card games, puppet role-plays, and puzzles). Types of interactions and exchanges are presented in Figure 3.1.

An engaging and telling interaction, for example, could involve a game, a storybook, or work with a laminated school or community scene. Similarly, an eliciting and evaluating interaction could involve activities based on a colorful children's storybook or on a set of sequence cards. Game-playing interactions were different from both engaging and telling and eliciting and evaluating interactions and typically involved activities centered around puzzles, board games or sequence cards. For each type of exchange (e.g., storytelling, game, sequence cards), we identified and classified moves and communicative acts produced by both volunteers and children.

Engaging and Telling Interactions

Volunteers who were comfortable providing what we termed a "steady stream of talk" engaged in engaging and telling interactions. These were interactions in which volunteers engaged youngsters in activities using extensive amounts of learner-directed language targeted at child L2 learners. These types of interactions sought to provide children with access to language by producing talk anchored in topics and objects to which both the child and the adult were attending jointly and made "comprehensible" by including repetitions, gestures, exaggerations, and other modifications.

The dialogue that follows includes an example of a transcribed engaging and telling interaction (see Appendix A for transcription conventions). In this particular example, the volunteer (labeled in the transcript as V) is a very skilled future elementary school teacher. The child (Adriana) is a first grader (labeled in the transcript as C) who was an advanced beginner and could already understand quite a bit of English and could respond to some questions. As will be noted in this interaction, the volunteer fills most turns of talk. She describes what is happening in the book and exaggerates and pantomimes to ensure the child's understanding. In turns 1 and 3, she pretends to sneeze. She also mimics being startled (turn 3) and pantomimes running by making running motions with her arms (turn 5).

1   V: okay? so at the beginning, they're taking the hamster out of the cage to look at that ((*turns page and gasps*)) but this girl sneezes ((*pretends to sneeze*)) ah choo, she sneezes and the air from her sneeze, makes the hamster jump away

2   C: why?

3   V: [the hamster jumps away, the hamster gets scared, because someone sneezes on her ((*pretends to sneeze on child*)) ah choo, and the hamster's ((*mimics being startled*)) oooh! and it jumps away

4   C: ((*giggles*))

5   V: okay? ((*turns page*)) and then it looks like they're chasing after the hamster ((*makes running motions with her arms*)) chasing remember?

6   C: ((*nods*))

7   V: chasing after the hamster, and before the hamster can get out of the door
        they close the door *((puts hands up like a closed door))* 'cause they don't want
        the hamster to run out do they?
8   C: *((nods slightly))*
9   V: that'd be bad *((turns page))* so the hamster's still in the room and it's
        running around over by the computer *((points to nearby computer area in the
        actual classroom))* right here
10 C: he's bad?
11 V: it's, is it bad?
12 C: **is that bad? he, he's going to the computer?**
13 V: **but is that bad? yes! you're right that's bad, because**
14 C: **[why?**
15 V: **good question, because he might chew on the wires** *((brings her hand
        to her mouth, then points to where the wires are in the classroom they're in))* **do
        you know what the wires are?**
16 C: no
17 V: okay, these *((they go over to computer and volunteer points out wires underneath
        desk))* this is a wire, this is a wire, this is a wire, where's another wire?
18 C: *((gets down on hands and knees))*
19 V: *((points under the desk))* those are wires aren't they?
20 C: *((crawls under desk toward wires))*
21 V: yeah, don't eat it! don't eat it! are you going to eat the wire?
22 C: *((crawls out from under desk))* oh no!
23 V: okay no you're not *((laughing))* you're not a hamster it's okay
24 C: xxx *((grabs at something under the desk))*
25 V: oh no no no leave that, okay, okay, so, that's why it's bad *((turning back to
        book))* so they have to get the hamster to go somewhere else don't they?
        so what they do, let's go back over here *((they walk back to their seats))* what
        they do is they pull out the chairs *((pulls on her chair before sitting down))*
        they pull all the chairs out, and that scares the hamster away, okay? if the
        little hamster's running along and then all of a sudden, it sees this big chair
        go *((gets up out of chair and pulls out her chair))* it got scared right?
26 C: *((nods slightly))*

The volunteer is interested in engaging the child, but she is also interested in determining how much the child understands. When the child appears confused about why it is bad for the hamster in the story to be near
the computer (turn 12), the volunteer attempts to explain and focuses on a
vocabulary item that she is not sure the child knows. In turn 15, she directly
asks the child if she knows what *wires* are. When she determines that Adriana
does not, she proceeds to crawl under the computer to point out the wires
to the child.

FIGURE 3.2. Sample Adult Communicative Acts in an Engaging and Telling Interaction

Moves	*Sample Communicative Acts*
Focusing	Marks transitions *(Okay now)* Calls on child to attend *(Let's look at this book)*
Engaging and telling Informing Modeling language Providing input	Narrates story Describes pictures and characters Explains, makes distinctions Models language *(ten little monkeys jumping on the bed)* Elicits *(Who called the doctor?)* Responds to his/her own elicits *(The mom called the doctor. See, she was worried about her children.)*
Expanding on aspects of the focus of joint attention Checking for comprehension	Elicits *(What was your favorite part? Was the book about monkeys or about bears?)* Gives clues *(Did you like the part where the monkeys fell down?)* Scaffolds *(My favorite part is when the doctor came.)*
Personalizing or linking to child's knowledge	Transitions *(So, how about you?)* Elicts *(Have you ever jumped on a bed?)*
Following up Evaluating child's understanding of story	Elicits *(What was this story about?)* Accepts *(Six monkeys, you're right.)* Comments *(These monkeys don't mind their mother.)* Evaluates *(Good job.)* Corrects *(Not "to" the bed, "on" the bed.)*
Responding Answering child questions	Provides information requested by child

Adult communicative acts in engaging and telling interactions. In engaging and telling interactions, volunteer moves might incorporate informing and narrating, modeling language patterns, checking for comprehension, linking to child's background knowledge, following up on children's responses, and responding to questions asked by the child. Figure 3.2 presents a summary of the moves and acts identified for an adult volunteer in an engaging and telling interaction involving a storybook exchange with the repeated pattern book *Five Little Monkeys*. Our analysis of such interactions determined that they typically began with a set of *focusing* moves by the adult with which he or she called on the child to attend. Such moves were followed by a second set of moves—engaging and telling moves—that informed, modeled language, and provided input. In this segment of the interaction, the volunteer typically narrated a story, used repeated patterns in the book, and asked and answered his or her own questions. These engaging and telling moves might be followed by either *personalizing* or *following-up* moves that included attempts to relate to the experiences of the child, expanding on aspects of the focus on joint attention, and traditional follow-up responses to comprehension checks (e.g., acceptance or evaluation of the child's answers). Finally, these types of interactions sometimes included answering any questions posed by the child. As noted in Figure 3.2, a volunteer working with a child on the book *Five Little Monkeys* typically narrated the story, modeled the repeated pattern, and might also model questions (*Who called the doctor?*) and respond to his or her own questions (*The mom called the doctor*).

We have labeled all adult communicative actions that request information or display of information *elicits*. These types of actions occurred in the various phases of these interactions including the segments labeled in Figure 3.2 as *engaging and telling, expanding, personalizing,* and *following up*. It is important to stress that the use of such elicit moves in all four of these phases of an interaction depended on the child's level of proficiency. A volunteer, for example, might try to link the story to the child's experience or assess the child's general understanding of the narrative, but if the child was very limited in his or her productive proficiency, he or she would not be able to respond appropriately. For that reason, volunteers frequently used yes/no questions (*Did the mom call the doctor?*) or multiple-choice questions (*Did the mom call the doctor or the teacher?*). These types of questions allowed children to respond easily and to participate in the interaction by filling their turns at talk. Personalizing moves were typically avoided by skilled volunteers with beginning English buddies because elicits that required children to talk about their experiences in relation to particular events in a story were extremely challenging. Children might very well understand the questions and yet lack the proficiency to talk about what they knew and had experienced. We will say more about these personalizing moves and children's responses to them in the sections that follow.

Children's communicative acts in engaging and telling interactions. Moves and communicative acts identified for ELL children in engaging and telling interactions, especially at the beginning of participation in the project, were primarily reactive. Children made participatory moves showing recognition of turn-taking signals. They made back-channel noises, gestured, repeated as requested, repeated spontaneously, labeled, and commented. They responded (sometimes very cautiously) to requests for display of information including shaking or nodding their head, choosing alternatives in choice questions, and sometimes masking their lack of understanding with ambiguous head gestures. As they grew in their ability to use English chunks and formulas, they negotiated, interrupted, and disagreed. They also requested information and attempted to narrate upon request. Figure 3.3 presents a summary of the types of moves and acts that were produced by young ELLs interacting with an adult volunteer in such an engaging and telling interaction.

In order to participate successfully in engaging and telling interactions, children needed to appear to be attending to the object or topic nominated for attention by the volunteer and to fill their turns appropriately during the interaction. In order for volunteers to participate effectively in such interactions, they needed to suspend their discomfort at talking to 5-, 6-, and 7-year-old children as if they were much younger. They also had to be comfortable in trying to make large amounts of talk comprehensible or, at least, engaging.

Eliciting and Evaluating Interactions

By comparison, eliciting and evaluating interactions primarily followed Initiation-Response-Evaluation sequences. They were made up almost exclusively of questions. Volunteers elicited replies to these questions and followed up by accepting, rejecting, and/or evaluating children's responses. Volunteers rarely provided additional information about the topic or object of joint interest, and they did not talk extensively, explain, or model language. Volunteers who engaged in such interactions often appeared worried about talking down to school-age children and, because they underestimated the impact of the ELL children's language limitations on the youngsters' communicative abilities, they also often attempted to relate to them with a series of "getting acquainted," "let's personalize the topic," "establish common ground" questions (e.g., *What kind of playground equipment do you have at school? Have you ever seen one of these? What kinds of things do you like to do at the beach?*) that the L2 beginners could either not understand or not respond to in age-appropriate ways in English.

FIGURE 3.3. Sample Communicative Acts Produced by Children in an Engaging and Telling Interaction

Moves	Sample Communicative Acts
Demonstrating attention	Demonstrates attention (Attends to materials, watches volunteer)
Participating in interaction	Recognizes turn-taking signals Back-channels (*um, hum*) Gestures Repeats (*ten little monkeys*) Labels (*bed, monkey, mama*) Comments (*monkeys jumping*) Negotiates (*Your turn*) Interrupts Disagrees
Responding to comprehension checks	Replies (nods or shakes head, selects from options given, responds in English, responds in Spanish)
Responding to attempts to link to background knowledge	Replies (nods or shakes head, selects from options given, or makes an ambiguous head gesture)
Requesting information	Requests information
Narrating	Narrates a story using pictures

One particular group of volunteers who generally engaged in eliciting and evaluating interactions struggled with our suggestions about the best ways to interact with young ELLs. Although we provided initial and ongoing training for volunteers and made available to them a *One-on-One English* manual with many detailed illustrations of the kinds of exchanges we hoped would take place, a good number of our volunteers found the role of "tutor"–as opposed to English buddy–much more comfortable. These individuals generally took on the role of traditional classroom language teachers and modeled their behavior on the only relevant experience they had had in attempting to acquire an L2: their foreign language study in high school and college. They thus saw themselves as responsible for teaching specific bits and pieces of language, for drilling students on vocabulary items, for teaching reading (letters and sounds), and even for correcting children's pronunciation.

Eliciting and evaluating interactions included a much narrower range of moves and acts than engaging and telling interactions for both children and volunteers and made different demands on the children. Figure 3.4 presents a summary of the types of acts produced by adults and children that we typically identified in such interactions.

In the following transcript of an eliciting and evaluating interaction, Fabiola and her volunteer are preparing to play a game of lotto. The child chooses the lotto boards and organizes the cards. The volunteer, instead of proceeding with the game, turns the interaction into a series of IRE-type exchanges that appear to "test" the child's knowledge of vocabulary. In the first part of this interaction, the volunteer is focusing on making certain that the child attaches the correct labels to objects found on the lotto cards. In turn 3, she shows the child a card and asks if she knows what it is. The child says no, and the volunteer proceeds to give her the answer. The child spontaneously repeats the label (*table*) provided by the volunteer. The volunteer still wants to make certain that the child has assigned the correct meaning to the label. She thus asks the child directly in turn 7 if she knows what a table is, but does not accept her response (*yeah*) in turn 8 indicating that she does know. She then translates the word into Spanish (*una mesa*) and asks her to point to a table in the room. When the child is able to do so making clear her understanding of the word, the volunteer accepts her reply saying *that's a table* in turn 11 and then moves on, showing her another card.

1   V: hold on, hold on *((collects cards))* okay, let's go through these first, ok?
2   C: yeah
3   V: okay, do you know what this is? *((shows Fabiola a card))*
4   C: no
5   V: **a table**
6   C: **table**
7   V: **do you know what a table is?**
8   C: **yeah**
9   V: **una mesa** *(a table)***, right? there's a table, where do you see a table in here?**
10 C: **uh** *((points to a table in the room))* **over there**
11 V: that's a table, what's this? *((shows Fabiola another card))*

In turn 12 of this same interaction Fabiola again tries to initiate the game, pointing to her board to indicate she has the item on her board and saying *me*. The volunteer, however, says they will play later and continues the vocabulary activity. She then proceeds to drill Fabiola on the vocabulary, holding up a card, having Fabiola name the object, and repeating it several times until it is pronounced correctly. In turn 21 she corrects the child's term *seat* and offers *chair* as the correct response. It is evident from the child's behavior (she gets up and moves elsewhere in the room, and she lies down on the floor holding the lotto board) that she is not engaged.

FIGURE 3.4. Eliciting and Evaluating Interaction

Adult Moves	Sample Communicative Acts of Adult	Sample Communicative Acts of Child
Focusing	Marks transitions (*okay*) Calls on child to attend *(Let's look at this book)*	Demonstrates attention
Initiating	Elicits (*What's this? Is this a tiger or a lion?*)	Replies (nods or shakes head, selects from options given, responds in English, responds in Spanish)
	Models language to be repeated (*The tiger is sleeping.*)	Repeats (*the tiger*)
	Directs (*Show me the tiger*)	Complies (*points*)
Following up	Reinitiate (*a tiger?*) Accept (*yes, a tiger*) Evaluate (*good job*) Comment (*tigers have stripes*)	Repeats (*a tiger*) Clarifies (*two*)

1   C: me! *((points at board))*
2   V: hold on, we're gonna do that later, what is this?
3   C: um, reloj *(clock)*
4   V: a clock
5   C: clock
6   V: where do you see a clock here?
7   C: *((points))*
8   V: **there's one, what's this?** *((shows Fabiola another card))*
9   C: **seat**
10   V: **a chair, right?**
11   C: **chair**
12   V: it could be a seat too, but a chair, where's a chair? there's one, you want to point to it?
13   C: um hum *((gets up, out of camera view))*
14   V: there it is, there's a chair, there's lots of chairs here, huh?
15   C: yeah *((lays down, holding her lotto board))*
16   V: do you know what this is? *((shows Fabiola another card))*
17   C: yeah
18   V: a bowl
19   C: bowl *((points to corresponding picture on board))*
20   V: bowl right? what about this? what do you use a bowl for *((flips back to bowl picture))* to eat?

21   C: *((nods))* eat
22   V: to eat, what about this? *((shows Fabiola another card))*
23   C: wa
24   V: umbrella?
25   C: uh, yeah
26   V: what's the umbrella for?
27   C: uh, watert
28   V: for when it rains?

Other examples of eliciting and evaluating interactions are perhaps more extreme in the minimal amount of language affordances they provide for the student. In some cases they actually resemble old-fashioned pattern drills. For example, the next transcript presents a storybook exchange between Selena, a newly arrived second grader, and a volunteer who believed strongly in modeling single sentences and having the child repeat them. In this interaction, they are working with the book *Corduroy*, a story of a teddy bear who loses a button and is sitting alone on a shelf in a department store. Rather than talking through the story, the volunteer expects Selena to repeat each of the narrative acts that she produces. The book is open in front of both Selena and the volunteer. Selena appears subdued, willing to comply with the wishes of her volunteer, but not deeply engaged in the activity.

1   V: he climbs down
2   C: he climb
3   V: *((holds book on the table and points to pictures))* the bear climbs down
4   C: the bear *((quietly, then again in a louder voice))* the bear
5   V: **climbs down**
6   C: **climbs down**
7   V: **the bear, walk, walks** *((points to picture on next page and moves finger back and forth to signal movement))*
8   C: **the bear, walks, walks**
9   V: **the bear can walk remember? the bear can walk,** and he's, he is looking for his button
10   C: xx
11   V: he is looking
12   C: he is, is looking
13   V: for his button . . . for his
14   C: for his
15   V: you know, pulling for the button he wants the button . . . does he want the button? *((pointing to page))*
16   C: *((nods))*
17   V: he wants the button?
18   C: yes

19   V: the bear wants the button
20   C: the bear

In this particular interaction, elicitation acts produced by the volunteer are limited to modeling sentences. In several cases she engages in a type of sentence modeling that was known in the teaching of language during the audio-lingual period as "backward buildup": *climbs down, the bear climbs down.* She breaks down longer segments into seemingly more manageable utterances and leads the child through various repetitions of the smaller segments before prompting her to produce the longer utterance.

The turns in the interaction above that are printed in bold illustrate that in this type of sequence, accept and evaluate acts may not be expressed directly. In turn 5, for example, the volunteer models the utterance to be repeated by the child, *climbs down.* In turn 6 the child repeats as requested, and in turn 7 the volunteer accepts the child's response by moving on to the next target utterance, *the bear walks.* In turn 8 Selena repeats the utterance as requested but communicates uncertainty: *the bear walks, walks.* The volunteer appears not to be entirely satisfied with the child's repetition of the modeled utterance and produces a rephrasing of the reply (*the bear can walk*) as a follow-up move. The volunteer then moves on to the next elicit.

In comparison to the language affordance (the quantity of input and the support for understanding) provided by the types of exchanges that we classified as engaging and telling interactions, in these pattern drill exchanges children were exposed to very limited examples of spoken English. Moreover, in such interactions volunteers had little evidence of whether or how well a child comprehended the utterances they were asked to repeat. However, as was the case during the audio-lingual period of language teaching, a child participating in such interactions did receive feedback to some degree on the form of her repeated utterances.

Game-Playing Interactions

Game-playing interactions were different from both engaging and telling and eliciting and evaluating interactions and typically involved activities centered on puzzles, board games, or sequence cards. In these interactions volunteers and children engaged in establishing rules for participation, in deciding on specific activities to be carried out, and in agreeing on game outcomes. Such interactions included the playing of the game itself as well as the use of organizational language needed to move the game forward (e.g., *it's my turn, I win, I have six points*).

As pointed out above, games and gamelike activities used in the project included animal lotto, memory games, ordering narrative sequence cards, finding objects in laminated scenes, total-physical-response (TPR) games such as Simon Says, and role-playing with puppets created for the project. Game-playing interactions varied widely in the amount of English that was made available to children while engaging in the game. The best games provided opportunities for volunteers to use language extensively, beyond the mere regulation of game activity. Most of the games used in the project, however, because they were not designed to scaffold language development, required adaptation and modification. For example, an animal memory game that required children merely to recall the spatial location of cards laid out on a table and to match pairs without using language, was adapted to require that children label or describe the animal before they were given credit for forming the pair. Figure 3.5 summarizes the types of communicative acts engaged in by adults and children that were identified in such interactions.

The following transcript of a game-playing interaction involves a guessing game between a volunteer and Elsa during the third year of her participation in the program. They are playing an adapted lotto game in which the player calling out the cards must describe the objects rather than merely label them. Elsa is attempting to describe an object to the volunteer, who is trying not to guess too quickly in order to motivate the child to say more.

1   C: **is something of you, is the, is raining you bring the?** *((pretends she's holding an umbrella and pauses for the volunteer to complete the sentence))*

2   V: okay it's raining, and so it's something for me to use, okay, uh, tell me something more about it

3   C: it's blue

4   V: okay

5   C: **the stick**

6   V: **there's a stick**

7   C: **a stick like that** *((makes shape of stick with hand))*

8   V: **a handle**

9   C: um hum

10   V: **so could I hold on to the handle?** *((pretends to be holding an umbrella))*

11   C: *((nods))*

12   V: okay, and what does it do?

13   C: to not be wet, wait, um, xx wait in the water

14   V: so it keeps the rain off me?

15   C: *((nods))*

16   V: is it an umbrella?

17   C: *((nods))*

Elsa attempts to produced the required description in turn 1: *is something of you, is the, is raining you bring the.* The volunteer recasts in turn 2 (*okay, it's*

FIGURE 3.5. Game-Playing Interactions

Adult Moves	Sample Communicative Acts of Adult	Sample Communicative Acts of Child
Focusing	Calls on child to attend	Demonstrates attention
Negotiating	Proposes beginning and ceasing of activity Accepts, establishes, negotiates rules Accepts, establishes, negotiates roles	Accepts volunteer's proposal Proposes alternative activity Accepts, establishes, negotiates rules Accepts, establishes, negotiates roles
Playing	Models game-regulation language (*my turn, you win*) Models language to be used in playing (*It's red and it's a fruit*) Repeats language used by child Recasts language used by child Requests clarification Requests additional information Evaluates Comments	Produces game-regulation language (*your turn, no fair*) Produces required language (labels, describes) Repeats Rephrases Clarifies Provides information requested

raining) and expands on what Elsa said (*it's something for me to use*). She also requests additional information (*tell me something more about it*). For the volunteer, who has the lotto card in front of her and can easily guess what the child is attempting to describe, the challenge is to scaffold the child's description of the object while providing language she may need. For example, in turn 10, after Elsa says that the object has a stick in turns 5 and 7, the volunteer expands on the label *handle* that she offered in turn 8 and says, *a handle, so could I hold on to the handle?* thus providing Elsa with additional information about the appropriate term for a stick that is part of an umbrella.

Except for the fact that the volunteer is pretending not to know the answer, this type of interaction is similar to those described in studies examining negotiation between adult classroom learners and native speakers reviewed by Larsen-Freeman and Long (1991) and Pica (1994). Note that in these types of interaction there was less attention given to the accuracy of the production and more attention given to developing the child's ability to describe objects by including several details.

Role-Playing Exchanges

Role-playing exchanges, by comparison with other games and gamelike activities, involved more extensive talk. In the transcript below Adriana and her volunteer are looking at a large laminated picture of children playing in a school yard. They focus on a group of three girls playing ball and choose puppets that correspond to the girls. Adriana chooses one puppet (Alison) and the volunteer takes the other two (Ting and Zoe). They then pretend to be the girls, enacting the scene and moving their puppets:

1   V: so I'm gonna say first *((pretending to be Ting))* Alison! why did you kick the ball so hard? now we're never going to get it back *((then switches to giving Adriana directions))* so you have to kick really hard and it's bouncing away

2   C: **because I want to, wa, want to, uh, I'm going to**

3   V: what did she want to do?

4   C: **to win, I wanted to win!**

5   V: you wanted to win the game?

6   C: **yeah**

7   V: well now you're gonna have to go chase that ball all across the playground

8   C: **if I don't want, if I not want it? xx**

9   V: you don't want the ball?

10 C: **no if xx, if I don't want it to go, with the ball, what happened to me?**

11 V: what happens to you if I go with the ball?

12 C: **no me** *((points to herself and then to her puppet))*

13 V: oh

14 C: **if I don't want it**

15 V: well why don't you go get the ball for us? will you go get the ball since you kicked it really far away?

16 C: **ummm** *((makes pensive face as if she were considering it))* **ok** *((moves puppet onto mat as if walking))*

17 V: thank you, now she brings it back

18 C: [**here it is** *((touches puppet to mat as if picking up the ball and returns to the group of other puppets))*

19 V: *((pretending to be her other puppet, Zoe))* hey, I want to play too kick the ball to me

20 C: **ok** *((gestures kicking with puppet))*

21 V: thank you so much, now I'm gonna be the teacher *((puts hand up to mouth as if speaking through a bullhorn))* girls it's time to come inside it's time to go to come to school *((pretending to be Ting))* oh no we have to go to class, who's going to take the ball back to where it belongs? who's gonna put it away?

22   C: um um um, me! *((waves puppet))*
23   V: you will? why do you have to put the ball away?
24   C: because I'm the leader, of the game

This type of interaction required that the child be able to engage in a pretend interaction between the puppets, that she comprehend the messages conveyed in each turn of the interaction, and that she be able to participate intelligibly in the pretend exchange. In this pretend exchange, the child enters into her role quite well demonstrating that she understood the volunteer's question in turns 2 and 4. She is able to explain why she kicked the ball so hard (*I wanted to win the game*), but has a harder time in turns 8, 10, and 12 at explaining that she does not want to chase the ball across the playground and at exploring the possible consequences of that action (*no if xx, if I don't want it to go, with the ball, what happened to me?*). Here again, the purpose of these interactions was not the production of accurate forms, but to offer children the opportunity to pretend to interact with fluent English-speaking youngsters. What mattered was that they were successful in participating in such interactions and that they could use their developing English language proficiency to engage in ordinary routines.

Role-playing exchanges were not attempted by all volunteers because they required a degree of comfort between the child and the volunteer as well as a willingness by the child to enter into imaginary interactions of various different types which, as made evident in the transcript, could move in unexpected directions. Our purpose in encouraging role-plays and in fabricating stick puppets was to provide opportunities for volunteers to help children use *interpersonal language* (e.g., answering and asking personal-information questions).[3] Ordinarily, little attention is given to such language in classrooms because it is assumed that children acquire this type of language in interactions with their peers. We had noted, however, that most children at Golden Hills Elementary were unable to engage in ordinary interactions of this type because they had very few same-age peer models to draw from.

Encouraging role-playing interactions was also an attempt on our part to provide more varied activities in the program and to move many volunteers away from an exclusive use of eliciting and evaluating interactions focused primarily on labeling. As was the case with many other materials that we experimented with, puppet activities were not considered sufficiently successful and were abandoned by the fourth year of the project.

Story-Telling Sequences within Engaging and Telling Interactions

In addition to the characteristics of engaging and telling interactions already mentioned, these interactions were central to developing children's ability to produce a narrative using pictures. We urged volunteers to use storytelling activities and to use pictures to model the language needed to tell stories. All pre- and posttests included a narrative task, and we frequently emphasized the importance of narratives in our regular volunteer trainings, selecting particularly effective examples of storytelling by both volunteers and children.

The following transcript is illustrative of an attempt by Marisol to tell a story immediately after her volunteer has modeled the entire narrative. This is a long segment involving a little girl who stops playing, takes her bath, puts on pajamas, and gets ready for bed, but does not fall asleep. We include the 88-turn sequence (in segments) primarily to illustrate the challenges faced by volunteers in trying to scaffold children's narrative moves effectively.

1	V:	you want to tell me this one? okay good
2	C:	one day, um, one day, the little house, and this is the dad, um little girl, and mom *((points at people in picture))*
3	V:	um hum
4	C:	[and then, it go, to the, clean
5	V:	um hum
6	C:	and then the dad go to the, the xx, dad is clean, but the girl is not clean *((turns page))*
7	V:	**she's not cleaning**
8	C:	**and then, eh, he, and then the, the, the girl is, is play**
9	V:	**that's right she's playing with?**
10	C:	with melon? *((points to picture))*
11	V:	with melon, good job!
12	C:	and
13	V:	what's that one called do you remember?
14	C:	*((shakes head))*
15	V:	napkin
16	C:	napkin
17	V:	uh huh
18	C:	and
19	V:	other stuff
20	C:	other stuff
21	V:	uh huh
22	C:	and then
23	V:	what does she make?
24	C:	**and then the girl, make, um**
25	V:	**do you remember? yeah? . . . b** *((makes b sound))*
26	C:	**boat?**
27	V:	**boat, good job**

In several places the volunteer recasts the child's utterances as in turns 7 and 9: (*she's not cleaning,* and *that's right she's playing with)* in order to help the child produce the narrative. The volunteer also frequently slips into an evaluative role. In turn 11, for example, she says, *good job,* commenting on Marisol's remembering the word *melon.* Moreover, at various moments in the exchange, the volunteer interrupts the narrative (e.g., turn 8) by focusing on a detail in the story or in the picture that might not have been the focus of the child's narrative direction.

At several points the exchange resembles an eliciting and evaluating interaction that focuses on vocabulary (turns 13–22) rather than the unfolding of the narrative itself. For example, in turn 24, after the child appears to have returned to the narrative (*and then the girl make um),* the volunteer responds to Marisol's hesitation by producing the elicit, *do you remember?* asking the child to recall the label for what the character in the story made. When the child cannot reply, she provides a hint so that Marisol can remember the word *boat.* Finally, she evaluates the production of the target word by saying *good job* when the child says the expected word.

In later segments of the storytelling sequence, the volunteer is much less intrusive, but still prompts Marisol for an additional detail in turn 39 asking, *what does the girl say?* She expands the child's utterances (*with your doll, with your bear)* in turn 43 and 45 but otherwise simply indicates that she is engaged and listening (turns 47 and 49).

28	C:	and then the mom he say, go to the, go put the pijama?
29	V:	pajamas on, uh huh
30	C:	and then, and then the mom is
31	V:	((pretends to brush her hair))
32	C:	((pretends to brush her hair and makes sound effect))
33	V:	((laughs)) brushing?
34	C:	brushing your hair
35	V:	[uh huh, uh huh
36	C:	but not brushing?
37	V:	but it's not brushing right? it's not going yeah
38	C:	and then the-
39	V:	**and what does the girl say?**
40	C:	[girl is ow ow ow
41	V:	[ow ow, you're hurting me you're hurting me
42	C:	((turns page)) then, brushing your hair with you, play
43	V:	**with your doll, uh huh**
44	C:	then you, you, you bread and xx
45	V:	**[with your bear, uh huh**

46 C: he say the mom, the, the little girl he say good night
47 V: good night
48 C: and then you dad
49 V: uh huh
50 C: the, he say, este *((uses Spanish hesitation marker))* go to the sleep
51 V: uh huh, time to go to sleep

In the final segment, Marisol's narrative momentarily breaks down in turn 56, and she communicates that she has gotten stuck in the middle of an utterance. She is rescued by the volunteer who asks her to remember what they saw in the book and provides her with a needed vocabulary item *(hug)*.

52 C: and then, we read the, the, the book and then the, the dad he say, good night little girl
53 V: good night little girl that's right
54 C: *((turns page))* but the girl is not asleep
55 V: no she can't sleep
56 C: **[and then, the mom go and**   *((long pause, leans head back))* **I don't know**
57 V: remember the book? the book that we read, and he says hug, hug, hug *((hugs herself))* so the mom gives, gives the girl a hug
58 C: hug
59 V: yeah
60 C: and then, he's going to sleep *((turns page))*
61 V: uh huh
62 C: and then the, the girl's not sleep
63 V: no
64 C: and then is, um the the, cómo digo? *(how do I say?)*
65 V: oh she puts the covers *((pretends to pull covers over herself))* uh huh
66 C: over your head
67 V: uh huh
68 C: and then the girl is runned, mom mom!
69 V: why is she running?
70 C: because is scared
71 V: 'cause she's scared that's right
72 C: [and then the, the, the girl is go to the dad
73 V: uh huh
74 C: and then the dad he say, it's okay and then
75 V: that's right
76 C: and then, la, go to the bed
77 V: yeah
78 C: [and then, but the dad is asleep

79 V: then the dad goes to sleep so silly look at him he fell asleep
80 C: then, the girl is put on your shoes
81 V: uh huh
82 C: [and go to the room with your mom
83 V: uh huh
84 C: but your mom is sleep
85 V: the mom goes to sleep
86 C: and then, and then, and then the mom sleep and then, your, your dad put
        the girl in the bed
87 V: uh hum
88 C: [and then, and then the girl sleep

Quite clearly, the narrative produced by Marisol is jointly constructed and rudimentary. It depends on strategic questions by the volunteer to move the action forward and to remind Marisol about particular details. An individual not familiar with the story who listens to her narrative might have difficulty following her account. For Marisol, however, the session provided her with the opportunity to attempt to tell a story in an interaction in which her tutor provided approbatory feedback as well as just-in-time assistance. We argue that opportunities to try out particular tasks in relatively safe contexts can be beneficial to children's developing ease in carrying them out in other perhaps higher stakes contexts. On the other hand, we also note that the greatest challenge for volunteers involved in these types of exchanges was refraining from diverting the child's intended narrative direction with questions on details that they, as adults, considered important.

COMMUNICATIVE CHALLENGES

Interactions between volunteers and children involved a number of communicative challenges to deal with including children's fatigue at the end of the school day, their eagerness to go home or to join the after-school program before snack time ended, distracting comings and goings of other children, and the noise level in the classroom where several volunteer-child pairs worked. At 5, 6, and 7 years old, ELLs could be charming, irritable, excited, and bored all within a very few minutes. Engaging in "conversations" with English-speaking adults was a new experience for them.

In order to provide access to English to these young ELLs, however, volunteers had to be able to control children's behavior under less-than-ideal circumstances by keeping them interested and engaged with materials and activities. Unfortunately, keeping children engaged and interested was much more difficult than it might seem. Except for occasional babysitting, many volunteers had little experience with youngsters. In order to function well in *One-on-One English*, they had to acquire skills that other volunteers who had young brothers and sisters had already developed: how to establish who is in charge, how to maintain joint attention, how to engage, cajole, play, and establish limits.

Moreover, as we pointed out above, it was not easy for volunteers to establish effective connections between the activities they were engaged in and children's lives and experiences. Because there was a clear disconnect between children's social and cognitive developmental levels and their proficiencies in English, it was difficult for volunteers to relate to ELL children as they might to fluent English-speaking youngsters. Attempts to link to children's background knowledge or lives (e.g., *Do you think you would like to have a pet rat?*) often failed because children could not understand unexpected questions about nonpresent or nonobservable topics. Few volunteers, however, were actually aware of these communication failures. They did not understand that because ELLs were eager to please and recognized turn signals, they felt compelled to provide some type of response to such questions, whether they understood them or not. In a surprisingly large numbers of cases, children produced what we have referred to as the *ambiguous head gesture,* a circular head movement that combines a head shake and a nod. For beginners, this gesture might indicate a failure to understand an unexpected, off-topic question, and for more advanced learners it could indicate an inability to express themselves effectively in English in response to questions about which they might actually have much to say.

The next transcript presents an example of the use of personalizing or linking moves by one volunteer. We describe this example in detail because we believe that comprehending and responding to such moves is one of the most difficult communicative challenges faced by all young ELLs in English instructional settings. They are used frequently in most classrooms, however, because teachers have been taught to bridge children's lives and experiences and classroom topics and to build on their background knowledge.

When they occur, personalizing or linking moves function as subsequences or parenthetical asides that depart from the main instructional topic. Interpreting such subsequences is difficult particularly for beginning English learners because they must recognize unexpected topic shifts at a point at which they are at the beginning stages of developing their ability to comprehend presentational classroom language.

In this transcript, Lino, a kindergartner who at the very early stages of his participation in *One-on-One English* is working with a volunteer who is attempting to carry out an engaging and telling interaction. The transcript contains several sub-sequences that illustrate the volunteer's attempts to personalize the story and to link in some way to Lino's background knowledge and experiences. These sub-sequences are presented in bold type.

1   V: *((opens book))* okay so here's a little boy *((points to picture))* he's walking
         back from school, and he's singing, **did you ever realize you can sing
         when we walk from school?**
2   C: *((nods))*
3   V: **yeah? I do too** *((turns page))* and he sees something, the little boy sees
         something *((points to object in the picture))* and he says, oh what is this? it
         looks like, it looks like it could be a r-
4   C: *((tries to turn the page))*
5   V: *((keeps her finger on the object she is pointing to, thus preventing Lino from turning
         the page))* is that a rock? or is it an egg? let's see *((turns page with Lino and
         gasps))* something cracks open, it's a bird *((points to next page where newly
         hatched bird is in the cracked shell))* **how did–remember the bird? from
         here** *((reaches for another book on the floor and starts to turn the pages))* **where
         is the bird?** *((turns more pages, finds page in the book and points to a picture of
         birds flying))* **remember the birds? they're coming** *((points back at baby
         bird in book they are looking at))* **he's a little baby bird, he goes peep
         peep peep**
6   C: *((Shakes his head several times))*
7   V: **remember?**
8   C: *((continues to shake his head))*
9   V: *((laughs and turns page))* and the little boy says, oh my goodness, I have
         my own bird, I have my own bird, he says peep peep peep *((both Lino
         and volunteer turn the page))* and he says well I'm leaving, he tells the bird
         ((points to the bird)) bye *((waves her hand))* I'm leaving and he's going home
         ((moves her finger across the page to indicate movement)) he's still walking, but
         the bird *((points to the bird))* he's, walking behind him *((makes walking
         gesture with fingers))* he keeps walking *((turns page))* and he says, no bird
         you have to stay *((puts out hand to signal stay))* I'm going home *((points to
         herself))* and he says, the bird says *((points to the bird in the picture))* please, I
         want to go home with you, and the little boy keeps walking *((makes moving
         motion with arm, taking it off the page))* and the, that man says *((points to
         a picture of a man in the book))* what is he doing? *((turns page))* this bird's
         following him, he can't leave him alone *((turns page))* and then his parents
         are here *((points to picture of parents))* **what happens if you brought
         home a pet?** *((looks at Lino))* **if you brought home a bird, would your
         parents be mad?**
10 C: *((Lino looks down and bows his whole body in what could be interpreted as a nod))*
         yes
11 V: yeah, my parents would be mad too

    In this exchange, the volunteer begins to describe the pictures in the sto-
rybook and to tell the story. She interrupts her own narrative in turn 1 and
begins a sub-sequence with a communicative act that we label *personalize:* (*do*

you realize we can sing when we're walking to school?). As is normally accepted school practice, she is attempting to make the story more accessible for Lino by linking what is happening in the book to his experiences. It is unclear, however, whether Lino actually comprehends.

In turn 5, the volunteer begins another sub-sequence, this time attempting to remind Lino that he is familiar with birds. This second sub-sequence includes several elicits: (*remember the bird? remember the birds?*) to which Lino responds by shaking his head. He does not immediately respond, but after the volunteer has made several other attempts to get him to reply, he begins to shake his head. It is not clear whether he has recognized the question, or why he is shaking his head so emphatically. It is unlikely that at this stage of his English language development, he would be able to comprehend a question that interrupts a narrative and focuses on a nonpresent, nonobservable topic. He gives little evidence of having comprehended the question asked by the volunteer or her broader pedagogical and communicative purpose.

Finally, in turn 8, Lino also displays what we take to be the recognition of a turn signal and a production of a reply in spite of his possible lack of understanding. In turn 9, the volunteer continues the narrative of the story. She indicates that the little bird follows the boy home and once again interrupts her descriptive narrative by asking Lino what his parents would do if he brought home a pet. At that point, he says *yes* bowing from his waist. The volunteer says *yeah* almost simultaneously and continues with her narrative.

VOLUNTEER-CHILD INTERACTIONS: A SUMMARY

Volunteer-child interactions in the *One-on-One English* after-school program provided young English language learners with a variety of affordances or "action possibilities" (Atkinson et al., 2007; Gibson, 1977; Van Lier, 2004) for using English in a social context to establish and maintain relationships with ordinary speakers of the language. Volunteers and children presented and performed identities in interaction, took part in turn taking, participation, and opportunity structures, and jointly accomplished the talk that unfolded between them (Goodwin & Goodwin, 1992). The many examples of talk that took place between children and volunteers that make up our data include a broad range of interactions. In many of these interactions, adult talk dominated and children listened and responded, often minimally. Nevertheless, they entered into what Atkinson et al. (2007) referred to as "coordinated interaction with the language being learned" (p. 172), and were supported by a broad range of different types of affordances: literacy tools (books and games); embodied tools (gestures, pantomimes, eye gaze, facial expressions); social tools (turn taking and interaction); individuals and their various roles (university students, church members, volunteers, tutors, ordinary speakers of English); socially defined participation structures (conversations, lessons, tutoring sessions); and historical trajectories (volunteer backgrounds, cross-cultural experiences, educational backgrounds). In Gee's (1995) terms, young ELLs participating in *One-on-One English* were "inserted" into social interaction as though they were speakers of English. In the best interactions they were scaffolded in their participation before "they could ever carry their own weight" (Gee, 1995, p. 336).

As we pointed out above, some children were embedded in rich and nurturing language activities with their volunteers. Others were exposed to much less language. Moreover, volunteers and children behaved quite differently at various times. The same volunteers sometimes engaged in engaging and telling interactions and other times in eliciting and evaluating interactions. Children who were sometimes silent were seen at other times taking rapid turns, commenting spontaneously on topics and objects of interest, and departing from the focus of the interaction planned by the volunteer. What is evident is that in their interactions with ordinary speakers of English in *One-on-One English*, ELL children engaged in a variety of spoken encounters in which the purpose of the interaction was to ensure both providing access to the language to young ELLs and also continuing the relationship of participants. Some of those conversations were reminiscent of parent-child communication with very young children, and others were similar to those normally carried out in instructional settings with older children. Like the infants and their parents described by Tomasello (2003), in engaging and telling interactions, children coordinated their behaviors "with both objects and people, resulting in a referential triangle of child, adult, and the object or event to which they share attention" (p. 21). Volunteers established a common ground, a joint attentional frame using program materials, and children "treated each communicative attempt as an expression of the adult's intention to direct their attention in ways relevant to the current situation" (p. 23).

Elicit and evaluate interactions were not strictly speaking exchanges of the same type. They were more similar to the three-part, predetermined sequences such as IRE's that are common in ordinary classrooms and in which the object of the interaction is very different from that found in parent-infant conversations. Moreover, these particular sequences did not necessarily have as a key purpose ensuring the continuing relationship of participants. Their key purpose involved what is often conceived of as "teaching," although fundamentally such exchanges seemed primarily to involve determining what children already knew. Instruction or teaching was limited to the small amount of information that was sometimes given in the feedback segment of the exchange (e.g., *no, it isn't a tiger, it's a lion*).

As was evident from the descriptions of interactions we provided in this chapter, access to both English and to different types of affordances varied for different children. It is reasonable to expect that the various patterns of language interaction that took place between children and volunteers created somewhat dissimilar contexts for "additional language learning" (Hellerman, 2008). The analyses included in the chapter that follows will describe the practices used by adult volunteers and young ELLs in accomplishing social actions and the changes observed in children's participation and interactional competence over a 2–3-year period through their engagement in interactions with ordinary speakers of English.

CHAPTER 4

The Development of L2 Interactional Competence

As we pointed out in Chapter 3, the children who were part of *One-on-One English* began their journey as English language learners by taking small steps. At the beginning of their participation in the program, some were cooperative but tentative, some were reluctant, and some were eager and curious. Their growth and progress in acquiring English was not linear. In this chapter we examine the changes that took place over time in the interactional competence of the nine children who participated in *One-on-One English* for a period of 2 or 3 academic years. By *interactional competence* we mean the ability to function in one-on-one interactions with adult speakers of English using their developing language resources.

In our analysis, we draw from video recordings of the children as they interacted twice a week with different volunteers. We describe the ways in which they first began to participate in English conversational exchanges, the challenges they faced, and the kinds of strategies that they used to take part in the volunteer-ELL after-school interactions. We also portray the ways in which children adapted to various interactional styles, types of exchanges, and the different expectations of the various volunteers.

GETTING STARTED

For the children who were absolute beginners, getting started in their trajectories as English learners and users by participating in on-on-one interactions with unknown volunteers presented numerous challenges. Some of these interactions required them to listen to volunteers' explanations and presentations, while others called on them to respond to various different types of questions and to participate in games and other activities. In analyzing children's beginning interactions with volunteers, we focused on describing the youngsters' participation in these exchanges in such a way that we might represent various different manifestations of their developing receptive and productive competencies. In this section we offer examples of behaviors in volunteer sessions and illustrate the various trajectories that we observed across all focal children, in particular types of youngsters, and in individual children.

The following interactions are illustrative of those that took place at the beginning of children's participation in the program. In the first interaction Elsa, a kindergartner (labeled in the transcript as C, for child) is looking at the book *A Very Hungry Caterpillar* with her volunteer (who is labeled in the transcript as V). The book tells the story of a caterpillar that ate different types of food and then emerged as a butterfly. The volunteer—who sees herself as a source of rich language—is utilizing small food-shaped props that accompany the book as well as a velcro glove on which food that is mentioned in the book can be placed. She is using a register of English that we refer to as *ELL-directed speech*. It has some features of child-directed speech as described by Ninio and Snow (1996), Ninio et al. (1994), and Snow and Ferguson (1977), and foreigner talk as described by Ferguson (1975). In this particular case, the register used by the volunteer includes the use of very short sentences (*He ate two pears, He ate three plums*), repetition (*Three? three. He ate three plums;* and *one orange, two orange, three orange, four orange, five oranges*), and questions that can be answered with a single word (*How many strawberries?*). The interaction proceeds as follows.

1   V: **he ate, two pears** *((has velcro glove on right hand, attaches two stuffed pears to glove))* these are pears *((makes munching sounds and pretends stuffed caterpillar is eating the pears))* **he ate two pears,** and how many are next? *((removes pears from glove and turns page))*

2   C: *((puts right hand on book to hold it open, looks up at camera and back at book))*

3   V: **three? three, he ate three plums** *((attaches plums to glove))* mmm, here he goes *((makes munching sounds and pantomimes caterpillar eating plums))* he ate three plums *((turns page))* how many strawberries? *((removes plums from glove))*

4   C: four

5   V: **four strawberries, four strawberries** *((attaches strawberries to glove))* wow that's a lot of strawberries, he ate four strawberries *((makes munching sounds and pantomimes caterpillar eating strawberries))* mmm, he likes eating strawberries *((removes strawberries))* what did he eat next? *((turns page))* he ate oranges, how many?

6   C: *((pointing to oranges in picture))* one, two, three *((points to final two oranges without saying numbers))*

7   V: xx five, he ate five of 'em, let's see *((attaches oranges to glove while counting))* **one orange, two orange, three orange, four orange, five oranges,** he ate five oranges so here's the caterpillar, he'll eat one orange *((makes*

munching sounds as she counts)) two orange, three oranges, four oranges, five oranges, yummy *((removes oranges from glove))* he was still hungry

8   C: *((starts turning page))*

9   V: *((takes page and continues turning it))* still hungry, oh we don't have those foods *((chuckles))* so he ate some cake *((pointing to food in illustration))* some cheese

10   C: sss *((attempts to repeat cheese?))*

11   V: some pie

12   C: *((looks up at camera))*

13   V: you're on camera *((chuckles))* some pie, and a cupcake

Throughout the interaction, Elsa remains engaged and looks at the book and at the velcro props as they are picked up and handled by the volunteer. She sits with her hand on the book, leans over it, points to objects, and occasionally turns pages. Elsa demonstrates that she can engage in interaction and attend to topics or objects nominated for attention by the volunteer. She clearly recognizes turn-taking signals and gives evidence in turns 4 and 6 that she both comprehends requests for display of information and can display the requested information.

By comparison, at the beginning of her participation in the project, Graciela, a second-grade student participated in an interaction with the same book with her volunteer somewhat differently. The video shows her standing up, taking possession of the book and quickly turning the pages, after commenting (in Spanish) that she is already familiar with the story and the book. The volunteer insists that they should look at the book, and the child points to various objects saying several words in English as she points (e.g., *moon, sun*). When the child is finally persuaded to sit down, they both look at the book together, and the volunteer begins an eliciting and evaluating exchange.

1   V: can you show me, can you show me the egg, on this page?

2   C: **((points to illustration))**

3   V: there's the egg, that's right *((points to illustration))* this is a little, little tiny egg *((gestures with fingers to indicate something very small))* little tiny

4   C: **es este, de aquí** *(it's this one, from here)* *((turns several pages and points to caterpillar))*

5   V: [on the leaf

6   C: **aquí viene, aquí** *((pointing to illustration))* **aquí, es la oruga** *(here it comes, here, here, it's the caterpillar)*

7   V: and he comes out of the egg, it's a caterpillar, can you say caterpillar?

8   C: xxx *((finger is in her mouth, responds in almost a whisper))*

9   V: it's a hard word, let's say it again, caterpillar

10   C: xxx
11   V: *((nods in a way that suggests child's repetition is not perfect but passable))*
12   C: *((points at something in illustration))*
13   V: *((points to caterpillar))* so here's the caterpillar, can you show me the sun?
14   C: **sun** *((points at illustration))*
15   V: [where's the sun? there's the sun, that's right
16   C: *((turns page))*
17   V: it's in the morning
18   C: mire la oruga se comió todo esto *(look the caterpillar ate all this)*

There is evidence in turn 2 (where she points to an object as requested) and in turn 14 (where she also points as requested and says the word *sun*) that Graciela comprehends more English than she can or is willing to produce. However, it is also evident, that in order to express a broader range of meanings than her English allows, Graciela responds and comments in Spanish (*es este, de aquí* and *aquí viene, aquí aquí, es la oruga*). This type of interaction was typical of four of the nine focal children whose language growth we will discuss in this chapter. Each of these children frequently used Spanish for various communicative actions including rejecting their volunteer's suggestions, teasing, taking control of the interaction, and translating in order to check the accuracy of their understanding of the volunteer's talk. We will say more about the use of Spanish by children in the sections that follow.

The experience of starting out was quite different for Lino. In his early sessions he was paired with a volunteer who understood her role as that of language teacher. She thus attempted to teach receptive and productive vocabulary directly to a kindergartner who was an absolute beginner. In the interaction transcribed below, the volunteer has just finished pointing to parts of her face, asking him to repeat the label for each part (*nose, mouth*), and giving him TPR-like commands (*touch your face, touch your mouth*).[1] She then wants the child to produce these same commands telling her what parts of her own face she should touch (turn 1). In this same turn, she determines that he does not understand what she says and therefore attempts to translate her request (*dígame, una cosa, en la cabeza, for- para mí*). The child responds by saying the word *eyes*, which the volunteer accepts (turn 3) by producing a physical response and touching her eyes and then asking *qué más?* Because of the volunteer's tendency to translate, it is not clear how much Lino consistently understood. There is evidence, however, that he did understand her question in turn 7 (*what do I use, Lino, what do I use to eat with?*) coupled with her pantomime of pretending to eat. He rubs his mouth in response in turn 8 and gives the Spanish term (*boca*) in turn 10.

1   V: **Lino, will you tell, tell me, what you want me to touch?** *((pointing to herself))* **can you tell me?** *((points to child, then herself))* dígame, una cosa,

en la cabeza, for- para mi *(tell me one thing in the head for me)* can you tell me?

2   C: **eyes**
3   V: **eyes *((touches her eyes))* qué más?** *(what else?)*
4   C: ears
5   V: ears *((touches and wiggles her ears))* what else?
6   C: *((looks away, at the floor))*
7   V: **what do I use, Lino, what do I use to eat with?** *((pretends to be eating))*
8   C: *((rubs mouth with hand))*
9   V: **what do we call it?**
10 C: **boca** *(mouth)*
11 V: the boca, sí, pero en inglés es? *(mouth, yes, but in English it's?)* *((pretends to be eating))* you call it the mouth
12 C: mouth
13 V: wonderful, you knew that one in, in Spanish right? and then, Lino, the last thing was the nose *((points to her nose))* can you touch your nose?
14 C: *((touches nose))*
15 V: wonderful

In this interaction Lino sits on the floor with his volunteer, and his attention wanders frequently. He complies with his volunteer's requests, recognizes turn-taking signals, and sometimes repeats spontaneously but appears disinterested and uninvolved.

RECEPTIVE PROFICIENCIES: CHANGE OVER TIME

Contrary to what has been suggested by a number of researchers, interpersonal interactions make a number of demands on both children and adults involved in such interactions. While it is true that interpersonal interactions occur in context and that there is an opportunity for participants to take advantage of a number of extralinguistic cues to support their understanding, the challenges involved—especially in comprehending spontaneous, unplanned spoken language—are not simple. Moreover, as Rost (1990) points out, one of the least understood aspects of second language acquisition is the development of the ability to understand spoken language, including rapid speech that may contain flaws, redundancies, fillers, self-corrections, and abandoned or incomplete utterances. For young ELLs engaged in face-to-face interactions with English-speaking strangers, "conversation" with their volunteers required that they participate in a joint activity in which they were expected to attend to the material nominated for joint attention, to show attentiveness, to recognize turn-taking signals, and to respond appropriately. As might be expected, in order to respond appropriately, youngsters needed to comprehend what their volunteers said or to guess intelligently about the probable content of the volunteers' language. The first step in their journey to becoming competent users of English, then, was not necessarily the ability to produce English, but rather, the ability to comprehend what was said to them in one-on-one or in many-to-one interactions.

In examining the development of interactive competence of the nine children that we describe in this chapter, we follow O'Malley, Chamot, and Kupper (1987) and take the position that comprehension is an active process in which a listener "constructs meaning by using cues from contextual information and from existing knowledge, while relying upon multiple strategies to fulfill the task requirement" (p. 434). Unfortunately, receptive competence is very difficult to evaluate in children. As Hurtado, Marchman, and Fernald (2007) argue: "Determining what young language learners understand in the speech they hear can be challenging, because the processes involved in comprehension are only partially and inconsistently revealed in children's behavior in everyday situations" (p. 228). As a result, researchers who focus on language understanding by very young children prefer what are called "online" measures, such as eye movements, to evaluate children's developing speech processing efficiency. In our case we relied exclusively on "off-line" indicators of comprehension, such as children's systematic responses to questions and requests of various types. The types of behaviors that we viewed as early manifestations of children's comprehension of their interlocutors' English included

- Attending to the topic/object nominated for attention by volunteer
- Recognizing common turn-taking signals
- Carrying out actions as requested (e.g., pointing to specific objects, repeating, standing, sitting)
- Recognizing and responding to choice questions (e.g., *Is this a bear or a cat?*)
- Recognizing and responding to yes/no questions (e.g., *Is he sleeping?*)

All nine focal children consistently displayed these behaviors during the first few sessions of their participation in the program. What this means is that children were able to figure out from the context what was expected of them, to take their turn as participants in the conversation, and to produce appropriate responses.

We are not prepared to say, however, that the children could consistently understand all or most of their volunteers' language. As we pointed out in Chapter 3 in our discussion of personalized or linking questions, when the conversation deviated from what children could predict given the topic or object of attention, they were unable to make sense of their volunteers' comments or questions. At the beginning of their time in the program, for example, most children did not understand questions that depended on unknown vocabulary, the meaning of which could not be deduced from the context. They clearly recognized that they were being asked a question and that a reply was expected, but if they did not know a particular key word, they could not guess intelligently at the possible meaning of the volunteer's question.

The next transcript illustrates the types of misunderstandings that often occurred when volunteers overestimated children's ability to follow rapid topic shifts. In this interaction, the volunteer was, in theory, talking about the book *A Very Hungry Caterpillar*. However, she engages in a type of exchange that involved numerous unrelated questions. This type of exchange was particularly confusing for beginning learners of English like Ernesto because talk shifted from one topic to another. Here the volunteer begins with colors and asks, in turn 1, (perhaps because no other examples of the color yellow are available to her) whether there is yellow in her eyes (*is there any yellow in my eyes?*). The child nods, but it is not clear how much he understands. The volunteer then moves to various illustrations in the book and asks Ernesto to identify a particular object (*how about this, what's this, big thing here?*). He replies appropriately with a single word (*sun*), and he is then asked conjecture about the sun's temperature (turn 7). The child again responds appropriately (turn 8) perhaps using the volunteer's physical actions to guess intelligently at the meaning of her question.

1 V: **is there any yellow in my eyes?**
2 C: *((looks at her eyes and nods once))*
3 V: some yellow? kind of green and yellow
4 C: [*((looks at camera then down at the book, nods slightly))*
5 V: *((looks at book))* **so, how about this, what's this, big thing here?** *((points to the illustration of the sun))*
6 C: sun
7 V: **sun yeah, and if you touched the sun, it'd be hot? do you think? hot or cold?** *((points to the illustration of the sun, points and removes finger quickly as if she were touching a hot object))*
8 C: **hot**
9 V: hot, ouch, hot *((touches the sun in the book, pretends that it is sizzling hot))* okay, so we have a bug here, right? *((points to caterpillar in picture))* the caterpillar?
10 C: *((nods))*

The conversation then moves to a focus on the caterpillar, the main character in the book that the two were working with. In turn 11, the volunteer asks what the caterpillar is going to do, and Ernesto responds, again appropriately. When the volunteer asks a personalized question (*are you hungry right now? are you hungry, Ernesto?*), however, the child appears confused and uncomfortable and does not respond.

11   V: what's he gonna do? *((turns page))*
12   C: eat *((smiles))*
13   V: eat, right, is he hungry?
14   C: *((nods))*
15   V: **are you hungry right now? are you hungry, Ernesto?**
16   C: ***((nods, switch in disposition, he was smiling but now seems uncomfortable))***
17   V: yeah? *((nods))* ok, so what's he gonna eat?

The majority of the focal children participated in interactions with their volunteers very much the way that Ernesto did. They either said nothing, or they attempted to produce as much English as they knew when requested to do so. Frequently, they masked their misunderstandings of their volunteers' questions or comments and continued to fill slots in the interaction as conversational partners.

Several children in the study, however, were what we refer to as strongly *Spanish preferent.* These children tended to revert to Spanish wherever possible in the interaction and were more reluctant to use English than were other children. We conjecture that this reluctance to use English had to do with the fact that English did not allow them to present themselves authentically as competent young people.[2] These children included three second graders (Graciela, Marisol, and Selena) who had very well developed first language skills as well as one kindergartner (Fabiola) who, for slightly different reasons, tended to resort to Spanish more than did the other children in the study.

The next transcript makes obvious the kinds of misunderstandings that could take place between these beginning learners and volunteers. In this case the misunderstandings are obvious because the child has insisted on using Spanish. In this interaction, Graciela and the volunteer are looking at a sticker packet of Disney princesses. As was her style, Graciela maintains Spanish for most of the interaction in which she talks about the resemblance between the princesses and members of her family. It is evident that she has some understanding of what her volunteer says, but it is also evident that both individuals have only a partial understanding of what is said by the other interlocutor.

1   V: she's a princess but do you remember what her name is? *((pointing at one of the princess stickers))*
2   C: *((shakes head))*

3 V: this is from Beaut-Beauty and the Beast and her name is Belle
4 C: mi, mi mamá dice que ella es mi hermana *(my mom says that she is my sister)*
5 V: oh yeah, she looks like your sister
6 C: [mi mamá quiere de, quiere que xx *(my mom wants xx)*
7 V: you're, you're Jasmine and your sister is Belle?
8 C: uh huh
9 V: okay, how many sisters do you have?
10 C: [y esta es mi prima *(and this one is my cousin)* cousin
       ((pointing at another sticker))
11 V: **your- your cousin? does she, does she have blonde, does she have
       blonde hair like that?**
12 C: mm *((nods))*
13 V: **she has blonde hair, she has blonde hair?**
14 C: [no, mi prima *(no, my cousin)* *((points
       at a different sticker))*
15 V: your cousin has
16 C: ese es mi prima *(that one is my cousin)*
17 V: **oh ok, so your cousin has brown hair?**
18 C: **no mi hermana, yo, mi prima** *(no my sister, me, my cousin)* *((pointing at
       three different stickers))*
19 V: **everyone has, this color hair?** *((touches child's hair))*
20 C: **no, liso** *(no, straight)* *((turns to girl on her left side))* **dile como tiene liso mi
       hermana** *(tell her how my sister has straight hair)*
21 V: oh
22 C: *((still addressing other girl))* **mi prima tiene liso el pelo** *(my cousin has
       straight hair)*
23 C2: he have, his hair um *((runs her hand over her own straight hair))* straight
24 V: [straight, straight like yours, like yours
25 C: prima *(cousin)*
26 V: [and yours *((referring back to Graciela))* yours is curly
27 C: yo soy esta *(I am this one)* *((pointing to sticker))*
28 V: oh yeah she's got kind of curly hair, do you know her name? *((pointing at
       another sticker))*
29 C: no yo soy las dos mejor *(no I am both of them, that's better)* *((points at two
       stickers))*
30 V: ahhh, those are the two best friends
31 C2: *((points at second sticker))*
32 C: esta es mi hermana dice mi mamá *(my mom says that one is my sister)*
33 V: Belle, that's, that's your sister?

What is particularly interesting about this interaction is that the child is
attending to hair texture in pointing out similarities between her sister and

her cousin and the Disney princesses, while the volunteer is focused on hair color. Differences in perspective such as this were often part of the challenge of communicating for both volunteers and English language learners. Often they had different views about the world that surrounded them, about what mattered, and about what was worth commenting on. In this particular bilingual, nonreciprocal interaction, Graciela maintains her primary language in every single turn of the exchange. She gives evidence, however, in turns 18 and 20, that she comprehends enough English to figure out that the volunteer has not understood her. Frustrated by the state of affairs, Graciela asks another child to tell the volunteer that her sister has straight hair (*dile como tiene liso mi hermana*). In this particular case even though the other child was only partially successful in communicating what Graciela wanted to convey, she does convey the word *straight*. In turn 24 the volunteer either guesses or understands that the characteristic that interests Graciela is hair texture rather than hair color. Throughout the interaction it is evident that what is important to this 7-year-old is actually communicating what she wants to say to the young adult with whom she is working, rather than simply "practicing" her English.

Children exhibited changes in their ability to make sense of their interlocutors' language over time. They moved from taking turns appropriately, guessing intelligently at meaning, and choosing elements in choice questions to behaviors such as

- Recognizing complex turn-taking signals
- Responding to indirect requests for information or action
- Responding appropriately to questions not based on the topic or object of joint attention
- Contradicting statements made by interlocutor
- Continuing narratives begun by their volunteer at the appropriate point in the narrative,
- Demonstrating understanding of explanations by asking follow-up questions
- Participating in subtle guessing games that involved comprehending descriptions of a particular object
- Responding appropriately to personalized questions

By the end of the second year, several children could respond to personalized or linking questions that sought to connect their personal experiences with the materials they were attending to. The next transcript shows Marisol and her volunteer engaged in reading a book about various kinds of bugs. Marisol recognizes and responds to a personalized question and shares her experience appropriately. In turn 3 the volunteer asks a personalized question: *have you ever had a bug land on you?* In turn 4 Marisol shares an incident involving a ladybug in response to the volunteer's question. Her response contains numerous false starts and hesitations, and her description depends to a great degree on gestures and pantomime; nevertheless, her answer makes it very clear that she understood a personalized or linking question which, at the beginning of her exposure to English, she and the other children in the program would not have been able to comprehend.

1   V: look at those, those are huge bugs *((pointing at bugs in illustration))* and that-

2   C: yeah

3   V: **butterfly, have you ever had a bug land on you?** *((touches Marisol's arm, like a bug landing on her))*

4   C: **one day uh um, is a like a little bit, um some, one day I xx, I, I see a ladybug, and then I was put like that my finger** *((sticks her index finger out))* **and then, I was like that and the ladybug go up** *((runs her other finger up her arm))*

5   V: and it tickles you whenever it's crawling on you *((moves her fingers like a bug crawling on her arm))*

As is the case in this example, over time children were able to comprehend questions that attempted to bridge their lives and experiences and classroom topics. Moreover, they attempted to respond to them with the rudimentary linguistic resources they had developed up to that point.

PRODUCTIVE PROFICIENCIES: CHANGE OVER TIME

As was the case with children's receptive competence, the children's ability to produce language also changed over time. The productive language behaviors that were observed in most focal children appeared in the following order:

- Responds to choice questions (single word or lexical phrase)
- Responds to yes/no questions
- Repeats as requested
- Responds to wh-/questions (*What is this? Who is sleeping?*)
- Labels objects as requested (*bear, dog*)
- Labels actions as requested (*sleeping*)
- Counts as requested
- Joins in repeating pattern (*five little monkeys jumping on the bed*)
- Uses known pattern independently (*You can't catch me. Are you my mother?*)

- Uses formula to fill turn (*I don't know*)
- Repeats spontaneously (words)
- Repeats spontaneously (phrases, multiword utterances)
- Comments spontaneously (one word)
- Comments spontaneously (multiword)
- Displays knowledge or information spontaneously (counts, labels)
- Requests information of volunteer
- Requests action of volunteer
- Contradicts
- Interrupts
- Retells book (says one word, points, and turns pages)
- Retells book (says pattern, turns pages)
- Retells book (multiword utterances, turns pages)
- Displays information about academic material
- Explains

In the rest of this section we present detailed summaries of the developmental trajectories of three very different children: Aracely, Ernesto, and Selena. We present segments of exchanges that contain one or more of the various behaviors listed above in order to illustrate how these behaviors changed over time. For each of these children we present a more complete list of communicative and interactive behaviors that they engaged in successfully. These lists were developed by drawing from the detailed descriptions of each of the video sessions recorded for each child. The descriptions noted the interactional behaviors observed in each child in each session. The lists included here present these behaviors in the order in which they appeared.

Aracely

Aracely was a very quiet child, who was either personally very shy or who had been socialized into ways of speaking that were very different from those normally expected in White middle-class children. She initially said very little. For the entire first year of her participation in the program, she participated nonverbally or with one-word responses to all questions and requests. Typically, she would not touch the book or the materials with which she and her volunteer were engaged. She was the epitome of a well-behaved little girl who paid rapt attention but who spoke minimally. She gave evidence that she comprehended what was said to her because she would point, nod, or shake her head appropriately, but when she spoke, it was barely above a whisper.

The transcript below gives an example of an early exchange between Aracely and her first-year volunteer. In this interaction her volunteer, Aracely, and another volunteer are at the table using a laminated house scene and lotto cards. Aracely has to identify which rooms the object on the lotto cards belong in. Note that Aracely gives evidence of comprehension, but she does not produce audible language.

1   C: *((picks up the next lotto card))*
2   V: hmm, what are those? can you show me how you use them?
3   C: *((looks at volunteer))*
4   V: how do you use scissors?
5   C: **((her hand is out of view, may have made a cutting gesture with her hand))**
6   V: very good, they're used to cut things right? *((makes cutting gesture with her hands))* cut things, and you might use them at school, hmm if you had scissors which room would you put them in? the kitchen or the living room *((points to kitchen and living room on the house picture))* what do you think?
7   C: **((points at living room with the card))**
8   V: in the living room you think?
9   C: *((nods))*

During the second year of her participation in the program, Aracely worked with a single volunteer for most of the year. She continued to display a strong interest in the materials that she engaged with. Most of the time she produced one-word responses, responded to yes/no questions, or responded using familiar patterns from pattern books (e.g., *The sky is falling*). In a few interactions, however, she surprised us by producing spontaneous comments. For example, in the next transcript, Aracely volunteers additional information about a character in the story in turn 4 (*the one mouse give him a dollar*) and then also contributes personal information about her ownership of a piggy bank in turn 8 (*I have one*).

1   V: he starts dreaming, what's he dreaming about?
2   C: the mom's getting xx candy *((points at illustration))*
3   V: yeah, he's dreaming, he's hoping for candy
4   C: *((turns page))* **the one mouse give him a dollar**
5   V: yeah, so he has a dollar, where does he put it?
6   C: *((points to illustration))*
7   V: yeah in his piggy bank, have you seen piggies like that *((points to illustration))* that have a little hole in 'em where you can put stuff in *((gestures a hole and putting something in a piggy bank))*
8   C: **I have one** *((points to illustration))*
9   V: you have one?
10   C: *((nods))*

11   V: you put your money in there?
12   C: *((nods))*

She is clearly interested in the topic and engages further by talking about her experience.

During her third year in the program, Aracely established a very close relationship with a third volunteer. This volunteer brought her books about castles and princesses, and together they would make up original stories about these princesses. Over time, moreover, the child felt comfortable enough with the volunteer to ask her personal questions and to share quite a bit of information about her own family. In the interaction included in the transcript that follows, the child asks the volunteer about her Thanksgiving holiday in turns 1 and 3. She is interested in finding out how many days of vacation the volunteer had. As will be noted, the form of her question is quite flawed (*um, do, the, when you were in your school, do they let you, five vacation of day?*), and the volunteer asks for clarification. Aracely is able to rephrase her question in turn 3 and to communicate her meaning more precisely

1   C: **um, do, the, when you were in your school, do they let you, five vacation of day?**

2   V: what? *((leans in))*

3   C: **when you were, in your school, in second grade, they don't let you five, they, in the turkey day, um, five days of vacation?**

4   V: oh no we didn't get five days of vacation we only got, we had the weekend, so we had two days, plus I think two more days

5   C: four?

6   V: four, but the, counting the weekend

In spite of her initial reticence, by the end of her time in the program, Aracely could talk about topics that she had learned about in school and make connections with her personal experiences. In the transcript that follows, the child is providing information about penguins, animals that she has learned about in class and has also seen at the zoo. In this interaction, Aracely is able to describe penguins quite well. She says that they live in the snow (turn 4), that they eat fish (turn 6), that they are like birds (turn 8), and that they don't fly (turn 10). She is also able to respond to a wh question in turn 14 (*is because the, the penguins eat, she eats fish, and then she jumped*).

1   V: okay tell me about these guys, who are they?

2   C: **they are penguins**

3   V: tell me-

4   C: [I know, where penguins, some penguin, **some penguins, they live in the, in the snow**

5	V:	*((nods))* they do like the snow, can you tell me anything else about penguins?
6	C:	**penguins, like to eat fish**
7	V:	*((nods))* and what kind of animal are penguins?
8	C:	uh, **like a bird**
9	V:	but do they do, is there something most birds do that penguins don't do?
10	C:	the birds fly and **the penguins don't fly**
11	V:	what do penguins do?
12	C:	xx, they, get in the rocks, and goes up *((pointing to illustration))* and, and go in sometime when I go to one um, one zoo, there were a lot of penguins and rocks, and, one penguin, get in a big rock, and then jumped, to the water *((makes jumping gesture with finger))*
13	V:	what did it do in the water?
14	C:	**is because the, the penguins eat, she eats fish, and then she jumped** *((makes jumping gesture with finger))*

As the interaction continues, she is also able to disagree with her volunteer's characterization of penguins in turn 17 (*it's like they fly underwater*) by insisting in turn 20 that penguins don't fly.

15	V:	so birds fly, what do penguins do?
16	C:	um, they swim,
17	V:	**yeah they swim some people say it's like they fly under water**
18	C:	*((shakes head))*
19	V:	because they use their wings
20	C:	**but they don't fly**
21	V:	yeah they're swimming but it kinda looks like flying sometimes, penguins are pretty cool, they live, in the South Pole, and Antarctica, and they live in South America, I don't know, if there's any other places they live

Finally, Aracely is also able to relate her knowledge of penguins to what she saw when she visited a local zoo. She talks about what she saw (turn 22) and displays a single lexical gap in conveying her meaning. She switches to Spanish to communicate this detail assuming the volunteer will recognize the word *resbaladilla*, which could be translated as *slippery* if it is a characteristic of the rock and as a *slide* if she is using the term to refer to a familiar piece of playground equipment.

| 22 | C: | **you know something when I go to the zoo, I see one penguin that, first I see one family penguin, and then I see a little penguin, and that penguin and that peng, little penguin, was in the, was in a rock, sit, sitting on a little rock, and it was in the rock, and the little um, penguin, fall but it was a rock like a, um resbaladilla?** *(slide)* |

FIGURE 4.1. Aracely's Communicative Behaviors Over a 3-Year Period

Initial Behaviors in Year 1	Behaviors Added in Year 2	Behaviors Added in Year 3
Responds nonverbally	Comments spontaneously (one word)	Takes turns narrating stories
Responds to choice questions (single word or lexical phrase)	Guesses and gives labels from descriptions of objects	Produces commands for game of Simon Says
Responds to yes/no questions	Responds to questions (multiword utterances)	Interrupts
Responds to wh-questions	Responds using patterns from books	Describes pictures
Labels objects as requested	Occasionally comments spontaneously (multiword)	Asks information questions
	Asks clarification questions	Gives details about objects
		Consistently comments spontaneously
		Gives details about personal experiences
		Talks about her family
		Asks personal questions
		Predicts actions in stories
		Displays information about content material
		Shares own experiences

> *((makes an S shape with her finger))*
> 23 V: I don't know that word

After a 3-year period, Aracely could communicate a variety of meanings; she could participate in complex interactions with a native speaker of English; and she could explain and contradict. She was also able to give details about personal experiences and to display information about content materials. Figure 4.1 summarizes the various types of communicative behaviors that we observed Aracely engaged in during her participation in the program. They include some of the sample behaviors mentioned previously, but more precisely illustrate changes in Aracely's interactional competence over time.

Ernesto

Compared to Aracely, Ernesto was far more outgoing when he entered the program. He was definitely a beginner, but he appeared to have developed a number of strategies for guessing intelligently at meaning during most of his initial interactions with volunteers. The interaction presented in Ernesto's transcript earlier in this chapter appeared to have been unusual in the number of comprehension challenges that it presented for him. What was not unusual is the manner in which he handled the interaction. He was a well-behaved, serious youngster who was respectful and compliant and did not cause problems for his adult volunteers.

As a kindergartner for whom many things at school were new, Ernesto seemed to have an enormous interest in books, especially books about animals of all types. This interest was evident in his enthusiastic engagement during interactions that focused on such books. In his third interaction as a participant in the program, for example, Ernesto produced a multiword spontaneous comment about an animal. The next transcript includes an example of this interaction.

This particular interaction shows Ernesto appropriately responding nonverbally in turn 2 by pointing to a giraffe. In turn 4, however, he responds incorrectly to a choice question (*Is he purple or brown?*) by nodding instead of choosing one of the alternatives. He also responds incorrectly in turn 6 to the clarification question (*Which one?*) referring to the colors purple, red, or brown) by pointing to the picture of a mouse. He does, however, comprehend and respond correctly to a wh- question (*what kind of animals are these?*) with the single word *lion* in turn 12.

1 V: What's he yellow all
2 C: ((**points to giraffe**))
3 V: and, yeah, and, he's yellow and there's some brown like spots on him, and what color is the mouse? is the mouse purple, red, or brown
4 C: **mm** *((nods head))*
5 V: which one?
6 C: *((**points to the mouse**))*
7 V: yeah, there's the mouse is he, purple, or brown?
8 C: **brown**
9 V: brown good job, and, is there a mouse over here somewhere? *((points to other page))* in this picture?
10 C: *((**points to the mouse**))*
11 V: yeah, he's right there he's looking at, what kind of animals are these? *((points at lions))*

12 C: **lion**
13 V: lions yeah, he's looking at the lions, and there are four lions right? on this
        train?
14 C: *((nods))*
15 V: yeah, let's see who else is on the train *((turns page))* oh my goodness, what
        are these? *((points to bears in illustration))*
16 C: I don't know
17 V: are they, rabbits or bears?
18 C: bears

At a later point in the interaction, in turn 24, he ignores the volunteer's
question and makes a spontaneous comment (*this is, this one bear, is sleeping.*)
He is clearly interested in the animals that are in the illustration and wants
to share what he sees with the volunteer. In turn 30 the child once again
makes a spontaneous comment about the mouse that the volunteer has just
mentioned.

19 V: bears, yeah, how many bears are there?
20 C: five
21 V: five bears yeah, and is there a mouse there too with bears? can you see a
        mouse?
22 C: *((points at illustration))*
23 V: are the bears, are the bears the same color as the mouse?
24 C: **this is** *((points at one of the bears))* **this one bear, is sleeping**
25 V: yeah this bear is sleeping, and all the bears are brown right? they're the
        same color as the mouse right there?
26 C: brown
27 V: yeah, they're brown, so the bears are brown and the mouse is brown, and
        there are five bears on the train, and what's over here? *((points at other
        page))* what are these?
28 C: crocodiles
29 V: crocodiles, yeah
30 C: **and he's sleeping, is the mouse** *((points at mouse on top of crocodile))*
31 V: yeah, so the mouse, is sitting on top of a sleeping crocodile?
32 C: *((nods))*
33 V: yeah? what are the other crocodiles doing? what's this one doing? *((points
        at another crocodile))*
34 C: he, he's do looking over there *((points))*
35 V: yeah, he's looking at the other crocodile, and, maybe they're talking, do
        you think they're talking? or is he just looking?

By the end of his first year in the program Ernesto showed that he had increased his receptive proficiency and that he was able to understand an indirect request for correction, contradict, and ask clarification questions. In the next transcript, the volunteer and the child are looking at a pop-up book in which Spot, the main character, opens a series of windows to reveal different baby animals. In turn 5 the volunteer asks Ernesto which animal makes the sound "moo." He gives the wrong answer, *cat*, but then recognizes the request for correction that follows in turn 7. When the volunteer repeats the word *cat* with a rising intonation, he quickly corrects himself and says: *no the cow*.

1   V: and he wants to go, the, this is the, the mommy says, Spot, I'm gonna
         show you some baby animals, so Spot is going to look for the baby
         animals *((turns page))*
2   C: *((sits up straight and points at page enthusiastically))* ooh let me
3   V: said moo
4   C: [moo moo
5   V: **what do you think? who says-**
6   C: **the cat**
7   V: **cat?**
8   C: **no the, cow**
9   V: cow, right *((opens flap on page))*
10 C: *((laughs))*
11 V: *((laughs))* did the cow have a baby?
12 C: nn nn *((no))*
13 V: noooo *((shakes head))*

Later in the same interaction, in turn 14, Ernesto uses game-playing language (*your turn, your turn, you say the, the names, okay*) to ask the volunteer to continue talking about the animals in the book. The volunteer refuses (*yeah, no you say the names*), but Ernesto then contradicts her by saying in turn 16: *no you*. The volunteer agrees to continue and does so in turn 17, but when she uses the word *neigh*, the child does not understand. He then asks the volunteer to explain the meaning of the word, saying: *what is the, neigh*.

14 C: **your turn, your turn, you say the, the names, okay?**
15 V: yeah, no you say the names
16 C: *((turns page))* **no you**
17 V: okay, we'll both say the names, okay, I'll say the sounds, okay so then
         Spot, is looking through the door and you hear the sound neigh, neigh,
         what's that?

18   C: **what is the, neigh, what xx?**
19   V: neigh, you know what animal says neigh?
20   C: nn *((shakes head no))*
21   V: horse
22   C: horse

By the middle of the second year Ernesto's receptive and productive proficiencies had changed impressively. For example, he was able to take part in role-playing interactions such as the one included in the next transcript. This particular exchange involves Ernesto and his regular volunteer. As the video begins, the child and the volunteer are holding stick puppets of characters seen in the laminated school and community scenes used in the project. Allison, Diego, and Tommy were characters in a set of materials that included laminated scenes of various places and settings (e.g., playgrounds, schools, street scenes). In this interaction both the volunteer and Ernesto shake each of the puppets when they are supposedly speaking and move them around to indicate that they are carrying out different actions. The particular exchange is complicated and requires that Ernesto speak for various characters and create the talk produced between them.

In turns 1, 3, and 5 Ernesto talks for his puppets and interacts with his volunteer who is also speaking for her puppets. He responds to her puppet's question: *where'd you get all the money from?* by saying: *Um, from, my dad giving the money.* In turn 7, he creates talk for two of his own puppets (Diego and Tommy) and at several points finds it necessary to add explanatory comments (*and then, this, this Diego said to Diego*) to indicate who is saying what to whom.

1   C: okay *((pretends one of his puppets gives food to one of her puppets))*
2   V: thanks Diego *((now speaking for another puppet))* I want a pizza
3   C: pizza *((pretends one of his puppets gives pizza to one of her puppets))*
4   V: thanks Diego, where'd you get all the money from?
5   C: um, from, my dad giving the money
6   V: your dad gives you the money?
7   C: yes, um, Tommy, Diego, Diego *((these are his three puppets' names))* what you want? *((holds up Tommy puppet))* Tommy I, I want, uh, soda *((one of the Diego puppets gives the Tommy puppet a soda))* thank you *((speaking for Tommy puppet))* you're welcome *((speaking for Diego puppet, then enacts conversation between his two Diego puppets))* **and then, this, this Diego said to Diego** what you want? um, ice cream *((one Diego puppet gives ice cream to other Diego puppet))* thank you, you're welcome *((then speaks for the other Diego puppet))* **and then this Diego said to him,** what you want Diego? I want ice cream too *((puppet gives ice cream to other puppet))* thank you

8 V: yeah, the ice cream is really good, right Diego? *((speaking for one of her puppets))*

9 C: mm hmm *((yes))*

Like other children in the program, by the end of his third year Ernesto also frequently engaged in conversations about the materials that he and his volunteer were attending to and brought into these conversations details about his personal experience. The transcript below includes an interaction between the child and an older volunteer, who, knowing his interest in animals, often brought well-illustrated animal books for them to share. In this particular interaction, the two are engaged in examining a book that contains pictures of many marine animals. The volunteer is pointing out particular aspects of the various sea creatures. In turn 2 the child adds a detail to a description of a starfish (*and he don't got hands*) and in turn 4 he shares the fact that his sister encountered one of these animals.

1 V: you want to see something? this says something really, strange and different, this is a starfish, it doesn't have any uh, heads, it doesn't have a head *((grabs Ernesto's head))* it doesn't

2 C: **[and he don't got hands *((pointing to starfish in picture))***

3 V: no, but right here at the tippy tip tip of the point *((pointing to starfish))* it says that that's, they have an eye, right there, that each tip is an eye *((points to each tip of the starfish))* isn't it strange?

4 C: **ooh my sister, got one of those *((pointing to starfish))***

5 V: she has a starfish?

As the interaction continues, Ernesto takes on the challenge of explaining, in turns 6, 12, and 20, how his sister's starfish was pulled back into the ocean by a wave. This was not a simple task because it involved the phenomenon of the wave motion that most second-grade children do not entirely understand. Not surprisingly therefore, Ernesto attempted to describe what happened in several different ways.

6 C: **he got it, then uh, the water come, and, my sister get in the water, and the starfish he go into the ocean**

7 V: is this Cathy?

8 C: *((shakes head))* nah

9 V: [no, which sister?

10 C: **Fabi**

11 V: F-, Fabi?

12 C: **he want to get, then the, the water come and the water, uh, keep it**

13 V: took the starfish back?

14   C: *((nods))*

15   V: well

16   C: **and he touch it a little bit** *((touches picture of starfish quickly))*

17   V: yeah, that happens, she's lucky she got to see it

18   C: **and she touch it**

19   V: she touched it?

20   C: **he grab it** *((pretends to grab with hand))* **and then the water come, and then, when you, the water come, you see like you're moving** *((moves his torso back and forth))* **but you're not moving, and he, he was in and he move, he throw the starfish, down** *((points down))* **and then the water grab it** *((starts turning page))*

21   V: and it went out with the water, with the, when the wave went back the starfish went with the wave?

22   C: *((nods))*

23   V: was it a wave?

24   C: uh huh

25   V: [Ernesto?

26   C: *((nods))* a wave

27   V: a wave, it happens

In sum, as was the case for Aracely, Ernesto's productive and receptive competencies changed impressively over the course of the 3-year period that he participated in the program. Because he was a well-behaved and friendly child, he was liked by all of his volunteers. Several of them went out of their way to bring special materials and to engage him in interactions that appear to be particularly rewarding and engaging. Figure 4.2 presents a summary of the types of communicative behaviors that we observed during each of the years that he participated in the program. In comparison to Aracely, Ernesto displays a broader variety of communicative behaviors in the first year and continued to exhibit many additional behaviors over the course of the next 2 years.

Selena

In comparison with the two children we have already examined in this chapter, Selena's experience in the program was very different. To begin with, Selena was a second grader, rather than a kindergartner, and her interactive proficiencies in Spanish were very well developed. She had a sense of herself as a competent student who had done well in her native Mexico, and thus her placement in a grade below the grade she had exited the previous year was probably disturbing. However, Selena was a pleasant child who also knew that she was an absolute beginner in English.

FIGURE 4.2. Ernesto's Communicative Behaviors Over a 3-Year Period

Initial Behaviors in Year 1	Behaviors Added in Year 2	Behaviors Added in Year 3
Repeats as requested	Comments spontaneously (multiword utterances)	Expresses delight
Responds to choice questions	Does not respond to hypothetical questions (says *I don't know*)	Volunteers information about experiences
Responds to wh-questions		Asks detailed questions about objects and topics
Repeats spontaneously	Paraphrases characters' dialogue in books	
Labels colors	Adds to volunteers' explanations (makes causative statements)	Narrates more extensively
Responds nonverbally		Attempts to explain complex occurrences
Comments spontaneously (multiword utterances)	Invites volunteer to attend to other topic/object	
Uses formulas to fill turns (*I don't know*)	Narrates segment of story prompted by volunteer	Argues
Describes as requested	Narrates stories independently	Negotiates game rules
Translates spontaneously for another child	Role-plays using puppet figures	Conjectures about causes of events
Responds to ambiguous questions	Gives directions	Corrects volunteer's understanding of questions he asks
Recognizes indirect requests for correction	Conjectures about locations of pictures	
Self corrects	Responds to questions and points to books to support answers	
Makes requests of volunteer	Adds details to volunteers comments	
Contradicts		
Interrupts	Attempts to clarify own comments	
Expresses likes and dislikes		

In part because she was older, we worked hard to match her with an appropriate volunteer. After a few unsuccessful sessions, we paired her with a volunteer who believed very strongly in direct instruction. As a result, she spent much of the first year in the program engaged in interactions that resembled pattern drills. (We included a transcript of one of these interactions with Fabiola in Chapter 3.) Nevertheless, in spite of her focus on direct teaching, the volunteer had many strengths. She spoke Spanish natively, and she understood that she could not treat Selena as though she were a very young child. She engaged her, therefore, in a number of activities that involved instruction on prepositions and other grammatical elements, but she also attended very early to the development of Selena's ability to narrate.

It is important for us to stress that Selena was strongly Spanish preferent. She sought to present herself as an intelligent person in her interactions with those around her, and she consistently used Spanish to express her reactions, her thoughts, and her feelings. She was not satisfied with expressing herself in elementary English. In many ways, the language was a challenge for Selena. At the beginning of her participation in the program, for example, she even struggled with (or resisted) repetition. On one occasion a member of the project staff asked the child to participate in a total physical response (TPR) activity. The volunteer repeated commands such as "touch your nose" and "touch her head" many times. She also modeled the behaviors expected of the child by doing them herself. She was unsuccessful, however, in getting Selena to consistently produce the entire command. The child insisted in producing only the label for each body part (*head, eyes, mouth*) and not the desired full utterance (*touch your head*).

As was the case for other children in the program, it was not always clear that Selena comprehended what the volunteer wanted to say to her in English. In the next transcript, for example, the child and the volunteer are playing with lotto cards and having a conversation about the objects found on the cards. The volunteer wants to associate the objects with different meals and times of day. Selena, however, becomes quite confused during the interaction. At this point in her language development trajectory, she is still responding primarily in Spanish, and the volunteer is attempting to use as much English as possible. In turn 1 the volunteer asks the child to tell her the time in which the meal she is describing took place (*what time was it? yeah what time was it?*). She is under the impression that they are talking about breakfast. Selena responds in turn 2 that the people she was describing started to eat at 3 o'clock sharp. The volunteer then attempts to ascertain whether the time is 3 o'clock in the morning or 3 o'clock in the afternoon. In subsequent turns it becomes evident to the volunteer from both the child's verbal and nonverbal behavior that she has not understood what has been said. The volunteer attempts to clarify and asks in turn 7: *Do you know what morning is?*

1   V: **what time was it? yeah what time was it?**
2   C: **xx empezaron a comer, puede ser esta hora?** *(xx they started to eat, can it be this time) ((picks up card with clock on it and points to clock face))*

     empezaron a comer a las tres en punto *(they started to eat at exactly three o'clock) ((looks at volunteer))*

3   V: okay, but remember we said breakfast in the morning?

4   C: *((looks at volunteer))*

5   V: remember we said we eat eggs and we eat hotcakes and, orange juice in the morning? for breakfast, so is is three o'clock the morning? *((shows three fingers))* is three o'clock, nighttime or, is it in the morning? three o'clock *((shows three fingers))*

6   C: *((looks down))*

7   V: **do you know what morning is? morning**

8   C: *((shakes head no))*

    The volunteer is committed to using English with the child and thus attempts to give her a description about what happens in the morning. In turn 13 she defines the word saying: *morning is when the sun, the sun comes.* Selena then understands what the volunteer wants. She displays this understanding in Spanish with an utterance (*ooh cuando ama-*) that is immediately interrupted by the volunteer. The volunteer realizes that Selena intends to say *cuando amanece* (at dawn) and therefore moves on to asking whether the child understands the word *night.*

9   V: ni- do you know what night?

10   C: ahora? *(now)*

11   V: night, do you know what night means?

12   C: *((shakes head no))*

13   V: **morning is when the sun, the sun, comes**

14   C: **[ohh cuando ama-, cuando**

15   V: **[and night is when the sun**

16   C: cuando oh, cuando el sol sale y se pone como soleado todo *((moves arms to indicate sunrise))* y empieza en la mañana *(when oh, when the sun comes out and everything becomes sunny and it starts in the morning)*

17   V: **[so you're sleeping en la mañana morning,** okay? so three o'clock *((points to card Selena has and shows three fingers))* not is not in the morning

18   C: no

19   V: so what time is the morning? like seven? remember we said seven?

20   C: **[seven, a las, a** las siete *(at, at seven)*

    It is important for us to emphasize that the problems in comprehension illustrated in the previous transcript were not unique to Selena. We conjecture that the same types of misunderstandings occurred in most interactions between volunteers and children. It is only because Selena worked with a bilingual volunteer and insisted on using Spanish and expressing herself extensively, that we were able to see the challenges that other children faced in communicating in English at the point at which they were absolute beginners.

In terms of language production, Selena's experience makes particularly evident the supporting role that a first language can have in the acquisition of a second language. As we noted above, Selena's volunteer (although she herself clearly insisted on using English) was able to use what we term "just-in-time Spanish" in many interactions. Moreover, after an initial period in which she moved the child through drill-like pattern activities, she allowed Selena to engage in their exchanges as a meaning-making interlocutor. We conjecture that in part because Selena was allowed to engage in exchanges in which she was helped to express what she wanted to say by code switching into Spanish and by being scaffolded strongly by her volunteer, she made considerable progress in the second year of her participation in the program.

The following transcript includes an interaction that took place in the second year of Selena's participation. It illustrates the ways in which code switching into Spanish for specific lexical items allows the volunteer to scaffold Selena's vocabulary development while she is also developing her ability to retell stories. In this interaction, the child and the volunteer are sitting on the floor next to each other. The volunteer has the book *Walter's Magic Wand* in her lap and they are looking at the book together.

In turn 8 Selena responds to the volunteer's question about what the librarian has in her hands by saying that these are objects that she refers to using the Spanish word *hongos* (mushrooms). The volunteer repeats the word in the next turn and seems amused. She laughs because she realizes that Selena is referring to small tacks, which are shaped to some degree like little mushrooms. From the volunteer's continued narrative, Selena quickly catches on to what tacks are and, in turn 18, comments: *yeah it like como, it's like cla-, clavos* (nails).

1   V: do you think the tiger's happy? look at-
2   C: no
3   V: do you remember her, who she is? *((pointing to illustration in book))*
4   C: like like, yeah the the the teacher like the library?
5   V: the, the librarian?
6   C: yeah
7   V: the lady who works at the library, look what she has in her hands
8   **C: is sh, he have like, like um, like like what do you say, on English**
      um, hongos *(mushrooms)*? but this is like hongos *(mushrooms)*?
      ((points to illustration))
9   V: hongos *(mushrooms)*?
10 C: [yeah hongos *(mushrooms)* yeah it's hongos *(mushrooms)*

11 V: *((laughs))* they're little they're like little tacks *((uses fingers to indicate something small))*

12 C: yeah

13 V: that poke you *((gestures poking with fingers))*

14 C: *((nods))*

15 V: and so she throws them to the tigers, because everybody's afraid up here *((points at illustration))*

16 C: [ohh I
know what is that

17 V: you know?

18 C: **yeah it's like como** *(like)*, **it's like cla-, clavos** *(nails)*

The volunteer continues the narrative in turn 19 and is joined by Selena in turn 20 explaining that the *clavos* are on the floor. The volunteer then gives Selena the English word *nails* (turn 21) for the object in question, and Selena appropriates the use of the term *nails* when she continues the retelling of the story in turn 22.

19 V: uh-huh kind of like that but little, and so the tigers are all, look at they're stuck in their foot, see

20 C: [like sl- like sad because because he's, because the, because them, the clavos *(nails)* is in the in the floor?

21 V: **yeah the nails**

22 C: and then, **the nails** is in the floor, and then the, the tiger put, the feet and then he said, aaa because he have lots

It is clear from this interaction that Selena is comfortable code switching into Spanish in order to talk about the events that take place in a story. Code switching allows her to communicate to her volunteer not only her understanding of the narrative itself but also the dimensions of her particular lexical needs.

The use of the first language in Selena's academic language development is further made clear in the next transcript, where Selena has said that the title of the book they are reading is: *"the bear is bicycle."* (The actual title of the book was *The Bear's Bicycle.*) When her volunteer corrects her, the child attempts to argue with her in English about the use of the apostrophe. She goes to the whiteboard and writes the sentence "the bear is" to demonstrate that the word *is* can be substituted by an apostrophe:

1 V: what's the story? what's the title?

2 C: the bear is bicycle

3 V: the bear is bicycle? the bear's bicycle

4 C: the bear is bicycle

5 V: not th-, the bear's bicycle *((points to title))*

6   C: [yeah, because it's comma *((points to apostrophe in "Bear's"))*
                   and this mean, like this look *((grabs marker and stands up to write on*
                   whiteboard)) **that means, it's like when you write like when you,**
                   when you write like, the bear, the bear is *((writes "the Bear is" on*
                   white board)) **and, and if you don't want like long, you only do it,**
                   you only do like that *((erases the "is"))* **you like if it is, if you put like**
                   that it, is

7   V: ah huh

8   C: **you take, this thing**

9   V: ah huh

10   C: **and you take the i**

11   V: ah huh

12   C: **and you only put** *((turns it to "the Bear's"))*

Selena does not know that the apostrophe in English can to be used both
to show possession (the bear's bicycle) and to show contraction (the bear's
gone). The volunteer uses translation into Spanish to make evident the distinction in meaning to Selena:

13   V: apostrophe, right, that means that, but do do you know how that translates
           into the bear is bicycle, do you know what that means in Spanish?

14   C: um, la, el, el oso, su bicicleta? *(the bear, his bicycle)* no *((erases board))*

15   V: **the bear is bicycle means el oso es bicicleta** *(the bear is bicycle),* **that**
           doesn't make sense right? *((pointing to title))* **so the difference here is**
           that this means that the bicycle the bike, is is the bear's

16   C: [the bear's bike

17   V: it belongs to him like, that backpack *((points to Selena's backpack))* is
           Selena's, Selena's backpack, that means it belongs to you right?

What is impressive is that Selena attempts a complex explanation in
English and that she attempts to argue about its use and meaning with her
volunteer in this language. This attempt says a great deal about the child's
personality, but it also says a great deal about the ways in which her production and comprehension of English has changed over a 2-year period. Figure
4.3 summarizes Selena's changing interactional abilities from the time that
she entered the program to the time that she left 2 years later to return to
her mother in Mexico. We include her use of both English and Spanish communicative behaviors for the first year. All behaviors are listed in the order
in which they appeared. Behaviors listed as attempted are those that Selena
attempted and either abandoned or completed only with much support from
the volunteer.

Figure 4.3. Selena's Communicative Behaviors Over a 2-Year Period

Initial Behaviors in Year 1	*Behaviors Added in Year 2*

English

Repeats as requested	Repeats storybook pattern (*catch me if you can*)
Responds to commands	Repeats spontaneously
Gives single-word commands	Responds to questions with phrases and patterns
Attempts to repeat more complex phrases	Attempts to answer speculative question in English
Produces set pattern sentences (*the bird can fly, the dog can walk*)	Constructs descriptive sentences following learned pattern
Counts in English	Participates in guessing game (guesses objects from descriptions)
Responds to choice questions	Provides descriptions of objects for game
Comments spontaneously (formulaic multiword utterance)	Narrates original story with strong scaffolding by volunteer
Gives wrong labels for objects.	Narrates storybook with code switches into Spanish
Describes in English (uses rehearsed pattern sentences)	Narrates using sequence cards alternating with volunteer
Describes her own actions (*I going up. I and top.*)	Gives explanations
Builds word-for-word sentences with volunteer's scaffolding	Gives opinion about character in book
Attempts to provide personal information in English with scaffolding	Participates in limited role-play
Attempts to describe in English with scaffolding	Responds to personalized questions on tastes
Attempts English narrative (original story based on vocabulary cards)	Explains (what to do in the library, how an apostrophe is used)

Spanish

Uses Spanish to give rationales for choices	Contributes personal information about herself and family
Uses Spanish to verify understanding of what volunteer said	Paraphrases what teacher says to students
Counts for herself in Spanish	Attempts to summarize book
Uses Spanish to explain game rules	Gives synonyms
Uses Spanish to contradict	Explains a grammatical point
Narrates in Spanish (original story)	
Uses a combination of English and Spanish to narrate basic story	

INDIVIDUAL DIFFERENCES, VARYING OPPORTUNITIES, AND CHANGE OVER TIME

As might be expected, the nine focal children whose interactions we ana-lyzed in detail were both similar and different. All of the children were Eng-lish language learners, the sons or daughters of recent immigrants, and most were also members of families that faced many economic challenges. They lived in crowded small houses or apartments with parents who worked long hours and had little disposable income. Most adults were new to the area and to the country and thus had little knowledge of schools. The children's lives, then, shared many commonalities.

Nevertheless, the children were different in all of the ways that children normally differ. They were different in their behavior, ability, intelligence, personality, appearance, motivation, and interests. Several children, for ex-ample, were good-looking and fair-skinned and appealed to both our young undergraduate and our community volunteers. A number of children were strong-willed and difficult to manage, others were docile and quiet and eager to please.[3] Aracely, for example, whose progress we have tracked above, was unusually pretty, quiet and sweet, and responded well to all of her volun-teers. Ernesto was curious and interested in the world that surrounded him. He was also well-behaved and cooperative. Both of these children were easy to pair with volunteers, and they established strong relationships with their buddies during the course of each academic year. Selena was older, and usu-ally had much to say in Spanish, but with a strong enough volunteer who established her authority, she fell into a routine and over time made a great deal of progress.

Of the other six children whose interactional competence we studied over time, Adriana, Marisol, Elsa, and Lino were generally cooperative and easy to work with for most volunteers. Except for Lino, each of these chil-dren made progress similar to that reported for Aracely and Ernesto. Two other children, Fabiola and Gabriela, presented a number of challenges to project staff and to volunteers. In the section that follows, we briefly describe each of these six children and summarize their experiences and the ways they engaged in interactions with English-speaking adults during the period that they participated in *One-on-One English.*

Adriana

Adriana was the most advanced of all the children at the beginning of her work in *One-on-One English.* She had very strong listening comprehension skills and was able to engage in joint narrative activities with her volunteer even in the first year of her participation in the program. At the end of her

2 years in the program, Adriana could role-play effectively as evidenced by the interaction included in her game-playing interaction related in Chapter 3. She could clearly recognize questions she could not respond to, comment spontaneously, paraphrase dialogue between characters in books, ask personal questions of her volunteer, ask for general information, share her own personal experiences, and propose a conclusion to a story. At the end of her participation in the program, Adriana appeared self-confident in her ability to use English. With the benefit of hindsight, we conjecture that Adriana profited from the program to some degree, but that because of her already developed proficiency, she might have profited more from involvement in other activities and interactions. It is evident that she made progress and that she was exposed to more English than she normally had access to at her school, but it would have been interesting to have explored ways in which we might have made available to her various other types of affordances.

Marisol

The niece of a bilingual teacher at the school, Marisol displayed many typically middle-class behaviors and inclinations and made rapid progress over the time she was in the program, moving from a strong dependence on Spanish to eagerness to engage in various English language games and activities. Marisol was a strikingly pretty, fair-skinned second grader who was especially fortunate in that she was "adopted" by a single undergraduate volunteer who doted on her and went out of her way to engage and entertain her. This volunteer also tended to use a great deal of Spanish, rather than using only a just-in-time amount of Spanish that we considered ideal. During the first year, Marisol tended to use Spanish with her volunteer to ask questions and to obtain clarification of activities. Spanish also appeared to be her fall-back language and she reverted to it at the least sign of nervousness or insecurity. At the end of the first year, Marisol could repeat as requested, participate in joint singing of the end of a repeated pattern (The wheels on the bus, go *round, round, round*), respond to yes/no and choice questions, count in English, provide labels for some common objects, and recognize turn-taking signals of various types.

Several of her videotapes at the end of her second year show her participating in various activities including narrating stories previously modeled by her volunteer with occasional switches into Spanish (such as the sequences included in Chapter 3). She also engaged in extensive role-playing (librarian, waitress), describing and narrating using sequence cards, interrupting her volunteer, and asking for information. She frequently tended to search for the right expression in Spanish either to express her meaning more exactly or to ask for help with a specific lexical item. Interestingly, Marisol displayed a concern about the linguistic accuracy of her utterances. For example, on one occasion she self-corrected her own use of the feminine pronoun *she* to the masculine pronoun *he* to refer to a snow angel.

For Marisol, *One-on-One English* was a setting in which she had additional access to English. Because of her family background, both she and her newly arrived mother had regular contact with speakers of English. The program provided her with additional resources and opportunities to use and hear English at school and to grow in her interactional proficiency.

Elsa

Elsa was a slightly chubby, dark-complected child who smiled frequently and was eager to please. While very pleasant, by the end of the second year, she required firm control. We conjecture that Elsa's English language proficiency was beyond some of the activities that she was involved in and that therefore she was often mischievous and quick to move the interaction to more interesting activities. In comparison to other children in the project, Elsa was always conscious of the video cameras and inevitably smiled or turned to the camera with some regularity during her sessions. We were unsuccessful in pairing her with regular volunteers, and so, over the course of her 3 years in the program, she worked with many different undergraduates and senior volunteers. She entered the program as a kindergartner who appeared to have had some preschool experience in English. She was familiar with repeated pattern books (e.g., *Five Little Monkeys*) but was otherwise a beginning English learner.

Toward the end of her third year in the program, Elsa could comfortably engage in a variety of interactions with different-age volunteers. She could also describe objects in lotto guessing games (as evidenced in Chapter 3), use other game-playing language, use various formulas for different purposes (e.g., *I've got one, this is the last one*), narrate stories using sequence cards, and narrate stories using picture books. She typically made many spontaneous comments about things that interested her, and could also disagree and argue with her volunteer. She could also negotiate about what activities to take on and respond to unexpected personalized questions.

Lino

As compared with many other children who participated in the program, Lino was perceived by his volunteers to need very direct teaching of vocabulary. For that reason, there were a number of sessions that either directly engaged him in vocabulary drills and/or interactions limited to labeling activities using books designed exclusively to teach vocabulary such as picture dictionaries. As we attempted to make evident in Chapter 3, in extended connected discourse involving the telling of stories, children have access to English that is quite different from that available to them in interactions primarily concerned with labeling objects, places, and people. As noted in Lino's first transcript early in this chapter, his participation in an eliciting and evaluating interaction with his first volunteer offered very limited opportunities for engaging with rich language. For different reasons, his interaction in an evaluating and telling interaction focusing on a book also proved to be frustrating because it involved a series of incomprehensible personalized questions. Fortunately for Lino, by the end of his second and final year in the program, he had the opportunity of working during several sessions with a young male undergraduate whom he liked very much. In those interactions, Lino displayed a number of interactive competencies including responding to yes/no and choice questions appropriately, complying with requests for action, spontaneously volunteering information (in minimal terms) about favorite possessions (e.g., a batman bicycle), participating in rapid back-and-forth exchanges on books, expressing likes and dislikes, and producing patterns on cue. On one occasion, he appeared quite engaged in the book selected by his volunteer, and he attempted to talk about what was happening in the illustrations. He pointed, produced several sentence-like utterances, and paraphrased what the characters might say.

In sum, as compared to other children in the program, Lino had fewer opportunities to work with skilled volunteers and to participate in engaging interactions. He was quiet and somewhat timid and also very young. He did not have Ernesto's self-confidence or Aracely's and Marisol's good looks. He was serious and was the eldest child of newly arrived Mexican immigrants, which meant that he did not have older siblings who had started school in English. More important perhaps, he was a boy in a program that tended to attract more female than male volunteers. He did not, therefore, have the opportunity of establishing a strong bond with a compatible volunteer. In retrospect, it was not entirely surprising that although Lino participated in interactions with several volunteers, these interactions provided a somewhat limited space for him to become an effective communicator and sense maker.

Fabiola

By comparison to the other children in the program, Fabiola was difficult to work with. She fidgeted almost constantly, was easily distracted, and focused more on running out of the classroom to buy afternoon snacks than on interacting with her volunteers. Over the course of her 3 years in the program, it was challenging to find volunteers who worked well with her. Because she was both manipulating and controlling, she typically got the best of the adults who worked with her. It was a struggle to keep her focused on materials, to get her to do much beyond labeling objects with single words, calling out colors, counting objects, and imitating pantomimes. She often repeated spontaneously filling her turns appropriately, pointed to objects as requested, and showed evidence of comprehension in various ways. She occasionally joined in the joint repetition of a repeated pattern book, but was more interested in playing games. Not surprisingly, she liked ordering sequence cards but would not respond to requests for narrating or describing in the course of a game. It was not unusual for Fabiola to ignore her volunteer, to get up and walk around, and to reach for a book other than the one selected for attention by her volunteer. She often appeared to deliberately misunderstand a question or instruction and respond with incorrect information (colors, labels) that she had produced correctly almost immediately before. Occasionally she had tantrums and outbursts in response to a volunteer's insistence on particular activities, behaviors, or choice of materials.

Our analysis of her taped interactions reveal that except for two occasions at the end of her second year and at the end of the third year in the program, Fabiola did not consent to jointly narrating stories with her volunteers, that is to participating in the retelling of a story previously modeled by her volunteer. These two tapes of such attempted retellings, involving interactions with a project staff member (Alvarez) who is an experienced elementary teacher, reveal that Fabiola was able to participate in this type of endeavor to a limited degree and to produce a rudimentary narrative by using single words, repeated patterns, and even some multiword utterances while she turned pages and was prompted in her narrative by the adult interlocutor. Tapes from the third year with a less skilled volunteer show her producing one-word responses to choice questions, labeling of objects, and singing along with her volunteer. We have some evidence, however, that she made progress in her receptive abilities in English and conjecture that she was able to produce much more English than we saw in interactions with volunteers.

Figure 4.4 summarizes Fabiola's communicative behaviors over a 3-year period. We include a summary in the case of Fabiola as an example of the differences in her communicative behaviors and those of Aracely, Ernesto and Selena for whom we have already provided summaries.

Few new behaviors were added to those originally listed for the first year of her participation. Fabiola primarily interacted with volunteers using the set of initial behaviors listed for all the children: responding physically to requests, to yes/no questions, to choice questions, and to requests for labeling. Many of her volunteers—in order to get her to produce English—focused on asking questions about colors, on requesting labels for different animals, and on asking her to count various objects. As a result, a far more limited number

FIGURE 4.4. Fabiola's Communicative Behaviors Over a 3-Year Period

Initial Behaviors in Year 1	Behaviors Added in Year 2	Behaviors Added in Year 3
Responds physically to request for display of information	Repeats patterns (*no more monkeys*) at inappropriate points in story	Comments spontaneously (adds detail to story narrative: *wants to eat the goats*)
Imitates animal sounds		
Repeats as requested	Struggles to repeat complete patterns as requested	Uses formula (*I don't know*)
Subvocalizes as volunteer counts in English		
Responds to yes/no questions	Displays problems pronouncing words (*umbrella*) and is sensitive to corrections	Contributes multiword utterances to joint narrative
Comments spontaneously (labels color)		
Responds incorrectly to wh-questions about colors.	Protests and complains using ambiguous sounds (*naaah*)	Repeats modeled utterances to move narrative forward
Responds to choice questions		
Imitates physical actions of volunteer	Calls volunteer's attention to object (*says look and points*)	Describes lotto card (one word)
Produces ambiguous responses to personalized questions	Participates minimally in joint narrative strongly scaffolded by program staff (turns pages and says single words)	Produces formulas for participating in game.
Labels objects (single word) as requested		
Counts objects as requested		
Comments spontaneously (single word, focusing on objects in illustration)		
Ignores volunteer's request		
Repeats spontaneously (one word)		

of affordances were available to her than were available to other youngsters in the program. We conjecture that because of her behavior and her focus on doing the program "her way," we had few opportunities to capture her actual interactive competence on video. Her occasional unguarded comments and utterances, however, suggest that Fabiola was much more competent than our list of communicative behaviors suggests.

Graciela

Graciela, who entered the program in second grade, was also a challenge, but her oppositional behavior was much more subtle than Fabiola's and was thus easier to work with for most volunteers. Graciela did not necessarily misbehave, but she structured her interactions with volunteers in such a way that she appeared to cooperate to some degree but at the same time made clear that her wishes had to be catered to. Her weapon of choice was the use of Spanish. In almost every interaction, with all her volunteers including project staff, Graciela responded minimally in English and used Spanish when she wanted to say something "real." Graciela was not a child who had much tolerance for approximate meanings. She wanted to say what she wanted to say, not practice English or impress other people by using more English. Graciela was not willing to play the "please the volunteer" game.

Several other reasons also come to mind in explaining her "resistance" to English: (1) It was her way of establishing control; (2) she was not willing to sound unintelligent by using a language that did not help her present herself authentically; (3) she had particular difficulties with English pronunciation; and (4) she had particular difficulties imitating language that she heard. There is evidence on several tapes that Graciela reacted negatively when she was corrected directly or indirectly or made to repeat an English utterance that she had just produced.

The first interaction transcribed earlier in this chapter, which involved Graciela and her regular volunteer in a discussion of the sister's and cousin's resemblance to Disney princesses, is illustrative of her other interactions throughout her participation in the program. As compared to Fabiola whose behavior resulted in her receiving very restricted access to connected discourse, Graciela was fortunate in working consistently with the same volunteer during her first year, a young undergraduate who persevered in using English in spite of Graciela's clever tricks (e.g., writing on the board, asking a related question in Spanish, disagreeing with the volunteer's description of a character in Spanish, sharing a favorite possession in Spanish, searching for objects in her backpack) and her attempts to derail the carefully planned activities. The tapes, however, offer clear evidence of Graciela's increasingly sophisticated receptive abilities when she challenges or contradicts her volunteer.

This final session of the first year did not show much production of English by Graciela. She knew a lot of words that she used occasionally. She also seemed to know some formulas that she used from time to time. She was very skillful at shifting the joint attentional frame of interactions, but she received consistent exposure to connected discourse as produced by her volunteer who had a tendency to expand on her comments and descriptions.

We noted in our retrospective analysis that this volunteer did an extraordinary job of providing access to the language. Interestingly, at the time that she was in the program, possibly because of our own largely unexamined concern about Graciela's refusal to use English, we were not aware of how much English surrounded the child in these interactions.

During the second year, Graciela worked with a volunteer who focused on drilling sentences. She typically used sequence cards and produced sentences for each card, asking Graciela to repeat them. Several tapes show Graciela describing sequence cards using these phrases and sentences. That year Graciela also had several sessions with the program's most skilled undergraduate male volunteer, a very handsome young Latino. Graciela's most extensive use of English occurred in interactions with this volunteer, and indeed the only example of her use of series of multiword utterances was produced in a jointly produced narrative with this volunteer.

At the end of the second year, Graciela carried out some actions as requested, responded minimally in English to yes/no and choice questions, occasionally repeated as requested in English, produced a limited number of drilled expressions (*the dog is on the fence, the dog is under the fence*), used some formulas (*I don't know*), shared limited personal information in English when asked, read in English and translated what she read to display her understanding of the material, participated in a joint analysis of two versions of the *The Three Little Pigs,* and used some spontaneous English utterances (*like that, what is this, he's saying come here come here*). During the final session of the second year, she produced the rudimentary retelling of a story that we mentioned above in which she attempted to communicate a particular version of the narrative that differed from the original. She produced a series of phrases and multiword utterances, and although she switched to Spanish at several points, she made evident that she had indeed developed some productive competence.

CHILDREN'S DEVELOPING L2 PROFICIENCIES

In sum, individual differences in children and varying opportunities for interacting meaningfully in English with volunteers who were ordinary speakers of English had a direct impact on the change that we were able to trace over time in each of the children. Children's personalities, experiences, abilities, and appearance made an important difference. Volunteers' skills in managing children and their ability to support, scaffold, and extend children's knowledge also made a significant difference in the opportunities that children had to interact in English and in the ways that they appeared to perceive themselves as speakers of this new language. As we made clear in both

Chapter 3 and in this chapter, the quality of "assisted performance" varied, as did the opportunities afforded by the elements of the program to various children. We were successful in recording change over time in all nine focal children, but there was much variation in the kinds of development that was manifested by different youngsters. In some cases, the changes appeared minimal after initial manifestations of growing comprehension because their participation did not include clear examples of advances in productive competencies. In other cases, however, interactions did provide continuous evidence of children's growing ability to respond to questions and suggestions, to make requests for joint attention, and to contradict and disagree.

In the chapter that follows, we view children's developing L2 proficiencies from an additional perspective, this time focusing on their performance in the pre- and post-elicitations that were conducted twice each year. There is much evidence from children's performance on these elicitations that even in spite of some children's reticence and/or resistance in interacting with adults, growth and change did take place in some of the very activities and behaviors on which the project focused.

CHAPTER 5

Growth Seen from a Combined Perspective

The Challenges of Measuring Children's Language Production

In Chapter 4 we described how over time we saw many changes in children's ability to participate in different interactions with their volunteers. Children grew in their ability to understand what the volunteers were saying to them and in using English to communicate ideas, tell stories, and talk about their experiences. In this chapter, we focus on changes in children's linguistic system as they participated in *One-on-One English* over 2 to 3 school years. We begin by discussing the challenges of measuring language proficiency and growth. As we explained in Chapter 2, we developed an elicitation procedure to assess students' English proficiency in the fall and spring of each school year. In particular, our analysis in this chapter focuses on one task within this elicitation procedure–the retelling of a familiar picture book. We describe the interactive nature of this retelling task in practice, and document children's developing role in the coconstruction of the narratives. We examine the linguistic changes observed in children's retellings along several dimensions, including narrative structure, cohesion, use of reported speech, language choice, turn length and type, sentence structure, lexical variety, verb morphology, and grammatical accuracy. Finally, we conclude with implications for the assessment and measurement of language development of young English language learners.

THE CHALLENGES OF MEASURING LANGUAGE GROWTH

There are many challenges that continue to surround the measurement of language growth. As Larsen-Freeman and Long (1991) point out, there are continuing debates about the definition of language proficiency, about whether syntax occupies a central position in linguistic proficiency, about whether proficiency can be divided into unrelated skills (speaking, listening, reading, and writing), about whether proficiency is a unitary or indivisible trait, and about whether we should be concerned about communicative competence as opposed to linguistic proficiency in studying second language acquisition. There are also strong differences of opinion about the point at which a particular feature or form is acquired in a second language. Some researchers consider a form to have been acquired if it is produced a certain percentage of times in all obligatory contexts (Hakuta, 1974). Other researchers (e.g., Meisel, Clahsen & Pienemann, 1981) consider the first appearance of a form to signal its acquisition. Finally, there are serious concerns about the type of language that can be produced by learners on language tests and on different types of tasks.

The measurement of language growth should, ideally, be grounded in an understanding of children's language development. Wells (1985) points this out with regard to L1 development:

> Ideally, of course, what is required is an instrument which is based on a thorough understanding of the developmental process and which gives due weight, at each stage or level, to those systems or features of language which are at the cutting edge of development. It should also give adequate representation to the various dimensions of language on which development is simultaneously taking place. Unfortunately, in the present state of our knowledge, such an ideal is far from having been attained. (p. 125)

Given the paucity of longitudinal research on young second language learners, such an ideal is even further from existence to describe children's *second* language acquisition. To date, a second language index of development such as that called for by Larsen-Freeman (1978) has not been created, which "will allow us to give a number value to different points along a second language developmental continuum . . . as learners proceed towards full acquisition of a target language" (p. 440). Different researchers have used scores on standardized examinations (such as the TOEFL) or proficiency scales developed for other assessment purposes as measures of language proficiency. According to Brindley (1998), however, the theoretical foundations of these scales have been questioned, and there is much concern about their validity as indicators of language ability. What is needed, according to Larsen-Freeman and Long (1991) and Bachman (1998), is a procedure such as that described by Clahsen (1985) that can address both language development and variation. This is important because, according to Bachman (1998), "accuracy will vary as a function of both the regular developmental sequence and individual variations across that sequence" (p. 190). While approaches to the measurement of language growth and development are still rare, some efforts have been made in this direction.

In examining the issues involved in assessing language proficiency in young English language learners, August and Hakuta (1997) argue that "most measures used not only have been characterized by the measurement of decontextualized skills, but also have set fairly low standards for language proficiency" (p. 118). They point out that, while examinations focusing on particular grammatical structures should not be entirely abandoned, such instruments must correlate with a variety of language proficiencies that have been found to be essential to classroom activities. Citing the work of Valdez-Pierce and O'Malley (1992), they list assessment procedures such as oral interviews, story retellings, simulations, directed dialogues, and the like as more difficult to administer and to score but as more accurately reflecting the multifaceted nature of language proficiency.

Questions of how to measure language proficiency have especially high stakes for English language learners in U.S. schools, affecting their classification as ELLs, placement in different tracks or courses, their instructional experiences in school, and the assessment of their achievement (Abedi, 2007). Title III of the No Child Left Behind Act requires that states assess ELL students' English language proficiency (ELP) using "reliable and valid measures" that are aligned with the state ELP standards. However, given the challenges defining and measuring language proficiency, it is not surprising that ELP assessments operationalize English language proficiency in different ways. In his review of classification systems for ELLs, Abedi (2008) describes how the ELP assessments used by different states are in fact based on different views of language proficiency and measure different uses of language.

THE NARRATIVE ELICITATION PROCEDURE

As described in Chapter 2, the elicitation procedure we used consisted of three components: personal information questions, receptive and productive vocabulary knowledge, and the comprehension and production of a narrative. Children were assessed individually in the fall (or whenever they entered the program) and in the spring at the end of the school year. In this chapter, we focus on the final component of the assessment, the retelling of a picture book. This task sought to determine children's ability to narrate using a set of pictures, a task that is also required by the California English Language Development Test (CELDT) administered to all ELLs in California. To provide a model for the child, the examiner produced a narrative that summarized the story line using the illustrations in the book, rather than actually reading the text. Care was taken to make certain that the child engaged in the story by using exaggerations and repetitions and pointing to particular pictures. The examiner then asked the child to retell the story he or she had just heard or to choose between two or three books to narrate. For this task, the examiner was to prompt the child by turning pages and asking appropriate questions, such as *And then what happened? What happens in the house?* This task was not attempted if it appeared that the child was unable to carry out the earlier segments of the assessment procedure. For this reason, many children (including four of the six children described in this chapter) did not complete this task until their second assessment.

Over the five years of the project, changes were made in the overall elicitation procedure based on our observations and analyses of the previous year's assessments. Figure 5.1 outlines changes made to the retelling task.

In the first 3 years, there were changes to the picture books used. In the second year, we used the story in *A Chair for My Mother* because this book was also used for the vocabulary portion of the assessment. During the year, however, project staff realized that the illustrations in this book were not conducive to telling a connected story, but tended to stand alone. Therefore, we returned to *The Three Bears* and *The Three Little Pigs,* because the illustrations in these books could carry a narrative. In the final 2 years of the project, the examiner did not model narrating in the spring assessment, because children were now familiar with the task of narrating a story from the illustrations (as opposed to reading the text). This task had been modeled in their initial fall assessment and was a frequent activity during their *One-on-One English* sessions.[1]

ANALYSIS OF CHILDREN'S NARRATIVES

In analyzing children's responses to the language elicitation procedures of the type we conducted, we were particularly conscious of the fact that we did not follow a standardized elicitation method. Rather, following Bachman and Palmer (1996), we sought to "encourage and enable test takers to perform at their highest level of ability" (p. 13). We knew that our rephrasings of requests for information gave children every opportunity to display their acquisition of English however slight. We were also conscious of the fact that children's responses are influenced by a number of other real-life factors: (1) the assumptions the child makes about what the listener already knows, (2) the assumptions the child makes about the inferential capabilities of the listener, (3) the child's previous experience in carrying out similar tasks, and (4) the specifics of the exchange itself (e.g., Was the child interrupted? Was the examiner nodding or frowning? Did the examiner use a language form that required a full sentence response by the child?). Finally, in the case of children whose first language is not English, a number of other issues must be taken into account. To begin with, it cannot be assumed that children's exhibited competence in English within the elicitation session is representa-

FIGURE 5.1. Changes to Retelling Task Over 5 Years

	Examiner modeling	Children's storytelling
Year 1 2003–04	Choice of *The Three Bears, The Three Little Pigs,* or *Little Red Riding Hood*	Choice of *The Three Bears, The Three Little Pigs,* or *Little Red Riding Hood*
Year 2 2004–05	*A Chair for My Mother*	*A Chair for My Mother*
Year 3 2005–06	*The Three Bears*	Choice of *The Three Bears* or *The Three Little Pigs*
Year 4 2006–07	*The Three Bears* No modeling in the final assessment.	Choice of *The Three Bears* or *The Three Little Pigs.* Retold same story in the final assessment
Year 5 2007–08	*The Three Bears* No modeling in the final assessment.	Choice of *The Three Bears* or *The Three Little Pigs.* Retold same story in the final assessment

tive of their control of the language under other, less stressful circumstances.

The elicitation procedure used in the study can be classified as a type of Language Proficiency Interview (LPI) in which a learner engages in spoken interaction with a proficient speaker of the target language. The purpose of an LPI is for the proficient speaker to assess the communicative proficiency of the learner, that is, the ability to participate in the interaction, speak about topics selected by the proficient speaker, and display the degree to which he or she can use various elements of the target language. Structured to resemble ordinary conversations, LPIs differ significantly from actual conversation in ways in which turns and topics are managed. The main purpose of an LPI, moreover, is to obtain a ratable and hopefully representative sample of the learner's language. Recent work carried out on LPIs from a discourse perspective by He and Young (1998) argues that "the LPI is an interaction between two persons who influence each other and react in relation to each other. LPIs do not simply sample an ability that exists in the learner prior to the interview; rather they actually produce or fabricate the abilities they supposedly measure" (p. 8).

In the rest of this chapter, we will describe the linguistic growth seen in children's production of the story retellings, focusing on six children who participated in *One-on-One English* over 2 to 3 school years and for whom we collected three to six narratives: Marisol, Selena, Ernesto, Fabiola, Elsa, and Aracely. Three other focal students–Adriana, Graciela, and Lino–are not included in this chapter because we only had two narratives for each child. Most of the narratives children produced were of *The Three Little Pigs* and *The Three Bears,* though Selena and Marisol both produced their first narrative for *A Chair for My Mother.*

In our analysis, we build on Clahsen's (1985) recommendations to describe second language development in terms of multiple dimensions, rather than reducing it to a single numeric score such as the mean length of utterance (MLU). In addition, both Clahsen (1985) and Cook (1999) caution SLA teachers and researchers against measuring second language development against a native speaker standard, an approach that would simply cast our focal students as deficient native English speakers. Therefore, we sought to describe children's developing linguistic competence as L2 users on their own terms. We will begin by analyzing the shifting role of the examiner and child in constructing the narrative and then describe children's developing production of the genre, including an analysis of their use of narrative structure, cohesive devices, and reported speech. We then move on to reporting changes in various dimensions of language: use of Spanish and English, turn types, sentence structure, lexical variety, verb morphology, and grammatical accuracy. In looking at different aspects of language, we attempt to capture the complexity and nonuniformity of second language development, as well as the individual differences between children's developmental trajectories.

Examiner and Child Participation

Theoretically, the story retelling could be viewed as a monologic task, in which the child independently moves through the illustrations and narrates a complete story. However, given that our focal children were beginning English language learners, they were often not able to complete this task independently in their early assessments. While examiners began with a general prompt (e.g., *What's happening here? Can you tell me what happened in the story?*), as the interaction progressed, they engaged in multiple practices in an attempt to scaffold children's production. This examiner participation included giving reprompts, asking more specific questions including labeling and choice questions, offering vocabulary, and recasting and elaborating on any attempt made by the child to narrate. What follows are excerpts from Selena's first narrative, in which she retold *A Chair for my Mother* (the examiner's turns are marked with an E, and the child's with a C).[2] The examiner begins with a general prompt in turn 1, but then provides possible completions to Selena's sentences in turns 3, 5, and 11, which Selena takes up in her subsequent turns. Selena's uptake of these completions and her use of the examiner's language suggests some comprehension and demonstrates her ability to repeat.

1	E:	Okay Selena, now you tell me the story. Let's start over here. So what's happening here?
2	C:	The the mom is asleep in on the chair and and
3	E:	**and the grandma and the girl?**
4	C:	**And the, and the girl is** is putting the the the money in the
5	E:	**in the jar**
6	C:	**in the jar**
7	E:	in the jar, very good. Okay so, so what happens here?
8	C:	One day the the mom, the mom and the and the girl is walk on the home.
9	E:	And then when they get home what do they see? What happened?
10	C:	The the person is "come come, look, the hurry the"
11	E:	**"The house is on fire."**
12	C:	**"The house is on the fire."**

In addition, in early assessments, examiners sometimes asked specific questions of children, rather than allowing them to proceed with an independent narrative. For example, later in Selena's retelling, in turns 14, 16, and 18, the examiner asks questions about aspects of the story she sees as important: the family's neighbors and changing coins into dollar bills at the bank.

13	C:	And the person is, "Move move the the house."
14	E:	**And what do the neighbors do? These are all the neighbors, and what do they do? You know what neighbors are? Vecinos (Neighbors)**
15	C:	Vecinos *(Neighbors)*. And this is, this is the the the, this is toy.
16	E:	A toy, yes absolutely. Okay, so the neighbors bring a lot of things to the family right? **And then what do they do? Where do they go? What's this?**
17	C:	The bank
18	E:	The bank. **What do they do at the bank?**
19	C:	The money
20	E:	Mm hmm, they change money.

The result of examiner interventions, therefore, was not a monologic narrative produced by the child, but a coconstructed narrative produced in interaction between the examiner and child. Given the examiners' extensive participation in children's early retellings, these narratives do not stand alone as narratives; their interpretation requires looking at both the child and adult's turns.

In contrast, in later assessments, the examiners gave only an initial prompt for the child to retell the story from the illustrations and then handed over the narrative task to the child. In these later retellings, examiner turns consist of affirmation and back-channel cues, as well as general prompts for the child to continue narrating (e.g., turning the page and asking, *And then what happened?*). For example, a year after her initial narration, Selena retold the story of *The Three Little Pigs*. In contrast to Selena's first narrative, the examiner provides only back-channel cues, and the text of Selena's narrative is comprehensible on its own. When examiners do provide support in later retellings, it is almost always for a specific lexical item and often at the child's request, as in turn 7 when Selena asks: *this is a straw?* In turn 1, Selena referred to the pigs as "bears," but the examiner did not question her and Selena self-corrected in turn 7.

1	C:	Once upon a time there were three bears? And, and they they don't have like um um home?
2	E:	Uh hum
3	C:	to live. And they came, they were like, they came to her mom.
4	E:	Uh hum
5	C:	Because they don't have like um house to live.
6	E:	Uh hum
7	C:	Then first the little pig saw a man with a donkey um having like um . . . **This is a straw?**
8	E:	**Uh hum**
9	C:	Um, and the first, the first little pig said to the man, "Please man, um can you give me the straw?"
10	E:	Uh hum
11	C:	And the man said, "Okay." And then when he came, he first picked a a um a place to where he's going to build his h- his house.
12	E:	Uh hum
13	C:	And then he he make his house. And then and then came, then the bird, I mean the wolf was in the um them. The little the first little pig was doing his house.
14	E:	Uh hum
15	C:	And he saw, and then he came. And he was a um, he was knocking. And I don't, and then he was, "In a huff and I puff and I blow your house."

Narrative Structure

In examining children's assessments during the time that they participated in the project, we found considerable change in the structure and elaboration of their retellings. There was also noticeable variation between individual children in their production, both when they entered the program and in their final retellings. As examples of this spectrum, we present two children—Fabiola and Ernesto—who represent a range in both their initial and final production. In discussing these changes, it is important to remember that in addition to learning English, our focal students were also in the process of developing their understanding of narrative genre in their first language, and in general. Studies of first language acquisition have found that children show considerable change in their production of narratives over elementary school as they begin reading and writing and gain experiences with the genre in school (Berman & Slobin, 1994). Both children's narratives are presented in paragraph form, with examiners' participation omitted, in order to focus on the changing nature of their narratives as texts. (The numbers refer to lines rather than turns.)

Fabiola's first retelling of *The Three Bears* took place in the spring of her kindergarten year. She begins with a series of single words in English to introduce or label the three bears and later labels the girl, Goldilocks. Fabiola relates key events of the story with single verbs in English and Spanish (e.g., *sit, broke, viendo*) and repeats, *oh what happened?* from the examiner's prompting. She uses Spanish for the bears' direct speech (lines 3–6), a common feature of the narrative genre and a traditional component of this particular story, which the examiner had modeled in English. She concludes her story with an English sentence (*coming she go*) and Spanish word (*vió*), describing Goldilocks's fleeing of the house and that the bears watched her leave.

1   One two three. Bears. Bear. Little. Bear. Big. Book xxx. Sleeps. Go. Girl.
2   Viendo *(Seeing)*. Viendo *(Seeing)*. xxx. Yummy. Sit. Broke. Big. Ca, cam.
3   Bore bore. Oh what happened? Mmm yummy yummy. Co, "él que él se comió
4   mi comida" *("he, that he ate my food")*. "Quién se sentó en mi silla?" *("Who sat*
5   *in my chair?")* Yeah. Broke. "Ella se subió en mi cama" *("She got up on my*
6   *bed")*. "Ella se subió en mi cama?" *("She got up on my bed?")* Bears. Coming
7   she go. Vió *(Saw)*.

In contrast, 2 years later, Fabiola retells *The Three Bears* again and produces a more complete narrative entirely in English. She begins with the conventional story opener *once upon a time* and introduces the main characters and setting. Fabiola then describes their actions in the story as a series of chained events, which Berman and Slobin (1994) describe as typical in the narratives of young children across different first languages. At times Fabiola also refers to and labels or describes the actual illustrations (e.g., *here's the big one,* in line 4), departing from the storytelling genre. This mixing of picture description and narration has also been found in young children's narration from pictures in their first language (Berman & Slobin, 1994). The events Fabiola relates—the bears going to sleep, taking a walk, Goldilocks's arrival, the bears' return, and Goldilocks departure—are temporally linked with *then, and,* and *and then.* In contrast to her previous narration, Fabiola is now able to recount the bears' speech in English in lines 14–17, though she does not use conventional reporting clauses. She closes her narrative with a resolution, that Goldilocks ran, and announces: *the end*. Fabiola then attempts to add some information about the bears' internal state, that they were sad, but appears to self-correct that they were happy.

1   Here's the little pigs. Once upon a time was a, the three were bear. Bears.
2   Um no xxx, the in they house. Swinging with the xx. Then the the little pig was
3   um, the little tiny bear bear and the big big one and the bigger. Then the little,
4   then here's the little one. Here's the big one. Here's the biggest. How the two
5   these two. He have, he have, he have the book. And then he have the book and
6   this. Then, then all the bears went to sleep. And then, the, they, then the going
7   to the um, the xxxx walk. Here's the, I forgot that name. Goldilocks went to the
8   house. Then Goldilocks looks the mama's plate, the big one, the big ones, the
9   medium, the big one. Then we can read um *The Three Little Pigs?* And then he
10 he eat all the big one and it hot. And then him eat all um cold. And here's more
11 better. Then she went to the chair, then the other chair. Then she went to the
12 little one and broke it. The baby, the baby was big, xxx, that. Here is a the arh, I
13 forgot the name of that, the. Goldilocks went to the big one, then the medium,
14 then the most smaller. Then "Who eat my who eat my-" I forgot this. Porridge.
15 "Who eat my porridge?" "Who eat all my porridge?" "All my who ch-" I forgot
16 the name, chair. "Who get my chair?" "Who get my chair?" "Who broke my
17 chair?" "Who was in my bed?" "Who was in my bed?" She was in all the
18 place. Then he she went running all day. The end. Yeah. Then we was sad,
19 happy.

In sum, Fabiola's final retelling is more interpretable on its own as a narrative text than the one she produced 2 years before and relates more of the events of the original story. The events are not causally linked or connected to an overarching plot structure, but rather are conveyed as a series of chained events. Fabiola does not provide background information to explain and connect key events, such as why the bears take a walk, that they return, or why Goldilocks leaves.

All the children who participated in *One-on-One English* were deemed "beginning" English language learners when they entered the program and had been rated as level 1 (on a 1–5 scale) for speaking/listening on the CELDT in the fall of their first year in the program. However, there was significant variation in the initial narratives they produced. Below is Ernesto's first retelling of *The Three Bears*, also produced in kindergarten. Clearly, Ernesto is able to produce much more in English than Fabiola did in her initial retelling. Like Fabiola in her final narration, Ernesto mixes picture description with storytelling, especially in the beginning of his story. As he proceeds to tell the story, Ernesto provides a chain of temporally ordered foregrounded events, also similar to Fabiola's final retelling. He does not provide background information and causal links for these events, which is also common in young children's L1 narratives (Berman & Slobin, 1994). For example, in line 4 Ernesto says the bears go to the *bosque*, or forest, but does not explain why. Ernesto uses reported speech in English at several points in the story and, unlike Fabiola, prefaces this direct speech with the characters' name or the characters' name and the speech act verb *say*. He attempts to resolve the story, but it is unclear from his ending which character leaves.

1   The papa bear and the momma bear is seeing the baby. And the papa bear and
2   papa bear is, I don't know. And is deserxxx. And the sleep. The books. Oh the
3   the little book he he he *((excited and laughing))*. And he's a sleeping the. And
4   the papa bear is, "aaagh." And they go on the bosque *(forest)*. And it said, "I
5   going to have the three bears." And this is sleep this. And this is, is um. I don't
6   know. I don't know. Comió *(Ate)*. Eating. And is say, "too hot." And the mom
7   is too. I don't know. I don't know. Frío *(Cold)*. Too cold, and the baby yummy
8   yummy. "I need is a sleep is." Se sentó en la silla *(She sat in the chair)*. And
9   this, y lue- y luego se sentó en la silla de de, la de la mama bear *(and then she sat*
10 *in the momma bear's chair)*. And and the baby bear, and he's cr-. Y lue- y,
11 and they str-. I don't know. This is in that in the. I don't know. The bed the papa
12 bear. And the, and the momma bear and the baby bear is a sleeping. And the,
13 and the bear, she's go in the house. And the, and the papa bear, "Somebody
14 eating my cereal." And the momma, "Somebody's eating no, eating my cereal."
15 And the baby, "Somebody eating all all my cereal." And the papa bear,
16 "Somebody's sitting in my chair." Then momma, the momma say, "Somebody's
17 sitting in my chair." And the baby say, "Somebody sitting in my chair." And the
18 papa bear, "Somebody, it is is, is in, I don't know, is in my bed." And the
19 momma say, the momma bear say, "Somebody sitting no, in is in my bed." And
20 the baby say, "Somebody sit in. I don't know. I don't know. Somebody sleep in,
21 somebody over here is in my bed." And the papa bear, no, the papa bear and the
22 mama bear leaves the, and leaves and is like that and is jump over there. I don't
23 know. And they run. No er no er, I don't know. Leave.

Two years later, Ernesto also retold *The Three Bears*. Unlike Fabiola, Ernesto does not use a conventional story opener, but rather begins his retelling with a picture description, using the frame *I see . . . .* However, after this initial picture description, the organization of his narrative is more developed than the one he produced in kindergarten. While in kindergarten he produced a chain of events, Ernesto now provides more causal linkages and explanatory background information conveying a clearer, overarching plot. In line

5, he explains that the bears are waiting for their *soaps* (soup), then in line 10 explains that they take a walk because the soup is not ready, providing what Berman and Slobin (1994) refer to as the plot onset. He then relates the plot's unfolding, as he describes Goldilocks's actions and the bears' return. Again, Ernesto uses direct speech for dramatic effect at the story's climax, and then provides a plot resolution in describing how Goldilocks ran away and *never came back*. Finally, he explains that the bears watch her leave and will send her away if she attempts to return.

1 The daddy is swinging the the little bear. And the mommy looking at them. And
2 the momma looking at, she's looking at playing. And then owl seeing me. I see
3 a little bear with his teddy bear and the mom bear and the dad bear. I see one
4 soap little and another. And I see a a big a a almost big plate with soap and a big
5 big plate with soap. **And the three little bears, they're waiting for their soaps.**
6 And they are reading. The little one is reading a little book in his chair. And the
7 mom she's reading the a big book with her chair. And wow, this is change little
8 big big. The little one bear, he's sleeping with his teddy bear. Um he's sleeping.
9 And the mom, she she's seeing his dad, the dad. And the dad is. I don't know.
10 They're walking home when the xxx, **because the soap is not ready.** And
   they
11 want to go out to to play. Then the girl come to the har, to they haws, the house
12 of the three little bears. And she got flower. And then she see the window. And
13 then she see the soaps. And then she eat the big soap. And it's really hot. And
14 the, and the momma soap is really cold. And the little one is is not cold and hot.
15 She eat it all. And then she she go to the big chair, then to the mom chair, and
16 then to the little one. And she loved the little one. And then she braked it. Then
17 she get up on the big big bed, and then in the mom bed, and the mom's bed. And
18 then she got in the little one bear. And she like it. **And the three little bears are**
19 **coming.** Then they say, "Who is, who it was eating my soap?" And then the the
20 mom she was like, "Who somebody was eating my soap?" And the little one
21 say, "They eat all my soap." And then the dad said, "Somebody sit in my chair."
22 And the mom said, "Somebody sit in my chair." And the little one said,
23 "Somebody broke my chair." And then then the dad said, "Somebody has been
24 in my bed." "Somebody has been in my bed," said the mom. And then the little
25 one said, "Somebody is in my bed." And the dad and the mom and the little one,
26 they are looking at her. **Then she run out the window and never came back.**
27 **And then they are seeing for for if she come back, they're gon- they're**
   gonna
28 **tell her to go out, the out they house.**

While there is change in both children's narratives, they clearly start and end in different places in their production of an English narrative. Such individual differences have also been found to be significant in other studies of both first and second language acquisition (Clahsen, 1985; Clark, 2003; Meisel et al., 1981; Myles, 2003). To some extent, students' different starting and ending places represent their different experiences with and access to English outside of school and *One-on-One English*. In addition, given that our focal children entered *One-on-One English* at different ages and with different school and home experiences in Spanish, they also drew on different L1 linguistic abilities and experiences with the narrative genre. Any attempt to map a trajectory of L2 development is a much more challenging task than doing so in an L1, when one could start with a group of infants who are all not yet producing any language.

Cohesion

In their analysis of children's L1 narrative development, Peterson and McCabe (1991) describe cohesion as the linguistic relationship between the clauses that make up the narrative, or "how the surface linguistic elements of a text are linked to each other in order to create a cohesive whole" (p. 30). Although various linguistic features are used to achieve cohesion, here we will describe children's use of two cohesive devices: temporal markers and conjunctions. Not surprisingly, children organized their narratives chronologically, following the temporal order of the story's illustrations. At different points in their development, all children began to use temporal markers to advance their narratives and relate events to each other in time. Figure 5.2 summarizes children's use of temporal markers in English, as well as Spanish (in italics) and indicates in parentheses how many times children used each marker.

Overwhelmingly, the most common temporal marker used is *then*, which has also been found in the narratives of native English speaking children (Berman & Slobin, 1994; Peterson & McCabe, 1991). Children also used conventional story openers, such as *once upon a time* and *one day*, as well as other markers that signal a temporal sequence, such as *first, next,* and *later*. In addition, three children (Ernesto, Fabiola, and Elsa) used the Spanish temporal marker *luego* in their early narratives before they began using English markers more frequently. This suggests that they were drawing on their knowledge of the narrative genre in Spanish and using their L1 to help perform the genre.

Children also began using conjunctions to relate story events together and create cohesion in their narratives. Conjunctions were seen at the beginning of a sentence or turn to relate that utterance to their or the examiner's preceding turn, as in this example from Selena's final retelling of *The Three Little Pigs*:

1   C: . . . And they came, they were like, they came to her mom.
2   E: Uh hum
3   C: **Because** they don't have like um house to live.

More frequently, students used conjunctions to create a compound sentence conjoining two or more shorter sentences as Selena does in the following excerpts from the same narrative:

1   And then he said, "And I huff and I puff and I blow your house." And then he was making it, **but** he can't make him.
2   And then the wolf was very angry **because because** he he don't he was like he can't blow this house **because** it was a bricks.

As seen in Figure 5.3, five of the six students began using conjunctions other than *and* in their third or fourth retelling.[3]

The most frequently used conjunction was *but* (13 uses), followed by *because* (10), *so* (7), and *if* (5). Through these different conjunctions, children communicated different forms of cohesion or relationships between events in the story, including negation, causation, and conditional relationships.

Reported Speech

Reported speech often serves as an important component in narratives, advancing the story line and highlighting dramatic moments (Peterson & McCabe, 1997). Goodell and Sachs (1992) explain that reported speech includes two distinct systems in English: direct speech in which the original statement is adjoined to a reporting clause (e.g., *The little one said, "Somebody is in my bed."*) and indirect speech in which utterances are reported second hand with syntactic and often semantic adjustments (*The little one said that somebody was in his bed*). Direct and indirect speech are often appropriate for different situations or purposes within a narrative. Indirect speech is used to communicate the message content, while direct speech can create a theatrical or dramatic effect and is used when it is relevant to provide the speaker's exact words. Peterson and McCabe (1997) cite their previous (1983) work, arguing that reported speech often serves as a form of complicating action in children's narratives. In the traditional accounts of *The Three Bears* and *The Three Little Pigs*, it is clear that direct speech serves this role (e.g., when the bears return home from their walk, when the wolf threatens the pigs) and the examiners modeled using reported speech in their own narratives. At different points in their assessments, all six focal children incorporated reported speech in their retellings, providing evidence of developing competence with this feature of the narrative genre.

FIGURE 5.2. Children's Use of Temporal Markers

| Child | TEMPORAL MARKERS IN EACH NARRATIVE | | | | | |
	1	2	3	4	5	6
Marisol	0	once one day (1) then (15)	once upon a time (1) first (2) then (27)	N/A	N/A	N/A
Selena	one day (1)	one day (2) then (12)	once upon a time (1) then (39) then one day (1) then first (1) then the next day (1)	N/A	N/A	N/A
Ernesto	*luego* (1) then (1)	0	then (39)	once upon a time (1) then (20)	then (18)	N/A
Fabiola	0	*luego* (1)	0	0	once upon a time (1) then (17)	N/A
Elsa	then (2) *luego* (3)	*luego* (1)	*luego* (2)	second (2) later (1)	one day (1) first (1) then (1) now (3)	then (1) next (1)
Aracely	0	then (4)	0	then (1)	then (23)	then (1) one day (1)

As they learn to use reported speech, children must develop competence with the devices used to mark a direct quotation or indirect speech and communicate appropriate changes in perspective for their listener. Goodell and Sachs (1992) investigated the use of reported speech among 4-, 6-, and 8-year-old children, as well as adults, and found that with age, children more consistently used reporting clauses (e.g., *he said*) to mark direct speech and

FIGURE 5.3. Children's Use of Conjunctions

| Child | CONJUNCTIONS IN EACH NARRATIVE | | | | | |
	1	2	3	4	5	6
Marisol	0	0	so (5) but (5)	N/A	N/A	N/A
Selena	0	0	because (6) but (1)	N/A	N/A	N/A
Ernesto	0	0	because (3) if (1)	0	because (1) if (1)	N/A
Fabiola	0	0	0	0	0	N/A
Elsa	0	0	but (1)	0	but (1)	but (1)
Aracely	0	0	0	but (3)	so (2) if (2) but (1)	if (1)

make these changes in vantage point clear to their listeners. Younger children preferred to use direct speech, often mimicking dialogue without reporting clauses. In contrast, adults used indirect speech more often, saving direct quotations to add excitement or drama at high points in the plot. Goodell and Sachs also found that young children overwhelmingly use generic speech act verbs, while adults employ a wider range of verbs to communicate the relevant illocutionary force of the reported speech (e.g., *complain, demand*). The use of reporting clauses is complex, and requires that the narrator infers the intended meaning of the original discourse and chooses an appropriate speech act verb.

Marisol, Selena, Ernesto, and Fabiola used reported speech in their first assessments with different conventional and unconventional strategies to mark changes in vantage point. Marisol, Ernesto, and Selena introduced reported speech with *is*, as in the following sentence from Marisol's retelling of *A Chair for My Mother*: *And the mom is the, "what what what's happening?"* In his first retelling, Ernesto also used conventional dialogue carriers like *say* and *said* in some instances or provided the character's name and reported speech without a dialogue carrier. Both Marisol and Fabiola used Spanish to relate reported speech in their first narratives. Marisol began using conventional dialogue carriers (*say* and *says*) in her third narration, and Selena did so in her second narration, though she did not always provide them. Although Ernesto almost always used conventional markers, including *say, said, asked, was saying,* and the colloquial *was like,* he sometimes omitted them up to his penultimate narrative. Fabiola began incorporating reported speech in English in her fifth and final narrative, but never used any introduction or dialogue carrier in either language. Elsa and Aracely both began using reported speech in their second narratives. Both used dialogue carriers like *say* and *says* from the beginning, though they did not use them consistently until the sixth narrative for Elsa and the fourth narrative for Aracely.

In sum, over the course of their retellings, five of the six focal children became much more consistent in their use of conventional dialogue markers. Even when students omitted dialogue carriers and/or characters' names, their reported speech was still often marked by changes in intonation. The children overwhelmingly used what Goodell and Sachs (1992) term "generic speech act verbs," primarily different conjugations of *say,* as well as less frequent use of *ask* and *tell.* In addition, some children used colloquial dialogue characters such as *was like.* The only focal student who used a nongeneric speech act verb was Elsa, who, in her final assessment, used *call* to describe how the little bear spoke to his parents when he found Goldilocks: *And the little bear call, "Mom, dad, a girl's right here my bed."*

In addition to using direct speech, Aracely and Ernesto incorporated indirect speech into their later narratives, which they introduced with *tell* or *told.* Here are four examples from Aracely's fifth and sixth narratives, in which she retold *The Three Little Pigs:*

1 And he tell the man, can I, can he get some of this to him so he can made a house.
2 And then the little pig told the man can if he can give the pig some sticks so he can make a house.
3 One day, the mom tell the little pigs that they have to go and build their own house.
4 And the third pig sees a man with bricks. And he told the man if he could get them

In all their uses of indirect speech, Aracely and Ernesto appropriately used third person pronouns to communicate perspective change, instead of using first person as one would in a direct quotation. They incorporated the indirect speech syntactically into the overarching sentence, often with the connectors *if* or *that.* The morphological adjustments required in verb tense appeared more challenging. Aracely used verbs unconventionally in almost all cases of indirect speech, either mixing verb tense and person markings as in lines 1 and 3 above, or using simple present rather than conditional tense as in line 2. In line 4, however, she did employ the conditional *could* to integrate the reported speech into the syntax of the larger sentence.

Changing Use of Linguistic Features

Language use. In their early narratives, five of the six children used Spanish for specific lexical gaps as well as to give complete sentences of narration. The examiners all spoke Spanish and often used Spanish initially in the assessments to explain the procedure and put the child at ease. Therefore, it was reasonable for children to rely on their L1 as needed to complete the task. For example, in Marisol's first narrative, she retold *A Chair for My Mother*. In turns 1 and 3, Marisol switches to Spanish to provide narration, and in turn 5, she begins in Spanish and switches to English. The examiner provides recasts in English and in turns 3 and 7, and Marisol is able to incorporate these recasts into her subsequent turns.

1 C: And the mom brother and the brother is the is the house house on the **se está quemando**? *(it is burning?)*
2 E: It's burning. Yes, it's burning. **It's on fire.**
3 C: **On fire, on fire.** And the ca- house and brother is the is the **le está diciendo que-** *(he's telling her that-)*
4 E: What's he saying?
5 C: **Que que que este que se está quemando** *(That that that this that it's burning),* on fire on the, on the house.
6 E: The house, **the brother's saying, "Come on come on."**
7 C: **"Come on."** And the house and the, and the fire.

In later assessments, children only used Spanish for one or two individual words within an otherwise English sentence or to ask for help or negotiate the interaction. For example, in Marisol's second narration, she uses a single Spanish word *(está)* within an English multisentence turn.

1 Once one day **está** *(is)* little bear, the little bear, the middle bear, and big bear.
2 This is little bear, middle bear, big bear. One bear is the one bear is the *((four*
3 *second pause)).* The little bear is sit in little chair. The middle bear is sit and little
4 chair. The middle bear is sit on middle chair. The big bear is the sit in big, big
5 chair.

In her next turn, Marisol uses the invented word *comma* for *bed,* attempting to create a cognate from the Spanish word *cama.* Similarly, in his sixth assessment above, Ernesto uses the word *soap* for *soup,* drawing on the Spanish word *sopa.*

Across children's assessments, there is a decreasing use of Spanish to the point where all but one student (Selena) narrate entirely in English in their later assessments. For example, in Marisol's final assessment, she retells the entire story of *The Three Bears* in English. Although she encounters difficulty with the word *porridge*, her strategy for compensating for this lexical gap differs from her previous assessment. Initially, she substitutes the word *bread* and continues her narration. She then asks for the word in English, repeats it to check her pronunciation of it, and incorporates the term into her narration in turn 9.

1	C:	So Gold, she eat. Um he he has hungry, so he eat the **bread** the bear. **What's that?**
2	E:	porridge
3	C:	porri
4	E:	porridge
5	C:	porridge
6	E:	porridge
7	C:	porridge
8	E:	uh hum
9	C:	Then then, first he eat the big **porridge**, but it's so hot. Then he eat the the medium size bear. And then he went over. It's so cold. Then he eat the the little one that is so good! So it such um good. And then, and then he she um eat all the porridge.

Her strategy for dealing with lexical gaps has changed as she is able to negotiate the interaction entirely in English.

Turn types. Examining the types of turns children took in the retelling interaction also provides insight into the changing nature of the interaction over time as children became more proficient with English and the genre of retelling stories. For this analysis, children's turns were coded in five different categories: single-word turns, phrase turns, sentence turns, phrase and sentence turns, and multisentence turns. For the sake of brevity, we present changes in children's use of three turn types (see Appendix B for complete table):

1. Single-word turns: These turns consisted of a single word in English (e.g., *Bears*).
2. Sentence turns: These turns contained an English sentence, defined as containing a subject and predicate both in English. (e.g., *And he do the house; The papa bear and the momma bear is seeing the baby*.).

3. Multisentence turns: These turns contained two or more English sentences (e.g., *They go to sleep. And the three bears come back to the house. Then the mom said, "Who" um the dad said, "Who get my my food?" And the mom said, "Who get my food?" And the little bear said, "Who eat all my food?"*).

A *turn* itself was defined as a speaker's talk without interruption by the interlocutor; a turn ended once the interlocutor spoke. Figure 5.4 summarizes the changes in children's turn type over the 2 or 3 years they participated in *One-on-One English.*

For all six children, there is an increasing use of longer turns with more sentence turns and multisentence turns over the assessment rounds and a decreasing use of shorter turns (i.e., single word and phrase-length turns). In at least one of their later assessments, five of the six students reached a point at which over half of their turns (ranging from 58–93% of total turns) were multisentence turns. Changes in turn type reflected the changing roles children and examiners took in constructing the narrative. When children's turns were largely single words and short phrases and sentences, the examiner provided extensive recasting and prompting. Interpreting the child's production as a story required looking at it in tandem with how they were prompted and recast by the examiner. As children produced longer, sentence-length, phrase and sentence, and multisentence turns, they held the floor and constructed their own narratives.

However, there is considerable variation across the children both in their starting place and ending place. Some students started using longer turns earlier than others, with two students—Aracely and Ernesto—using multisentence turns in their first assessment. In contrast, even in her final assessments, Fabiola only used multisentence turns 15–16% of the time. In addition to this between-child variability, there is also variability within children such that their growth is not always uniformly upward in this dimension. While Marisol and Selena demonstrate considerable and consistently upward growth in their use of multisentence turns, the patterns for the children who participated in the project for a longer duration are less uniform. Ernesto and Fabiola seem to plateau in their use of multisentence turns after their third and fourth retellings, and Elsa produces a high of 75% multisentence turns in her fifth retelling, only to produce many fewer (32%) in her final retelling. Moreover, Aracely's trajectory is up and down, producing a large percentage of multisentence turns in her second (83%) and fourth retellings (93%), and a majority of shorter turns in her third, fifth, and sixth retellings. These shorter turns are still sentence-length turns that are interpretable on their own, and the examiner's participation consists simply of affirmations and back-channel cues. This decrease in turn length is not explained by her production of an

FIGURE 5.4. Summary of Children's Turn Types

CHILD/TURN TYPE	TURN TOTALS/TURN TYPE PERCENTAGES FOR EACH NARRATIVE					
	1	2	3	4	5	6
Marisol	49 turns	11 turns	26 turns	N/A	N/A	N/A
Single-word turns	18%	9%	8%	N/A	N/A	N/A
Sentence turns	14%	27%	35%	N/A	N/A	N/A
Multisentence turns	0	55%	58%	N/A	N/A	N/A
Selena	20 turns	27 turns	33 turns	N/A	N/A	N/A
Single-word turns	5%	0	3%	N/A	N/A	N/A
Sentence turns	55%	60%	18%	N/A	N/A	N/A
Multisentence turns	15%	15%	58%	N/A	N/A	N/A
Ernesto	31 turns	10 turns	14 turns	6 turns	9 turns	N/A
Single-word turns	6%	0	0	0	0	N/A
Sentence turns	39%	40%*	29%	17%	33%	N/A
Multisentence turns	23%	0	64%	67%	67%	N/A
Fabiola	30 turns	20 turns	27 turns	32 turns	33 turns	N/A
Single-word turns	50%	25%	11%	16%	9%	N/A
Sentence turns	7%	5%	15%	25%	61%	N/A
Multisentence turns	0	0	4%	16%	15%	N/A
Elsa	26 turns	37 turns	15 turns	33 turns	16 turns	31 turns
Single-word turns	0	5%	13%	3%	0	0
Sentence turns	27%	54%	33%	58%	13%	45%
Multisentence turns	0	11%	27%	21%	75%	32%
Aracely	15 turns	6 turns	11 turns	14 turns	10 turns	11 turns
Single-word turns	7%	0	0	0	0	0
Sentence turns	80%	17%	55%	7%	40%	73%
Multisentence turns	0	83%	27%	93%	60%	18%

Note. Percentage totals do not add up to 100% because other turns existed that were not coded, including turns exclusively in Spanish and unintelligible turns, and we have excluded phrase turns and phrase and sentence turns from this table. See Appendix B for the complete table.
*All Ernesto's sentence turns in this assessment consisted of the repeated formula *"I don't know."*

increasing number of turns, as the number of turns is similar across her final three retellings.

Finally, from the beginning, all students were able to produce turns considered to be English *sentences,* defined as having an English subject and predicate. Children produced sentences between 7 and 80% of the time in their first narratives. This evidence suggests that beginning ELLs are not building from part to whole in language development, mastering smaller pieces of language—words and short phrases—before putting them together into larger chunks. Instead, our focal students attempted and produced some sentence-like turns from the beginning. However, the number of sentences they produce in their narratives increased dramatically over their assessment rounds, as did their use of multisentence turns.

Sentence structure. Although children use what we have considered sentences (an utterance with an English subject and predicate) from the beginning, the composition of these sentences changed over time. Overwhelmingly, across assessment rounds and children, sentences are in a conventional subject-verb, subject-verb-object, subject-verb-adjective, or subject-verb-prepositional phrase order. This pattern of use suggests that word order may come relatively early in second language acquisition, as it does in children's acquisition of English as a first language (Brown, 1973). Four students produced a very small number of sentences with verb-subject order. Of the six children, Fabiola produced the most sentences with verb-subject order, though they made up only four of a total of 52 sentences across her five retellings. In her first retelling, the only sentence she produced was *Coming she go,* and in her third retelling, one of her nine sentences was *Is here apple.* Of the 19 sentences in her third retelling, Fabiola produced two with verb-subject order: *Is sad baby* and *Goes run the girl.* Her final two assessments did not include any sentences with verb-subject order. In her second retelling, Aracely produced one such sentence (*Is coming the three bears*), out of a total of 23 sentences. Selena and Elsa also produced one and two verb-subject sentences, respectively, in their later assessments. However, these sentences could be viewed as stylistic variation typical of the narrative genre. One of Selena's 75 sentences in her final retelling was *And then came then the bird,* and in her fourth and sixth retellings, Elsa produced two similar sentences: *Come a big wolf* and *Come a little girl.* Two students also produced a few sentences in which they introduced the object first (e.g., *The first one he tried; Then the third one he like it.*), which could also be seen as stylistic variation in word order.

Aside from the above exceptions, as stated before, students began using sentences with conventional word order (e.g., subject + verb) early on. Over time, however, they added a variety of components to their sentences, such as modifiers, possessives, adverbs, prepositional phrases, and compound verb forms. Five of the six students began producing compound sentences in which they used conjunctions such as *if, but,* or *because* to conjoin two or more sentences. Marisol, Ernesto, and Selena began doing so in their third narratives, Aracely in her fourth narrative, and Elsa in her fifth narrative. Students also frequently used *and* to string together sentences. At different points in their narratives, five of the six students began embedding sentences within larger sentences through the use of reported or rephrased speech. This use of embedding could be seen as acquisition of syntactic complexity or as a formula students have learned (e.g., subject + say + reported speech). Fabiola was the only student who did not construct compound sentences or embedded sentences. Only one child, Marisol, used relative clauses to embed sentences in her final retelling (*Then he saw that nobody is in there*).

Lexical growth. To examine our focal children's lexical growth, we counted the number of word types—that is, different words or lexical items—they used in each retelling. We did not count multiple occurrences or tokens of a single word separately (e.g., *pig*), but only counted each word type once. Word types may appear in different forms; for example, *walk* may appear as *walk, walks, walking,* or *walked.* In these cases, we counted the word type *walk* once, rather than counting each token. In general, we observed an upward trend in students' lexical diversity over their participation in the project. Figure 5.5 summarizes the number of word types students used across narratives. Darker lines between columns indicate the break between school years. For example, in the case of Ernesto, during his first narrative in the spring of 2006, he produced 55 different word types. The following fall, his second narrative included 12 word types, and that spring (2007), his third narrative contained 85 word types. The next fall Ernesto produced 71 word types in his fourth narrative, and in the spring of 2008 his fifth narrative contained 93 word types.

Similar to the patterns with other linguistic features, this trend is not consistently upward. As in Ernesto's case, students often used fewer word types in fall assessments than they had in the previous spring assessment, perhaps because they had less access to English over the summer months. In addition, the intervals between narratives were not constant—3 months over the summer, compared to 9 months over the school year.

Emergence of verb system. Over their participation in *One-on-One English,* children used an increasing number of different verbs in their retellings. Figure 5.6 summarizes the number of different verb types children used. As in other dimensions of language growth, there is considerable variation across our focal children. For example, in her final narrative Fabiola used 12 different verbs, the number of different verbs Ernesto used in his very first narrative.

In addition to the number of different verb types used, we also analyzed growth in verb morphology over time, summarized in Figure 5.7. From the beginning, children used more than one different verb form, producing an average of 4.33 different verb forms, ranging from 2 to 7 across students. In their first narrative, all six children used simple present tense verbs (e.g., *is, make*), and all but one used present progressive verbs, either in a conventional (e.g., *is putting*) or unconventional (e.g., *is walk*) form. Present progressive has also been found to be acquired early in first language acquisition in English (Brown, 1973). In general, there was a slightly upward trend, with students producing an increasing variety of morphological forms over time. At their highest point, students produced between 6 and 9 different verb forms. However, these patterns are variable within children, as some students produced more verbs in one retelling, and fewer in a subsequent retelling (e.g., Ernesto and Elsa). Elsa, for example, produced the same number of verb forms in her first and final narrative.

In addition, over time children used a greater number of verb types in multiple morphological forms (e.g., using *say, said,* and *says*). This suggests that students have not simply memorized particular conjugations of verbs, but can use multiple morphological forms of one type. In their first assessment, five children used 0–2 verbs in multiple forms, while Ernesto used six verbs in multiple forms. There is also a range in students' verb use in their final assessments, with Selena using 13 verbs in different morphological forms compared with Fabiola using only 2 verbs in multiple forms. In addition, as seen in other dimensions of language growth, students for whom we have five or six retellings do not show a steady upward trend.

By their final narrative, all students used simple present, present progressive, regular and irregular past tense, and infinitive forms. Five students used third person present tense and modal/auxiliary forms with verbs (e.g., *can, can't, don't*), and some students used past progressive verbs. Within the past tense and third person forms, students used both regular and irregular forms. The irregular forms they used included general high frequency verbs such as *to be,* as well as verbs that were important within the particular story they had heard modeled and were retelling (e.g., the irregular past tense *broke* and *ate* in *The Three Bears*). Across all students' narratives, third person present was less frequent than other verb forms, such as present progressive, simple present, and past tense. The *-s* morpheme for third person present has been found to be acquired late in L1 English development, perhaps because this morpheme encodes multiple meanings and functions, making its mapping between form and meaning opaque (Beyer & Kam, 2009; Brown, 1973). On verbs, *-s* marks both number and tense, and on nouns it marks plural and possession. When narrating in present tense, children often marked tense

FIGURE 5.5. Word Types Across Retellings

CHILD	WORD TYPES USED IN EACH NARRATIVE					
	1	2	3	4	5	6
Marisol	62	40	91	N/A	N/A	N/A
Selena	36	35	110	N/A	N/A	N/A
Ernesto	55	12	85	71	93	N/A
Fabiola	19	8	26	34	72	N/A
Elsa	20	49	51	75	75	73
Aracely	22	40	41	70	61	66

FIGURE 5.6. Verb Types Used Across Retellings

CHILD	NUMBER OF VERB TYPES USED IN EACH NARRATIVE					
	1	2	3	4	5	6
Marisol	8	9	17	N/A	N/A	N/A
Selena	10	8	29	N/A	N/A	N/A
Ernesto	12	1	28	18	23	N/A
Fabiola	6	2	6	8	12	N/A
Elsa	5	12	13	21	17	18
Aracely	9	15	14	21	20	17

with simple present, without any person marking (e.g., *walk*), or with present progressive, which does not require person marking for third person.

Looking at students' changing verb usage raises questions of whether children have actually acquired particular verb forms and how to define acquisition itself. Although the focal students used an increasing variety of verb forms to mark tense and person, they did not use them accurately in all obligatory contexts. It not clear when children have productive, analyzed use of a particular form, are using it within a memorized chunk, or have simply learned that form of the word as a lexical item, without an awareness of its tense or person marking. For example, in their early narratives, children often used the verb *broke* when they came to the page in which Goldilocks breaks the baby bear's chair, which was the same verb form the examiner had modeled in her own retelling. However, it is unlikely that children had acquired this past tense form, as opposed to the present tense form *break*. Later, we see the same child use the form *breaked*, overgeneralizing the past tense *-ed* ending. Both this memorization of particular items and their extension into rules play a role in first language acquisition (Berman, 2004; Clark, 2003) and likely do in second language acquisition as well. Clark (2003) posits that first language acquisition includes a process of memorizing particular structures and using analogy to extend those models into productive rules.

FIGURE 5.7. Children's Use of Verbs in Multiple Forms

Child	Verbs Used in Multiple Forms in Each Narrative					
	1	2	3	4	5	6
Marisol	1 verb in 2 different forms	4 verbs in 2–3 different forms	7 verbs in 2–3 different forms	N/A	N/A	N/A
Selena	2 verbs in 2 different forms	1 verb in 2 different forms	13 verbs in 2–4 different forms	N/A	N/A	N/A
Ernesto	6 verbs in 2–4 different forms	0 verbs in multiple forms	11 verbs in 2–4 different forms.	6 verbs in 2–5 different forms	11 verbs in 2–3 different forms	N/A
Fabiola	0 verbs in multiple forms	0 verbs in multiple forms	2 verbs in 2 different forms	3 verbs in 2 different forms	2 verbs in 2–3 different forms	N/A
Elsa	2 verbs in 2–3 different forms	3 verbs in 2–4 different forms	4 verbs in 2–3 different forms	7 verbs in 2–3 different forms	7 verbs in 2–3 different forms	4 verbs in 2–3 different forms
Aracely	2 verbs in 2 different forms	4 verbs in 2–3 different forms	1 verb in 2 different forms	7 verbs in 2–3 different forms	8 verbs in 2–3 different forms	5 verbs in 2–3 different forms

In examining first language acquisition, Wells (1985) also poses the dilemma of setting a criterion for *acquisition* and problematizes the use of the term.

> The use of the term "acquisition" suggests an instantaneous, all or nothing event. But for many categories this is an inappropriate way of conceptualizing the learning process, for a considerable period may be involved during which the child's control of the category develops from correct use in a single, limited context to full mastery across all relevant contexts. (p. 131)

Instead, Wells speaks of "emergence" or "the occasion in our longitudinal observations when a child was first observed to use a category correctly" (p. 133). Also studying first language development, Berman (2004) describes "an apparent paradox in children's acquisition of their native language: the incompatibility between early emergence versus late mastery of linguistic knowledge" (p. 9). Similarly, Brown (1973) concludes that in first language development, the acquisition of grammatical morphemes does not occur suddenly and completely, and there is a considerable period of time during which a morpheme is sometimes present and sometimes absent in obligatory contexts. In our examination of children's developing verb use, it became clear that similar patterns hold for L2 development. While we see the "emergence" of many verb forms in our data, we do not see evidence that children have mastered all of these forms over the 2 or 3 years represented here.

Grammatical accuracy. Over time the six focal students used an increasing variety of linguistic forms—syntactic, lexical, and morphological—in their retellings. For our final analysis, we examined children's accuracy with these forms and noted disfluencies that are not a part of monolingual varieties of English. Such disfluencies include interlanguage forms reflecting partial acquisition of particular language features as well as features that result from a transfer of elements from the children's L1. Utterances that contained both a subject and verb and were considered well-formed were categorized as "targetlike sentences." Utterances that contained both a subject and a verb and contained disfluencies of various types (e.g., agreement, pronouns, lexical) have been classified as "flawed sentences." We also counted switches into Spanish for lexical gaps as disfluencies. Sentences with inaudible portions, repetitions of examiner speech, and abandoned sentences were omitted from the analysis. Figure 5.8 presents the number of flawed and targetlike sentences produced by each child in the initial and final narratives, as well as the percentage of sentences in each category.

As discussed previously, all students produced many more sentences—both flawed and targetlike—in their final narrative than in their initial narrative. However, the picture regarding the accuracy of students' sentences is more complex. For two students—Selena and Fabiola—we saw a substantial increase in the percentage of sentences that were targetlike, and Aracely produced slightly more targetlike sentences in her final narrative than in her initial narrative. In contrast, Marisol, Ernesto, and Elsa actually produced a greater percentage of targetlike sentences in their initial narratives than in their final narratives. In their final assessments the majority of children's sentences were not targetlike, except for Aracely who produced a majority of targetlike sentences from the beginning. Therefore, as children developed their proficiency with English, their speech did not necessarily become more accurate as a whole.

However, looking beyond the initial categorization of a sentence as flawed or targetlike, and examining the flawed sentences children produced actually illustrates their development. Figure 5.9 presents some of Elsa's flawed sentences in her first and final narratives. To begin with, Elsa no longer relies on Spanish in her final retelling. Moreover, the kinds of meanings she is communicating within these sentences changes. In her first narrative her sentences communicated a single idea (e.g., the pigs have bags, he's making a house, a boy is coming with sticks). In contrast, Elsa communicates and connects multiple ideas within one sentence in her final assessment (e.g., the bears made food and it was hot; they read books, but did so incorrectly). She is also able to use embedded sentences to provide reported speech with conventional dialogue markers. In her final sentence, she uses the nongeneric dialogue marker *call*, communicating the illocutionary force of the little bear's statement, as well as his actual statement.

The grammatical flaws in focal students' sentences included issues with morphology, pronouns, or prepositions. As described earlier, with very few exceptions, students used conventional English word order from the beginning. Brown (1973) also found this pattern in children's acquisition of English as a first language, and concludes that children's early acquisition of word order facilitates effective communication, despite inaccurate usage of grammatical morphemes. In our analysis of L2 English development, as exemplified in the examples from Elsa's final retelling, children's flawed sentences successfully communicated meaning, despite morphological "errors."

Further complicating questions of accuracy is the distinction raised by Meisel, Clahsen, and Pienemann (1981) "between what the learner has not yet acquired and what he/she is not yet able to use correctly in every context" (pp. 115–116). In order to communicate efficiently in real time, L2 learners will not always be able to display their complete linguistic abilities. As children's sentences and communicative intentions became more complex and they used a greater range of linguistic structures and features of the narrative genre, there was more room for students to make "errors." In contrast to the flawed sentences in Elsa's final assessment, students' targetlike sentences were often shorter and simpler, frequently relying on formulas. For example, 9 of Ernesto's 10 targetlike sentences in his first narrative consisted of "I don't know."

SUMMARY: WHAT CHANGE LOOKS LIKE

In this chapter, we have described the changes in children's retellings of familiar picture books that took place over 2 to 3 years. We have examined growth across multiple dimensions of language use to provide an in-depth portrait of young English language learners' changing proficiency in English. This change over time was not uniform, and there was a great deal of variation between the six focal students, even though they were all rated as

FIGURE 5.8. Children's Use of Flawed and Targetlike Sentences

Child		Flawed Sentences		Targetlike Sentences		Total Sentences
Marisol	First narrative	6	(67%)	3	(33%)	9
	Final narrative	39	(75%)	13	(25%)	52
Selena	First narrative	8	(62%)	5	(38%)	13
	Final narrative	39	(51%)	38	(49%)	77
Ernesto	First narrative	18	(64%)	10	(36%)	28
	Final narrative	29	(67%)	14	(33%)	43
Fabiola	First narrative	1	(100%)	0	(0%)	1
	Final narrative	17	(53%)	15	(47%)	32
Elsa	First narrative	4	(57%)	3	(43%)	7
	Final narrative	30	(68%)	14	(32%)	44
Aracely	First narrative	4	(36%)	7	(64%)	11
	Final narrative	8	(33%)	16	(67%)	24

FIGURE 5.9. "Flawed" Sentences in Elsa's First and Final Retellings

First Narrative	Final Narrative
Pigs are *bolsa.* Y *luego*, he's doing house. A boy is coming um *palos.* He's he make farming.	They do the food and is hot. And they read a little bit book, but they do it wrong. And the dad said, "Who sit in my in my bed?" And the little bear call, "Mom, dad, a girl's right here my bed."

"beginning" English language learners by the state's English language proficiency assessment. In addition, for those children who participated in the project over 3 years, change did not represent a simple upward trajectory in their uses of different linguistic features.

Despite this variation, however, we observed several general patterns across the six focal children. Over time, students were able to produce more independent, structured narratives in English without the support of an interlocutor. In doing so, they produced longer turns that were interpretable on their own, rather than in relation to the examiner's prompting and recasting, including increasing numbers of sentence and multisentence turns and a decreasing number of single-word turns. Children also began incorporating conventional features of the narrative genre into their retellings, such as temporal markers and conjunctions to achieve cohesion and reported speech to relate vivid narratives and highlight key moments in the plot. From the beginning, children's sentences overwhelmingly reflected conventional English word order, and they gradually incorporated more components and used an increasing variety of sentence structures. In addition, children employed a greater variety of verb types and verb morphology and showed an increased lexical range over their participation in *One-on-One English.*

Looking across multiple dimensions of language use, we see that children's linguistic growth was not part to whole, mastering small pieces of language before moving on to the next feature. Instead, change took place at multiple levels of language simultaneously: morphology, lexicon, syntax, and discourse. In their final narratives, children were able to express more meanings using a greater variety of linguistic forms across these four levels of language. As children took on a greater variety of linguistic structures and communicated more ideas, their speech continued to include disfluencies that mark them as nonnative speakers. For example, even though students produced an increasing variety of verb forms, they still did not use these forms accurately in all or even, for many students, most obligatory contexts. Therefore, we suggest that children's L2 development is more productively considered in terms of an increased variety of language forms, rather than in terms of accuracy.

IMPLICATIONS FOR ASSESSMENT

This picture of what growth looks like empirically in our focal students raises implications for the assessment of young ELLs in schools. In addition to the variation between our focal students, there was often dramatic variation within individual children's trajectories. The narratives we elicited over 2 or 3 years did not show a steady, linear improvement in the various features examined. This within-child variation suggests two conclusions about language development and its measurement. First, development is not linear and simultaneous in all features of language. Second, any attempt to measure a child's language is itself a complex social situation, which will necessarily affect the language produced beyond the child's language proficiency. The students for whom we have five or six retellings show ups and downs and plateaus in their production of various linguistic features. These patterns may indicate something about their developmental trajectories, but they may also reflect the social context established through these assessment interactions, such as their relationship with the examiner, distractions in the room, the particular story they retold, and perhaps boredom with a task they had now completed several times. Students' personalities or learned styles of interacting may also have affected their performance, especially for students like Aracely who appeared shy or reticent to narrate in their early assessments. Over time she may have simply grown more comfortable with or aware of the genre and expectations of the elicitation task. It is notable that her accuracy with English was very high initially, suggesting that she may have been much more proficient than her teachers or program staff realized when she was referred in kindergarten. In sum, what appears to be linguistic growth or lack of it may be an artifact of the elicitation procedure, materials, or the testing situation.

In addition, the patterns of change over time raise questions about the standards and rubrics used by different assessments to classify ELLs at beginning, intermediate, or advanced levels of proficiency. Figure 5.10 compares three such rubrics and standards used in different states to evaluate ELL students' speaking abilities in grades K–2:

1. California English Language Development Test (CELDT)–the rubric used to evaluate students' oral narration from pictures
2. World-Class Instructional Design and Assessment (WIDA)–the performance definitions outlined in the consortium's standards, which serve as the basis for the ACCESS assessment of English language proficiency
3. English Language Development Assessment (ELDA)–the performance level descriptors for K–2 speaking

For all three, we present the intermediate and early advanced levels[4] with the criteria that address issues of accuracy in bold type.

In creating holistic levels, assessment rubrics and standards make hypotheses about what aspects of language growth will coincide as children develop competence with English. However, this uniformity is not borne out in the developmental paths of our six focal students. For example, all six children used varied grammatical and syntactical structures and five used complex sentence structures (e.g., compound and embedded sentences), which would place them at a Level 4 on all three rubrics. Identifying their level of grammatical proficiency on these rubrics is not so straightforward. In describing acceptable errors, all three rubrics use the criterion of impeding or interfering with communication. In general, the focal students' errors do not "interfere with communication" given a context in which they are looking at illustrations with a supportive interlocutor who wants to understand them. The CEDLT provides more specificity about the "few" and "minor" grammatical errors that are permissible at a Level 4: errors with articles and prepositions. This criterion excludes our focal students, given that they all continue to make what are apparently "major" errors in agreement and tense.

The classification of errors into "major" or "minor" types seems arbitrary and not reflective of the language of developing English speakers. For example, even considering Aracely, a child who stands out as far more targetlike

FIGURE 5.10. Comparison of Proficiency Standards for Intermediate and Advanced Levels for CELDT, WIDA, and ELDA

	INTERMEDIATE LEVEL 3	EARLY ADVANCED LEVEL 4
CELDT	Story is coherent and includes explanation of major events, but does not provide much elaboration (e.g., explanations of details and context).	Story is coherent and effective, including explanation of major events, with appropriate elaboration (e.g., explanations of details and context). Contains more complex sentence structure.
	Vocabulary resources are generally adequate to perform the task. The student sometimes cannot find the right word.	Vocabulary resources are well developed. The student can almost always find the appropriate word. Uses precise word choice.
	Response is generally adequate grammatically. Errors rarely interfere with communication.	Response displays **few grammatical errors** and contains varied grammatical and syntactical structures. **Any errors are minor (e.g., difficulty with articles or prepositions) and do not interfere with communication.**
	Student may have an accent and/or make some errors in pronunciation, but pronunciation is generally accurate and usually does not interfere with communication.	Student may have an accent, but both pronunciation and intonation are generally accurate and do not interfere with communication.
WIDA	General and some specific language of the content areas.	Specific and some technical language of the content areas.
	Expanded sentences in oral interaction or written paragraphs.	A variety of sentence lengths of varying linguistic complexity in oral discourse or multiple, related paragraphs.
	Oral or written language with **phonological, syntactic, or semantic errors that may impede the communication but retain much of its meaning when presented with oral or written, narrative or expository descriptions with occasional visual and graphic support.**	Oral or written language with **minimal phonological, syntactic, or semantic errors that do not impede the overall meaning of the communication when presented with oral or written connected discourse with occasional visual and graphic support.**

FIGURE 5.10. Continued

| ELDA | Students . . . are no longer wholly dependent on practiced, memorized, or formulaic language. They restructure learned language to communicate on a range of subjects.

Their speech is still marked by **errors in modality, tense, agreement, pronoun use, and inflections. These errors seldom interfere with communication in simple sentences, but do interfere in complex constructions**.

Students are limited in vocabulary, especially academic vocabulary.

They can retell, describe, narrate, question, and give instructions, although they lack fluidity and fluency when not using practiced or formulaic language. They often use language to connect, tell, and sometimes to expand on a known topic. | Students . . . are able to restructure the language they know to meet the creative demands of most social and academic situations. They can supply mostly coherent, unified, and appropriately sequenced responses to an interlocutor. They use some devices to connect ideas logically and they use a range of grammatical structures.

They make **some errors in modality, tense, agreement, pronoun use, and inflections**.

Students have sufficient vocabulary to communicate in non-academic situations and most academic ones.

They can engage in extended discussions. They can often use language to connect, tell, and expand on a topic; and can begin to use it to reason. They are fluent but may still hesitate in spontaneous communicative situations. |

in both her initial and final narrative than others, we see inaccuracies with agreement and tense in her final retelling of *The Three Little Pigs:*

1 One day **the mom tell** the little pigs that they have to go and build their own house. And then

2 the first pig, he sees a man with a donkey with with straw. And he made a house with the

3 straw. And then the **wolf came and blow** the house of the pig. And the second pig sees a

4 man with sticks. And **he make** a house with with sticks. And **the wolf wolf came and blow**

5 his house. And the and the third pig sees a man with bricks. And he told the man if he could

6 get them. And then the wolf was outside. And **he blow and blow**. And he could not blow it

7 away.

Although Aracely uses a variety of verb forms and sentence structures, there are still several verbs in her narrative that are not used conventionally. On the other hand, she does not make any errors with prepositions or articles, which *would* be permissible of an advanced speaker on the CELDT.

The WIDA and ELDA both define advanced (Level 5) speech in terms of approaching a native speaker norm (see Appendix C). According to the WIDA, a student at Level 5 would use "oral or written language approaching comparability to that of English-proficient peers when presented with grade-level material." The ELDA describes an advanced ELL as using grammar and vocabulary "comparable to that of a minimally proficient native English speaker." Clearly, Aracely and our other focal children have not reached such a level. Even though they have begun using a greater variety of linguistic features, they continue to exhibit many disfluencies that distinguish their speech from that of native English speakers. As students move beyond the intermediate level, accuracy becomes a key criteria for reaching the "advanced" level and being reclassified as Fluent English Proficient. From our focal students, we cannot tell how long it would take a young ELL to reach a "native-speaker" level of accuracy in English as currently defined in language assessment descriptors. Examinations of CELDT scores over time show that the largest group of ELLs in California are concentrated at the intermediate level (Linquanti & George, 2007). Moreover, less than half of intermediate ELLs move up one level in a year, compared with two thirds of students at the beginning and early intermediate proficiency levels. It is unclear what factors or criteria prevent students from moving beyond the intermediate level and to what extent accuracy plays a gatekeeper role. However, stating accuracy as a criterion presumes that it is required for children to succeed in learning academic content in a mainstream, English-medium classroom.

Underlying any language measurement or rubric are implicit assumptions about the trajectory and end point of L2 development—assumptions that may not be reflective of ELLs' actual English language development. We suggest that these assumptions are unfounded and that much caution needs to be exercised in the design of programs and pedagogical approaches based on the expectation that accurate, nativelike production is easily attained and indicative of students' ability to use English to learn in schools. As we have pointed out in this chapter, the children who were part of *One-on-One English* manifested clear change over time in the acquisition of the linguistic system as well as in their capacity to use academic oral language to narrate. We maintain that they made notable progress; rather than describing their language as primarily characterized by "errors," it is important for teachers to be aware of how much academic content can be communicated through children's approximative systems (Nemser, 1971).

English language proficiency assessments have high stakes for children's placement in classes and programs and their access to academic content and English. If practitioners have unrealistic expectations about children's language attainment that are based on standards-setting procedures and the development of scales and descriptors used in assessment instruments (North, 1998) rather than on a research-based understanding of the stages of L2 acquisition for young children, they may inadvertently contribute to their marginalization. As we have argued previously, we do not currently have an empirically based index of development on which to draw for validly assessing children's L2 proficiencies. What our research suggests, however, is that L2 development is not a rapid process in children, it does not move to grammatical accuracy, and it is directly dependent on the eyes (or ears) of the beholder.

CHAPTER 6

Reflections on
On-on-One English

As we pointed out in the introduction to this book, seen against the enormity of the problem of educating children who do not speak English, the work carried out as part of *One-on-One English* was a very small attempt to make a difference in the lives of young English language learners. We did not expect that it would provide simple formulas for closing the achievement gap or offer quick fixes for teachers who must teach reading and math to children who cannot understand the language of instruction. We hoped, however, that what we learned could provide practitioners, teacher educators, and researchers with some insights about the process of second language acquisition and with a deeper understanding of the challenges faced by schools in creating a context in which English can be acquired. In writing this book, we hoped that it would provide information about the small steps that children take in their journey to learning English when they have frequent one-on-one contact with the language. We also hoped that what we learned might assist teachers, principals, and other school administrators in designing instruction for this group of very vulnerable youngsters. In this chapter, we reflect on the work that we carried out over a 5-year period including the concerns that led to its design and implementation. We focus on several main themes: (1) change over time in children's language, (2) how affordances mattered in *One-on-One English*, and (3) implications of the project for the education of second language learners. In discussing the third theme, we focus on the kinds of language that need to be acquired by immigrant children in order to succeed in school and offer a set of principles that might guide an integrated practice for educating English language learners.

CHANGE OVER TIME IN CHILDREN'S LANGUAGE:
A RETROSPECTIVE VIEW

Our retrospective analysis of change over time in children's language drew directly from our perspectives on interaction and interpersonal communication. We viewed children who were part of *One-on-One English* as involved in the very beginning stages of learning how to participate as dialogue partners when using a developing second language. Moreover, we also viewed them as taking part in interactions with adults who were originally unknown to them in communicative events that made it necessary for them to align with their interlocutors and to engage in activities that required them to participate jointly in conversations.

Garrod and Pickering (2004) define *interactive alignment* as an unconscious process by which people "align their representations at different linguistic levels at the same time" (p. 9) and make use of each others' choices of words, grammatical forms, and meanings. These researchers contend that conversation is a joint activity within which interlocutors work together to establish a joint understanding of their topic of focus. Moreover, they use—not explicit negotiation—but an unconscious process of interactive alignment, which actually involves imitation. Each speaker's production influences the other speaker's production at all linguistic levels, and each speaker generates utterances on the basis of what has been heard from the other speaker. Interlocutors in all conversations, moreover, build up a body of aligned representations or common ground and use an "increasing proportion of expressions whose form and interpretation is partly or completely frozen for the purposes of the conversation" (p. 10). According to Garrod and Pickering, "routinization greatly simplifies the production process and gets around problems of ambiguity resolution in comprehension" (p. 10). While not used extensively in this sense within the SLA field, we found Garrod and Pickering's description useful because it makes evident the importance of imitation in establishing common ground between participants. Within the SLA field, Atkinson et al. (2007) use the term *alignment* somewhat differently and emphasize that alignment includes "the learner coming into coordinated interaction in tandem with an array of sociocognitive affordances" (p. 172), not simply or exclusively with the language produced by an interlocutor.

As speakers of Spanish, young ELLs in our study had already learned how to align with same age and adult interlocutors in order to participate in age-appropriate interactions in their L1. They knew how to take turns, use preferred and dispreferred seconds (e.g., answer questions, respond to directives appropriately), and establish an implicit common ground leading to the use of similar expressions, linguistic structures, and lexical items in the course of the interaction. Through their participation in *One-on-One English* they grew over time in their ability to draw on similar mechanisms to function in English conversations. As we indicated in Chapters 3 and 4, ELLs participated in the program in the following ways:

- Engaged in jointly constructed interactions with their volunteers
- Engaged in opportunistic planning because they could not predict the direction in which the conversation would unfold
- Imitated the language of the adults
- Engaged in constant task switching (listening and speaking)
- Drew on a common goal (e.g., to talk about book materials)
- Relied on routinized expressions and formulas (*I don't know*)
- Guessed at missing information in full, elliptical, and fragmentary utterances

It was evident, however, that as opposed to most conversations between adult native speakers who are skilled at this alignment and who speak the same language, not all communication went smoothly. There were numerous and frequent breakdowns in communication. Children displayed an apparent lack of understanding of questions and utterances they had understood in other interactions. Sometimes children simply did not respond. Possible reasons for nonresponse were many, but some undoubtedly involved a child's inability to clear up miscommunication because of still developing linguistic and/or pragmatic proficiencies. Children's manifestations of developing interactive competence were not necessarily linear and consistent. Displays of what they could do in one interaction, for example, did not predict what they would continue to display in other interactions thereafter.

Children behaved differently with different volunteers even when using the same materials. Some were initially shy with strangers, and the chemistry between volunteers and particular children was sometimes less than positive. Some adults were experienced in managing tired and bored children, and others tried too hard to be liked and to be accommodating to children's wishes. Some children were mischievous, and others were defiant and strong-willed.

As we emphasized in Chapters 3 and 4, children received various amounts of exposure to the very different kinds of discourse and participation structures available in engaging and telling interactions, eliciting and evaluating interactions, and game-playing exchanges. Some children had large amounts of talk made available to them during their entire 45 minutes of each day's participation. Others heard mainly a series of requests for display of information and possibly confirming or disconfirming responses. Some children remained mainly passive participants in interactions and responded as directed by their volunteers to yes/no and choice questions. Other children grew over time to become active participants in their interactions with adults and contributed spontaneously to the interactions. Such spontaneous contributions resulted in much more balanced interactions between volunteers and children because both individuals contributed to the exchange more equally. Spontaneous contributions included:

- Comments and questions about topics of focus
- Calls for attention to other topics or materials
- Requests for action
- Expressions of like or dislike
- Contradictions
- Sharing of related experiences
- Personal questions about volunteer's life and experience

Typically, these types of contributions involved multiword utterances, which, although not always syntactically complete, most resembled ways in which White middle-class children are expected to interact when they are manifesting interest, engagement, and eagerness to learn.

As we pointed out in Chapter 5, even when change and growth were not clearly evident in interactions with volunteers, pre- and postassessments reveal that over time children were able to produce more independent, structured narratives in English without the examiner's support. Over time, in their story retellings students expressed more meanings using a greater variety of linguistic forms across four levels of language: discourse, syntax, morphology, and vocabulary. In their later assessments, focal children produced longer turns that were interpretable on their own, rather than in relation to the examiner's prompting and recasting, including increasing numbers of sentence and multisentence turns. Children also began incorporating conventional features of the narrative genre into their retellings, such as temporal markers and conjunctions to achieve cohesion, as well as reported speech. In terms of syntax, although from the beginning children's sentences overwhelmingly reflected conventional English word order, over time they incorporated more components in their sentences and used an increasing variety of sentence structures. In addition, children used a greater variety of verb types, verb morphology, and vocabulary in later assessments. However, as children took on a greater variety of linguistic structures and communicated more ideas, their speech continued to include disfluencies that marked them as nonnative speakers.

It is important for us to emphasize that the change over time was not uniform, and there was a great deal of variation between students, even though they were all rated as "beginning" English language learners by the state's

English language proficiency assessment. In addition, for those children who participated in the project over 3 years, change did not represent a simple upward trajectory in interactional competence or in the use of different linguistic features.

It is also essential for us to stress that we deliberately make very few claims about the relationship between children's change over time and their participation in One-on One English. We know that by participating in the program children had access to English in interactions with ordinary speakers of English who, to varying degrees, focused on engaging them in working with lively children's books and on retelling stories. We do not claim, however, that their change over time in their interactional and linguistic proficiencies was exclusively or primarily a result of such interactions. What we do suggest is that the structure of our program provided a set of affordances to children that are not generally available to young English language learners in typical classrooms. We have evidence that children responded to and interacted with these features of the environment, and we contend that these affordances contributed to some degree to changes in the children's productive and receptive uses of English that we have documented.

HOW AFFORDANCES MATTERED

As we indicated above, in *One-on-One English*, children participating in regular interactions with adult volunteers had available to them a range of affordances that included a socially defined situation (after-school sessions), interaction with adult volunteers, literacy tools (e.g., books, games, puzzles), and embodied tools (e.g., physical orientation, pantomimes, gestures, eye gaze). These affordances may have mattered to children in different ways, and it is thus useful for us to reflect on a number of the assumptions that we had made about these features of the design environment. Some of these assumptions proved to be unfounded, and several affordances themselves worked in ways that we had not anticipated.

The Socially Defined Situation

The situation that we defined as after-school "volunteer assistance" had been originally conceptualized as entailing actions that could be construed broadly as "teaching," including instructing, explaining, guiding, testing, questioning, assisting children in making connections, expanding, and scaffolding. In our original design, these activities, except for the teacher-to-learner ratio, were considered to be similar to those carried out in school classrooms. For a period of time, we even used the term *tutors* to refer to volunteers. Volunteer assistance, moreover, was viewed as instantiating particular identities for both participants engaged in the one-on-one activity. For the adults, these identities included "more knowledgeable other," and "caring adult," and, for the children, possible identities were thought to include "child," "less knowledgeable other," "novice," and "non-English speaker."

Simultaneously, we hoped that actions, stances, identities, and activities that were part of volunteer assistance activities would be similar in important ways to those present in one-on-one interactions between parents and children who are engaged in "teaching" or socializing their own offspring. We expected that these interactions—while not identical to those that take place between parents and their young children—would be reminiscent of them. We specifically envisioned interactions with supporting adults committed to these children's acquisition of English and to giving them access to an Anglophone middle-class range of materials, behaviors, topics, and world knowledge considered appropriate for children.

By the end of the first year, we concluded that our initial definitions of the situation were contradictory and that, therefore, the structuring of this particular affordance was problematic. To the degree that volunteers were part of an after-school tutoring situation, they saw their roles and their interactions with children as involving much direct teaching. Volunteer tutors as opposed to *English buddies*—a term that we emphasized strongly in subsequent years—saw their roles as "teachers" and were most comfortable engaging in eliciting and evaluating interactions and often in direct drilling and pattern practice.

Our attempts to redefine the situation and thus to make available a set of affordances that stemmed from a different definition may not have been entirely successful. It was not easy to move volunteers from their initial conception of themselves as tutors, particularly because many were closely affiliated with a campus tutoring center. We spent much time modeling one-on-one interactions that could provide L2 Latino children with rich access to English and in establishing a view of volunteers as caring adults who focused on playing the role of more knowledgeable others who could both monitor a child's current skills and support or scaffold the child's extension of knowledge. What did become patently clear to us is the importance of the initial definition of situations in design experiments and the potential of different situations to afford learners very different action possibilities, in this case involving language.

Interactions and Volunteers

During the 5 years of the project, our ideas and conceptualizations of what constituted successful interactions were refined and modified. These modifications impacted how we trained our volunteers and what we emphasized during trainings. From the beginning, our trainings and interactions with volunteers emphasized the importance of providing rich input for the students. The notion of rich input was grounded in two main ideas: (1) the reality that these students had very little access to ordinary speakers of English and (2) access to the language was a requisite for English language learning. Our goal was to provide students with the opportunity to hear English and interact and engage with books and other materials.

As one of the affordances that were part of the program, one-on-one interactions with volunteers invited a possible relationship for young ELLs within which they could engage in joint activities with competent members of the English-speaking community, that is, with adult, knowledgeable "ordinary speakers of English" who had committed their time to playing the role of more capable others. As we have already suggested, in interacting with children, volunteers faced a number of challenges. Their first challenge involved their viewing themselves in a role that would invite interconnections with young English language learners in ways that could best support the acquisition of English. This challenge involved communicating in age-appropriate ways with learners who were at the very beginning stages of acquiring English and who could not interact in this language in ways typical of K–3 children. As we noted above, our revised definition of the situation in which children and volunteers were involved imagined that these interactions would be reminiscent of those that take place between caretakers and young children. In such interactions children and caretakers engage in co-constructions of the ongoing exchange and adults adjust to the level of development of the children. By comparison, volunteers who had had little experience with ELLs varied widely in their ability to gauge the developmental level of children and therefore in their capacity to adjust their own language to that of their young learners.

As we emphasized in Chapter 3, one-on-one interactions between children and the volunteers varied enormously. Volunteers used a variety of different materials (e.g., books, lotto games, sequencing cards, paper puppets) and used them in a number of different ways. Some volunteers read the text of the books to students, while others "read" the pictures and ad-libbed stories. Some volunteers made up new rules for games, while other played the games by their traditional rules. Some volunteers used many materials during a session, switching activities often, while others used a book or a game for longer amounts of time. All interactions, regardless of the activity and the level of the student's English, included question asking by the volunteer. These questions encompassed choice questions, yes/no questions, questions embedded in the text (book or game) being used during the interaction, and questions that were requests for a display of information. In addition to asking questions, volunteers often answered their own questions. Question asking appeared to be a strategy used by volunteers to keep children engaged, to check for understanding, to make sure students were following along, to make personal connections with the students, and as a way to encourage children to produce language during the interaction.

Some of the interactions were characterized by the volunteer's allowing the student to lead the conversation and to dictate what was talked about. This included the volunteer's abandoning his or her language to follow what a student said, allowing the student to turn the pages of a book and dictate the pace of the talk, asking the student questions about a topic he or she had initiated, and allowing the student to change a volunteer's plan. During these interactions students appear highly engaged and the interaction felt more like the type of conversation in which two interlocutors collaborate in the exchange. In these instances, children's utterances were longer, and it appeared as if students initiated some of these exchanges.

Some of the interactions were characterized by an extensive use of gestures and animation while the volunteer was talking. The volunteer acted out his or her verbal language—explaining vocabulary or concepts through gestures. These interactions were also characterized by language that was grounded in the text being used (book, game). This included pointing to pictures while talking—indicating vocabulary, characters, and actions. This strategy appeared to direct the student's attention to the text and to help him or her in following along with the volunteer.

For our analysis, we sought to determine what kinds of language the students actually heard from volunteers and how we might determine if a particular session was successful or not. As program staff, we often had instinctive reactions to particular volunteers and their sessions and categorized them as successful or unsuccessful in our daily documentation of activities. Sessions with long stretches of silence, students who were clearly struggling to stay engaged, and an overemphasis on accuracy tended to send up red flags for the program staff. We would often try to intervene with these volunteers and model the kinds of rich language we were hoping they would use. We generally responded positively to sessions that had lots of talk by the volunteer and students who appeared engaged with the volunteers and the materials.

A critical component of every session was the volunteer's ability to establish and facilitate joint attention around a text (e.g., book, game, TPR). Many elements played into this: the experience of the volunteer, the volunteer's demeanor and attitude, the age of the student, the student's affect, and the appropriateness of the materials. It is important to point out that we determined that engagement and joint attention are not identical. A student could be engaged in an activity but might not be attending to books, materials, or other artifacts *jointly* with the volunteer. Students were engaged when they were somehow interacting with the text. For instance, they were turning the pages of the book; they were matching lotto cards with their game board; or they were putting sequence cards in order. These children were engaged with the task at hand, but they were not necessarily interacting with the text in a *dialogue* as defined by Garrod and Pickering (2004) and Pickering and Garrod (2004). We conclude that it is this social reciprocity that characterizes a dialogue, and we suggest that for ELLs, participating in a dialogue depends on actual joint attention to the topics nominated by one or the other of the two interlocutors. When children attended jointly to materials or topics with their volunteers, students also turned the pages of the book, matched lotto cards with their game board, or put the sequence cards in order, but they were doing so in reaction to and as a result of the joint construction of the activity with their volunteer.

As we noted in Chapter 3, it became evident that while volunteer sessions and interactions were affordances present in the children's environment in *One-on-One English* they varied in what they offered, provided, and furnished to young learners and in the ways in which different children perceived and interacted with them. An *affordance* is a relationship between an object in the world and the intentions, perceptions, and capabilities of a person. An affordance according to Gibson (1977) exists relative to the action capabilities of particular actors. In the case of *One-on-One English*, the properties of the affordance of volunteer-child interactions for L2 learners directly depended on the activities and capabilities of volunteers as well as on the abilities of young learners to draw from them the possibilities that they offered, provided, or invited.

Materials

Materials were a particularly important affordance for both children and volunteers. As we pointed out in Chapter 2, during the first year of the program we received a donation of many of the books and materials used by a local early literacy program, many of which had a multicultural orientation. However, within a very short time it became clear that not all beautifully illustrated books with ethnic themes lent themselves to the use of rich language during volunteer-child interactions. After the first year's implementation, books that appeared to work best were identified as ones that allowed volunteers to provide children with extensive language input because they

1. Told a story
2. Contained illustrations that supported interactions between children and volunteers
3. Allowed the story to be inferred from the pictures
4. Could draw more easily from the background knowledge of the ELLs

During the next 4 years of the project we continued to explore the use of various types of materials that could support good interactions between volunteers and their English language buddies and experimented with the use of a variety of games and puzzles and other activities representing a wide variety of genres. We concluded that not all materials worked equally well in providing affordances for language development for ELLs. The success of particular materials appeared to be dependent on the facility of the volunteers to be creative and flexible in using them to augment extensive language input. Our most successful volunteers were able to use games as well as books during their sessions with children. However, the majority of our volunteers struggled to use materials besides books as a vehicle for language input.

Affordances: A Summary

Viewed from Van Lier's (2000) perspective on the role of affordances in SLA, we conclude that a number of features of our design experiment offered opportunities for reciprocal relationships between children as actors in the environment and elements such as after-school sessions, volunteer conversational partners, and materials. For 45 minutes for 2 days a week, children were immersed in an environment that Van Lier would refer to as "full of potential meanings" (p. 246). For various children in the program, different elements became affordances for their language development. They interacted with these features and drew from them the language that was useful to them as part of the activities they engaged in.

IMPLICATIONS OF THE PROJECT FOR THE EDUCATION OF ENGLISH LANGUAGE LEARNERS

One-on-One English began because we were concerned about certain approaches and pedagogies that were being used with English language learners in other volunteer programs that we did not believe were appropriate for these children. Specifically, we were convinced that, in order to become good readers of English, children needed to develop at least a rudimentary oral communicative ability in English similar to the age-appropriate Spanish language facility that they had already developed in their first language.

Our views were congruent with those of Hoff (2009) who maintains that literacy builds on "earlier acquired oral language skills" (p. 355) and with researchers who work with Hoover and Gough's (1990) "simple view of reading" (SVR) and stress the importance of oral language development and particularly of linguistic comprehension in reading. As described by Durgunoglu (2009), the SVR contends that reading comprehension relies upon and is the product of decoding and linguistic comprehension (usually measured by listening comprehension). As children become proficient decoders, the role of decoding decreases and linguistic comprehension plays a more central role in facilitating reading comprehension.[1] While both decoding and linguistic comprehension are key to reading comprehension, ELLs usually catch up to native English speaking peers in decoding and other word-level skills (e.g., spelling, word recognition), but continue to fall behind in reading comprehension (Lesaux, Kida, Siegel & Shanahan, 2006). These findings suggest the importance of focusing on English language learners' oral language abilities—especially higher order comprehension—to support their English reading comprehension (Durgunoglu, 2009).

As we have pointed out, the children who were part of *One-on-One English* exhibited growth over time in their comprehension of English and in their facility to engage with, use, and enjoy quality children's books thought to be important in the lives of English-speaking, middle-class, American children. At the end of their time in the program, several children appeared ready and eager to begin to read in English. They understood that books were fun, that they contained interesting stories and exciting facts about people, places, and animals. Most important, perhaps, they had talked and learned about the world *in English* to a degree not normally possible in the kinds of classroom environments in which the children at Golden Hills Elementary spent their days. They had been exposed to the vocabulary typical of children's books as well as that used in gamelike activities and had many opportunities for incidental learning of receptive (and possibly productive) vocabulary though repeated uses of the same words in interactions, story retellings, and other activities. Many volunteers used high-frequency words with children in ways described by Nation (2001) in the case of native speakers of a language.

The work that we present in this book, while offering a glimpse of the ways in which English language proficiencies develop in newly arrived K–2 immigrant students over a 2- to 3-year period, also raises questions about existing expectations of rapid English growth in ELLs that are present among policy makers and practitioners, current practices and pedagogies thought to result in acceleration of the acquisition of English, and the preparation of teachers. It also challenges views of L2 acquisition that are implicit in state language assessment instruments such as the CELDT, ELDA, and WIDA. In the final sections of this book we draw from what we learned in the years of working with young ELLs and focus on the kinds of English that must be acquired for immigrant children to succeed in school, including the importance of conversation in developing classroom interactional competence, and offer a preliminary framework for conceptualizing the language needed by ELLs in academic settings. We also outline a set of key principles that might guide the development of an integrated practice for the education of English language learners.

THE KINDS OF ENGLISH THAT MUST BE ACQUIRED FOR IMMIGRANT CHILDREN TO SUCCEED IN SCHOOL

Over the course of many years, a number of researchers have examined the language demands of all-English classrooms and the effect of particular language teaching practices on academic achievement. From Wong Fillmore (1982), for example, we learned that in order to participate in the life and work of schools and in order to learn academic subject matter, immigrant students must develop two fundamental skills in English: (1) They must be able to comprehend the spoken language of their teachers as they explain and present instruction; and (2) they must comprehend the language of textbooks from which they are expected to learn.

The current *ESL Standards for Pre-K–12 Students* (TESOL, 2006) directly address the goals of English language study by delineating progress indicators of English language development for ESL teachers and administrators. These standards specify the language skills English language learners need in order to have unrestricted access to grade-appropriate instruction in challenging academic subjects and stress that learners need to develop English proficiency in order to participate in social interactions as well as to achieve academically in all content areas. Specifically, the three goals of English language learning involve: Goal 1: Use English to communicate in social settings; Goal 2: Use English to achieve academically in all content areas; and Goal 3: Use English in socially and culturally appropriate ways. The standards for Goal 2 stress that English language learners must develop abilities to achieve academically in all content areas and use English to

- Interact in the classroom
- Obtain, process, construct, and provide subject matter information in spoken and written form
- Use appropriate learning strategies to construct and apply academic knowledge

From the perspective of the TESOL standards, then, students must develop proficiencies in English that allow them to follow oral and written direction, ask and answer questions, paraphrase a teacher's directions, work successfully with partners, negotiate and reach consensus, compare and contrast information, read and get meaning from texts, gather evidence, prepare and participate in debates, and edit and revise written assignments. They must, moreover, be able to choose language variety, register, and genre as appropriate to the interaction, interlocutors, and setting, and they must also respond to humor, express anger, make polite requests, carry on small talk, and recognize and use idiomatic speech.

Similarly, writing about children's transition from multiparty discourse at home to school, Snow and Blum-Kulka (2002) emphasize that in formal learning settings, using language appropriately involves "knowing what to say, and knowing the rules of interaction that allow one to say it" (p. 328). At school native English-speaking children must learn skills that include knowing who has the right to speak, how to bid for the floor, whether or not the teacher wants an answer in "a complete sentence," how to participate in IRE sequences appropriately, and how to engage in verbal performances, such as sharing time, presentations of book reports, and the presentation of summaries of group discussions. Snow and Blum-Kulka note that practice in verbal performances in a home setting may promote children's ability to perform at school.

Interestingly, neither the TESOL standards nor the work of researchers such as Snow and Wong Fillmore are focused exclusively on aspects of language that are often subsumed under the label of "academic English" as it is currently being used. As we underscored in Chapter 1, the terms *academic English* and *academic language* are presently being defined narrowly by many researchers and practitioners whose main area of concern is the education of ELLs, and this narrowness of focus has directly influenced educational policy. In California, for example, English Language Development (ELD) instruction is now designed to develop "academic" (as opposed to conversational or oral) language and is almost exclusively limited to instruction in explicit grammar, phonics, and vocabulary (Thompson, 2009). Indeed, as Thompson notes in her in-depth examination of the textbooks approved for adoption for ELD instruction in California, state policies now require a 60-minute ELD block that, in theory, "will move English language learners as quickly as possible through stages of language proficiency and enable them to achieve mastery of the English–language arts content standards" (California State Board of Education, 2007, p. 274, as cited in Thompson, 2009). The California Reading/Language Arts Framework, moreover, specifies that ELD materials must provide "formal linguistic instruction, practice and opportunities for application" (California State Board of Education, 2007, p. 298, as cited in Thompson, 2009). According to Thompson, all ELD instruction is required to be direct, systematic, and explicit, informed by contrastive analysis, and strongly committed to corrective feedback. Texts now approved for adoption focus extensively on grammar and usage, vocabulary, oral reading fluency, and phonics, Some meaning-focused oral activities, however, are sometimes included as introductions to reading selections in order to build children's background knowledge.

Our work suggests that well-meaning as these policies are, the practices that they support are—by themselves—unlikely to result in the kinds of language and literacy development that policy makers and educators envision. As we emphasized in our descriptions of *One-on-One English,* although children were primarily engaged in oral interactions, they made clear progress in their acquisition of the kinds of language and knowledge that they will need in order to achieve academically. Ernesto's explanations about starfish, Selena's explanation of apostrophes, and Aracely's descriptions of penguins at the zoo with careful attention to their characteristics and activities was exactly what the TESOL standards for English language learners (2006) list as indicators of learners' abilities to use English to obtain, process, construct, and provide subject matter information in spoken form. Children's increasingly complex, independent, structured narratives in English were also examples of language needed to achieve academically.

It is important to emphasize, however, that our program provided students with sustained one-on-one interaction with a native English speaker. More specifically, these interactions focused on particular oral genres, especially narrating stories as well as talk about these stories, interpersonal talk, and game playing. Therefore, students, especially those with strong volunteers, had extensive opportunities to listen to and participate in telling stories from pictures and talking about these stories. Over time, children took on a greater role in narrating stories, talking about stories, sharing experiences, asking the volunteers questions, and negotiating game playing. It appears that students benefited from this repeated participation in similar speech genres, with an interlocutor who wanted to understand them and who modified his or her own participation to the child's growing competence.

This kind of interaction is different from what children would experience in an ELD class with a focus on explicit, systematic instruction in a series of language structures. Most obviously, children's interaction in the program was one-on-one, compared with a 20:1 or 30:1 ratio is most elementary classrooms. But beyond this, students were engaged in repeated social interactions in the same uses of language with someone they genuinely wanted to communicate meaning to. The entry point then was on the meaning and use of language, rather than its form. Instead of being taught the features of a genre, the children were socialized into this register of language, for example, by listening to stories and increasingly participating in telling stories themselves. In contrast, in an ELD class as currently envisioned in California, a child would have been taught the features of a narrative to use (e.g., setting, beginning, middle, end) and particular language forms (e.g., *once upon a time,* structures for reported speech, specific sentence frames). The purpose would be on practicing English rather than communicating meaning. They would have fewer opportunities to listen to competent models of the genre.

Perhaps the teacher would model a narrative before having children produce their own. The other examples of narratives children would hear would be those produced by their own classmates, also English language learners. If, as in many schools, children were grouped into leveled ELD classes, children would only hear narratives produced by peers at their level, such that the beginning ELLs in *One-on-One English* would only have the examples produced by other beginning ELLs.

Given that they were beginning ELLs, however, it is unlikely that a teacher or curriculum would ask these students to participate in story narrations, as this genre of language would be considered too difficult for beginning ELLs. Instead, instruction would be limited to smaller chunks of language, isolated sentences or phrases presented in sentence stems. Clearly, producing a narrative would have been too difficult for our focal children at the beginning of their participation in *One-on-One English*. However, their access to the language was not limited by their current productive capabilities. Even though they themselves could not tell a story completely in English, they were still engaged in numerous experiences listening to stories and participating as they could.

As we pointed out in Chapter 1 in our review of second language acquisition, there are many disagreements and debates about the process of second language acquisition. There continues to be much discussion about what it means to know a language and about the characteristics of contexts in which second languages are acquired. There is evidence, however, that time-honored views about ultimate attainment are shifting and that researchers are beginning to look at language as a dynamic system and second language development as a dynamic process. From the perspective of Dynamic Systems Theory (DST), for example, which De Bot (2008) describes as being informed by chaos theory and by complexity theory, second language development (SLD) is seen as a nonlinear process, the outcome of which cannot be predicted. As a dynamic system, growth in language is dependent on resources including input and output, encouragement, motivation, attention, feedback, time to learn, memory capacity, and modeling of language. All resources are interconnected. Larsen-Freeman (2002, 2007) highlights the nonlinearity of the process, the existence of backslides, stagnation, and jumps in acquiring a second language, and once again, the unpredictability of the entire process. Larsen-Freeman & Cameron (2008) point out that from the perspective of chaos and complexity theory, change and variability in SLD are fundamental. They further emphasize that "instead of single causal variables, we have interconnecting and self-organizing systems that co-adapt and that may display sudden discontinuities and the emergence of new modes and behaviors" (p. 203).

What this implies is that expectations of linearity in second language acquisition predictably moving toward greater complexity and/or accuracy may be seriously misguided. Moreover, what we learned from exposing children individually to English suggests that language does not become accurate or nativelike rapidly. Children's language production—even when they were engaged in complex interactions or in the production of quite sophisticated narratives—was not "error free" as expected by various state assessments.

We have many apprehensions, then, about the well-meaning implementation of practices that depend on "curricularizing" language for young children. We are not convinced that selecting, sequencing, and practicing its "bits and pieces" will result in the acceleration of the acquisition of academic English or for that matter of any other kind of English. Nor do we believe, as we pointed out in Chapter 1 in our review of the literature on SLA, that direct error correction is successful in restructuring learners' interlanguages.

Conversations and Interactional Competence

The interpretative framework used to examine the evidence of change (i.e., growth and development in the acquisition of English by K–3 children) was one in which the focus was on participatory or interactional competence rather than on the acquisition of the linguistic system. We sought to examine the ways in which children would begin to function as members of the broader English-speaking community by engaging in interactions with English-speaking volunteers (ordinary speakers of English). In designing our work, we sought to enrich the field's existing understanding of L2 acquisition by young children and to advance credible assertions about the ways in which young children function in one-on-one interactions with limited language, how they grow in their ability to participate in such interactions, and, to a lesser degree, what kinds of growing participatory competence are reflected by changes in the linguistic system.

In talking about what we learned in the course of our work, it is important for us to elaborate on interactive proficiencies in second language acquisition. Children engaged in interactions or conversations as special cases of *focused interactions,* the kinds of interactions that occur "when persons gather close together and openly cooperate to sustain a single focus of attention, typically by taking turns at talking" (Goffman, 1963, p. 24). As Goffman (1981) also indicated, conversation can be defined from two perspectives. From a sociolinguistic perspective, the term *conversation* is used in a "loose way as an equivalent of talk or spoken encounter" (p. 14). In everyday life, however, the term is used more narrowly. *Conversation* is defined as talk occurring when participants set aside instrumental tasks and engage in talk in which unequal statuses of participants are set aside, in which all talk is encouraged, and in which a key purpose of the interaction is to ensure the continuing relationship of participants. In most everyday definitions of conversation, the expectation is that no individual dominates the interaction and that all individuals are free to nominate topics and change the subject.

A number of scholars have argued that, as compared to conversations, classroom interactions are more academic and make many more demands of children. Indeed, within recent years, discussions focusing on the language to be acquired by English language learners in order to succeed in school have minimized the importance of the acquisition of "interpersonal" language and focused around the notion of "academic" language. According to some researchers (e.g., Alvarez, 2008; Valdés, 2004), the term *academic language* is ill-defined and used in contradictory ways by both researchers and practitioners. Nevertheless, academic language, as contrasted with conversational language, has become the focus of a number of programs designed to remedy existing language deficits. In some cases, researchers consider that academic language has both oral and written modes (e.g., Tong, Lara-Alecio, Irby, Mathes, & Kwok, 2008), but all too often, practitioners—perhaps misunderstanding Cummins's (1981) conceptualization of language proficiency— refer to *oral* or *conversational* language as though the two terms were synonymous. Many researchers and practitioners refer to conversational language as "mere" interpersonal or surface fluency and believe it to be of limited importance in academic settings.[2]

Our position is that the proficiencies required to carry out academic work in school settings include both oral and written language. Moreover, we view conversation as central to language development and agree with H. Clark (1996) who cites C. J. Fillmore (1981) in maintaining that "the language of face-to-face conversation is the basic and primary use of language, all other being best described in terms of their manner of deviation from the base" (Fillmore, 1981, p. 152, as cited in Clark, 1996, p. 8). The basic setting in which children learn to communicate and acquire their first language is in face-to-face interaction (E. Clark, 2003; H. Clark, 1996).

There is much evidence to suggest, moreover, that in spite of its supposed "contextualized" features, conversation is not simple. For example, Garrod and Pickering (2004) and Pickering and Garrod (2004) provide an analysis of the complexities of conversational interaction. They highlight various characteristics of conversations that make them particularly challenging. For example, conversational utterances are elliptical and fragmentary and, because speakers cannot predict how a conversation will unfold, they cannot engage in advanced planning. Additionally, speakers in conversation must make their contributions appropriate to the addressee, while paying close attention to when it is socially appropriate to speak or to be silent. Planning what to say happens at the same time that speakers are still listening to their interlocutors. They must both multitask and task-switch between listening and speaking.

Similarly, the work carried out on conversational analysis (Goodwin, 1981; Gumperz, 1977; Sacks, 1995; Schegloff, 2007; Taylor & Cameron, 1987) has identified the complexities of the interactive construction of talk-in-interaction including the demands of turn taking for speakers engaged in interaction, the knowledge they must have in order to choose preferred and dispreferred responses (e.g., invitation-acceptance, question-response, complaint-apology) in adjacency pairs, and the ways in which self- and other repairs can be used in the process of mutually constructing conversations. Overall, analyses of naturally occurring conversation suggest that participation in such interactions reflects the skilled merging of cultural knowledge, productive and receptive competencies, and cooperation. According to Lewis (1969), as cited by Pickering and Garrod (2004), "dialogue is a game of cooperation, where both participants "win" if both understand the dialogue, and neither "wins" if one or both do not understand" (p. 171).

In the case of L1 learners, researchers (e.g., Ninio et al., 1994; Ninio & Snow, 1996) have recognized that an adequate description of children's language development must include an analysis of the development of pragmatic skills. These researchers point out that the pragmatic system is dominant in early development and that skill in "conversational turn taking and communication with gestures and early words develops before any syntax or morphology" (Ninio et al. 1994, pp. 158–159).

It is our position that the same may be true in L2 acquisition. Drawing from recent work on second language acquisition from a sociocultural perspective, including recent examinations of interactional development (Hellerman, 2007, 2008), as well as from our analysis of children's interactions over a 5-year period, we contend that it is possible for young second language learners to participate in interactions with interlocutors using limited formal resources and demonstrate change over time in their ability to participate in face-to-face interactions. It is our position also that an increased understanding of how children use such limited or flawed resources in face-to-face communication with adult native speakers can inform our understanding of L2 development in children—including how syntax and morphology might develop from this initial interactional competence. More importantly, perhaps, such knowledge might be able to guide teachers in building on such resources in classroom contexts.

An Integrated Perspective on the Dimensions of School Communication

Given our position on the importance of oral language for classroom participation and collaboration, we propose a working framework that has been useful to us in conceptualizing the place of conversation and interactional competence at school as well as the importance of receptive and productive proficiencies in learning and displaying the learning of academic content. We maintain that such a conceptualization is essential if ELLs are to be supported in developing the range of proficiencies needed to succeed in school. Without such a guiding framework, both policy makers and educators may, with the best of intentions, focus on very narrow aspects of what they consider to be "academic" language.

Figure 6.1 outlines the various dimensions of language that are essential for students in academic settings and offers examples of various tasks, activities, and interactions involving language under each of these dimensions. The framework recognizes three communicative types: (1) Interpersonal, (2) Interpretive, and (3) Presentational. Each type of communication takes into account the number of interlocutors involved (one-on-one, one-to-many, present or distant) as well as the types of skills (receptive versus productive) required for each task.

The three types of communication presented here depend on the internalized knowledge of linguistic and pragmatic systems. The second, third, and fourth columns of Figure 6.1 figure depict three types of school communication: Interpersonal Communication, Interpretive Communication, and Presentational Communication. The row labeled "Use" explains the ways in which these types of communication are used in both oral and written language. The row labeled "Examples" gives several examples of each type of communication as it is used by both teachers and students. Interpersonal communication, for example, involves oral language in a variety of modes including using language with peers to complete small group work as well as communicating with the teacher. Within small group work, for example, students use interpersonal oral language to negotiate a shared understanding of the assigned task, delegate roles, discuss content, and complete the required product. This interpersonal communication may also involve making requests for information, materials, or assistance, as well as consulting more knowledgeable others. The spoken language may be informal in certain types of interpersonal interactions and much more formal in others, depending on the audience and context (e.g., talking through an assignment with classmates versus talking to the school principal). Interpersonal written language is also included in this category, as in the writing of informal notes and "friendly" letters of the type written in interactive journals between children

FIGURE 6.1. An Integrated Perspective on the Dimensions of School Communication

	INTERPERSONAL COMMUNICATION	INTERPRETIVE COMMUNICATION	PRESENTATIONAL COMMUNICATION
Use			
Oral language	Used in face-to-face oral communication	Used in comprehending spoken communication as a member of class, audience, or other group	Used in communicating orally with a group (face-to-face or at a distance)
Written Language	Used in informal written communication between individuals who come into personal contact	Used in comprehending written communication as a member of a general readership	Used in communicating in writing with an audience or general readership
Examples			
Oral language	Asking the teacher or a peer for information Defending a position in a small group Negotiating the division of work in a small group Requesting supplies to complete an assignment Asking for assistance with a task Asking and answering questions Explaining actions Elaborating other people's ideas	Understanding instructions Listening to a teacher's explanation to the whole class Listening to classroom presentations Watching a documentary Listening to the news on radio or TV Listening to announcements	Presenting a report to the class Summarizing small-group discussions Constructing charts and graphs for presentations Participating in debates
Written language	Passing notes to a friend Writing invitations to a birthday party Writing thank you letters Writing in an interactive journal with a teacher or classmate	Reading textbooks Reading stories and novels Reading electronic materials Gathering information from sources Taking standardized examinations	Writing a report to be read by the teacher and others Writing personal essays Writing narratives Writing summaries Drafting a flyer for a school event Editing and revising a written assignment

Note. This figure is adapted from the National Standard in Foreign Language Education Project (1996), Figure 5, page 33.

and teachers. This type of communication requires linguistic, sociolinguistic, and pragmatic knowledge. We argue that it is not necessarily less challenging or less important in school than the other three types of communication and is essential to negotiating daily life in a busy classroom.

Interpretive communication involves understanding what is communicated by others in both oral and written texts. When students read classroom content materials, literary texts, or listen to explanations or lectures, they are engaged in interpretive communicative activities. The abilities that are required for engaging in this type of communication are primarily the receptive skills of reading and listening. Like interpersonal communication, interpretative communication varies in terms of what registers of language students hear. For example, listening to the presentations of fellow students as compared to watching a documentary to learn new information are two distinct tasks, which require linguistic, sociolinguistic, and pragmatic knowledge particular to those activities.

Presentational communication involves communication with a group of listeners or readers. It can take place in both written and oral language. As will be evident, oral communication in the presentational mode is quite different from oral communication in the interpersonal mode. In the presentational mode, because one speaks one-to-many, there is little opportunity to read body language and to clarify or reformulate online. Oral communication in the presentational mode is, in fact, much like formal written communication in this same mode and requires a sense of the audience as well as planning and preparation in presenting an argument, explaining, or summarizing information. In a classroom, oral presentational communication includes oral presentations of reports to the class and summaries or share-outs from small-group discussions, as well as participating in debates. Before such presentations, students may create charts or graphs to help communicate their ideas with an audience. In its written mode, this communication includes written assignments of different genres—reports, essays, narratives, and summaries. It also includes the process of editing and revising written assignments to communicate more clearly and appropriately to an outside audience.

For students with a non-English background who must carry out academic work in a second language, this integrated framework of communication types makes evident the range of communicative tasks that children carry out at school using both oral and written language proficiencies. It also makes clear the ways in which both receptive and productive skills are essential for children in achieving academically. More important for our purposes, it makes clear that interpersonal communication, rather than unimportant and trivial in school settings, is very much central to children's everyday participation in today's interactive classroom communities.

Moreover, these different modes of communication build on each other in classroom activities and in children's processes of completing academic work. As an example, one can imagine a science lesson in an elementary school classroom. Students will need to use interpretative skills to understand the teacher's instructions for conducting the experiment, as well as her explanation of the purpose or key concepts they will be exploring through the experiment (e.g., how magnets attract and repel each other, what plants need to grow). As they work in small groups, students will rely on their comprehension of the teacher's preceding explanation and also use interpersonal communication to negotiate the tasks involved in the experiment, make observations, and possibly ask for help. There may be a whole-class discussion of what students observed and what conclusions they can draw, which will require interpreting the explanations of other students and of the teacher and presenting their own observations. Finally, students will be asked to present their ideas in writing, perhaps a paragraph summarizing the experiment or a simple lab report. Being able to accomplish this writing task requires that a student was able to make meaning of the preceding types of language in the activity and apply it to their own writing. For example, if a student never understood the teacher's initial explanation of the experiment's purpose or the small-group or whole-class discussion, he or she may struggle to write observations and conclusions that are conceptually appropriate.

In the section that follows, we offer a set of principles for practice, for teacher preparation, and for language assessment that draw to some degree from our work on *One-on-One English*, that are informed by the framework of communicative types that we presented in Figure 6.1, and that are based on our observations and study of English language learners in a variety of settings (e.g., Valdés, 1996, 2001, 2003). We strongly believe that in order to make progress in educating English language learners, the field must move beyond existing dichotomous views of language (e.g., BICS versus CALP, oral versus literate modes of expression, restricted versus elaborated codes, and conversational versus academic language).[3] We suggest, moreover, that we must give much attention to settings in which there is little access to fluent speakers of English and that we must seriously grapple with the challenge of educating ELLs in contexts in which language learners always outnumber the native speakers.

TOWARD AN INTEGRATED PRACTICE FOR EDUCATING ENGLISH LANGUAGE LEARNERS: KEY PRINCIPLES

By an *integrated practice* for educating English language learners, we mean:

1. The development of policies, practices, and pedagogies that are informed by a comprehensive view of language that encompasses linguistic, pragmatic, and textual competencies

2. A wide-ranging perspective on the education of ELLs that recognizes the interaction between teaching practices, teacher preparation, and language assessment

We outline a set of key principles below that we suggest might support such a practice and discuss the possible implications of each.

Principle 1. *In order to achieve in school, English language learners need to develop interpersonal, interpretive, and presentational communicative competencies.* Principle 1 suggests that all instruction directed at English language learners must have as its final goal the development of productive and receptive abilities that will allow children to participate as full members of an academic community. The design of standards, curriculum, and lesson sequences must be directed at helping children develop their L2 to communicate interpersonally with instructors, school personnel, and other classmates; to interpret oral and written texts; and to produce oral and written texts for presentation and broader distribution.

Both the success of the direct "teaching" of language as well as all efforts to create rich acquisition contexts for English language learners must be measured against the expectation that they will result in children's ability to use this language in order to acquire the skills that are considered essential in this country for becoming productive members of society.

Instruction in subskills (e.g., the teaching of vocabulary, the teaching of letter names and sounds, and the teaching of sentence starters) cannot be seen as ends in themselves. If such direct instruction is undertaken, its effectiveness must be continually evaluated by examining its resulting contribution to children's capacity to use language in its written and oral modalities in classroom and other real-life contexts and not solely by standardized assessments. The best measure of children's L2 acquisition is their ability to function in the language for both personal and academic purposes in real-life settings in all three types of communicative modes.

Both oral and written language are essential to academic achievement. Students will not succeed in classroom contexts if they cannot interact with their peers to exchange ideas, to collaborate on assignments, and to participate in discussions about the academic topics that engage them. Similarly, students will not succeed in obtaining an education if they cannot learn from teacher explanations, academic lectures, and written texts. They must learn to read and read well, and they must learn to use the written language to express themselves using traditional and new media in their interactions with the wider world.

Principle 2. *Language is acquired through meaningful use in a context in which there is access to speakers of the language.* Important as instruction is in educational institutions, we know that language is best acquired when learners can interact with ordinary speakers of the language and learn how individuals use language effectively to achieve different purposes, how discourse conventions work, how texts (oral and written) are structured, and how the language system operates. They must use all of this knowledge *together* in the process of transmitting and receiving meaningful messages and especially in order to continue to learn through the medium of English.

According to Wong Fillmore (1991), the necessary ingredients for second language learning include:

> (1) learners who realize that they need to learn the target language (TL) and are motivated to do so; (2) speakers of the target language who know it well enough to provide the learners with access to the language and the help for learning it; and (3) a social setting which brings learners and TL speakers into frequent enough contact to make language learning possible. (p. 52)

Principle 2 suggests that classrooms must become contexts for acquisition that can directly contribute to the expansion of students' pragmatic and linguistic range so that they can carry out face-to-face interactions; comprehend live, recorded, and extended oral texts; learn through written texts; and use language in written and oral form to present information to groups of listeners or readers. Implementing practice according to this principle, however, will unfortunately be challenging. Increasing residential segregation will continue to result in the linguistic isolation of newly arrived poor immigrant children. Moreover, policies that require homogeneous or leveled ELD groupings will make it difficult to ensure interactions between new learners and speakers of English who know the language well enough to provide them with access to the language.

What we learned in our program, however, is encouraging. The children in our program made progress, in part because they had access to ordinary speakers of English and because they came into frequent-enough contact with these speakers to make language learning possible. There may be many ways of structuring contexts so that children are exposed to many examples of oral and written language that is used for engaging and meaningful purposes. Using adult volunteers, or children from adjacent schools, or more fluent older students to provide sufficient exposure to English is one option, as is exploring the use of technology to bring the language more consistently into the lives of isolated ELLs. Increased awareness of what it takes to acquire a language will be essential to a fundamental rethinking of the conditions that are currently present in many schools and classrooms in which new immigrant children spend their days.

Principle 3. *Teacher education programs must prepare future teachers to structure their classrooms and their instruction to provide maximum access to English aimed directly at developing interpersonal, interpretive, and presentational proficiencies in students.* Given the growing numbers of English language learners in the country and their presence in areas in which they had formerly not resided, a very large number of teachers regularly have English language learners in their classrooms. A large number of these teachers are not prepared to work with such students because their teacher education programs have only recently begun to develop expertise in this area, often in response to new state regulations and political pressures to provide qualified teachers for English language learners. As a result, teachers often struggle to find ways of making instruction accessible to new learners of English and to students who have not yet been redesignated as fluent English speakers. Some try to develop their students' English, but most of the time, it is not clear to them what needs to be developed and how they might proceed to bring about that development at the same time that they are teaching elementary students to add and subtract and older learners the fundamental concepts of biology. If they have listened to the buzz around academic language, they often view their role as limited to developing what they understand to be the language of the discipline or what Nation (2001) has labeled technical vocabulary (e.g., respiration, latitude, oligarchy). When students have problems understanding instruction, they pair them with same-language peers who can translate for them. They do not realize that they are creating conditions where ELLs do not grow in their ability to understand spoken language and where their translating peers are burdened unfairly. They may also have no way of evaluating the quality or accuracy of the translated explanations. Similarly, when they put ELLs in small groups with other students as a strategy for English language development, they often do not realize that these arrangements may not always result in increased access to English. Groups that do not include fluent ordinary speakers of English will have few models of well-developed language that can be imitated and appropriated by new speakers.

Principle 3 suggests that in preparing new teachers to work with ELLs, teacher education programs should orient them to viewing the teaching of English learners as involving the teaching of academic content as well as the development of interpersonal, interpretive, and presentational communicative abilities in students. Such an emphasis would prepare teachers to improve on commonly used approaches to teaching ELLs such as SIOP or SDAIE[4] and provide students with extensive experiences in designing and implementing classroom activities aimed at developing all three communication types: interpersonal communication (comprehending instructions, stating opinions, making requests), interpretive communication (reading stories, reading text materials, using Internet sources, drawing information from videos and documentaries, using headings in texts to skim material), and presentational communication (structuring talks and oral reports, preparing multimedia and visual displays for presentation, writing academic papers to inform or explain synthesizing information from relevant sources).

However, what is critical is not the specific approach to teaching ELLs, because approaches have a tendency to go in and out of fashion, but the emphasis within the approach on developing particular aspects of interpersonal, interpretive, and presentational communication skills. For example, language objectives in a SIOP social studies class might focus on developing presentational skills in the genre of the persuasive argument. In California, for example, 10th grade students studying World War I might look closely at the arguments for entering the war from various perspectives. That would mean that over the course of a series of lessons, the teacher would focus on teaching the elements of persuasive argument, providing students with examples of the various arguments for and against the war, and ultimately on directing the process of writing a persuasive argument using effective, but possibly flawed, language. Students might have the opportunity to defend their argument first in a small group (interpersonal communication) as well as watching a documentary about the political and economical rivals of the time (interpretive communication). Students would write a persuasive paper that built on their interpersonal and interpretative communication opportunities and conceivably these papers would lead to their participation in a class debate (presentational communication).

In addition to preparing and supporting students in developing interpersonal, interpretive, and presentational communication skills, teachers also need to be trained and supported in assessing students in these various areas as well. We have mentioned throughout the book the pivotal role assessment plays in the learning opportunities of ELLs; and, given the narrow assessments teachers commonly use in their classrooms (e.g., CELDT, benchmark assessments from scripted reading programs, state standardized tests), learning how to provide multiple opportunities for students to demonstrate what they are able to do in the three different communication types is critical. Assessment cannot wait until the end of the year but must be a regular part of the life of a classroom. Moreover, assessment opportunities should reflect the whole academic task (e.g., narrating a story, explaining a scientific concept, writing a lab report) and provide information about students' abilities to perform this communicative task, rather than isolated linguistic skills.

The assessment in an SDAIE science unit, for example, might focus on assessing the development of asking and answering questions. In California for second-grade students studying life cycles, the class might look closely at the life cycle of a butterfly. That would mean that over the course of a series of lessons, the teacher would engage students in asking and answering questions, providing students with examples of the various ways in which scientists ask and answer questions (e.g., making predictions based on observations, making comparisons between objects and ideas). Students would have the opportunity to demonstrate question asking and answering through the three communication dimensions. Through interpersonal communication students might ask their teacher and/or peer a question, answer a question of the teacher and/or peer, and write or draw their observations and questions in a science journal. Through interpretive communication students might read a text in order to gather information related to their questions. And through presentational communication students might participate in the creation of a KWL chart articulating their questions and curiosities about the unit studies (Ogle, 1986). All of the experiences provide the teacher with information about the students' language use and development that can inform the future opportunities she develops for her students.

Principle 3 and our experiences preparing volunteers for *One-on-One English* point to the need to reconceptualize the role of support and experience in the preparation of teachers to support the language acquisition of ELLs. These understandings illuminate the need for a recalibration by teachers away from their own experiences as learners (i.e., where the emphasis on discrete production was privileged) and away from narrowly focused curriculum and assessment tools that overly stress bits and pieces of language and nativelike proficiency. Instead, we need to move to training and professional support that enables teachers to deeply understand and integrate into their practice the necessity of access to rich, descriptive, and plentiful English language for ELLs.

Principle 4. *English language assessments must focus on students' ability to engage in grade-level work without modifications or accommodations and not on the accuracy of their production.* As we pointed out in Chapter 1, a growing number of applied linguists and SLA researchers have many doubts about the rate of nativelike accuracy or fluency that is possible for most ordinary second language learners. Socially oriented theorists, in particular, argue that deficit perspectives that focus on learners' limitations and on their failure to become identical to native speakers are misguided. Critics of mainstream SLA point out that negative views about approximative systems, interlanguages, and nonnativelike ultimate attainment rests on the acceptance of a single native-speaker norm as the goal and the measure of the acquisition of a language other than the first. Cook (2002) argues for the term *L2 users*, rather than *L2 learners*, for individuals who "exploit whatever linguistic resources they have for real-life purposes" (p. 2). Firth and Wagner (2007), for example, offer examples of such L2 users from their own research, which "revealed people who were artfully adept at overcoming apparent linguistic hurdles exquisitely able to work together interactionally, despite having what at first blush appeared to be an imperfect command of the languages they were using. . . . Moreover, despite noncollocating noun phrases, verb-concordance, prosodic and morphosyntactic errors, and a host of other linguistic anomalies, they were buying and selling thousands of tons of Danish cheese . . . and maintaining cordial relations with one another" (p. 801).

In the case of young minority children who are acquiring English, reconsidering the importance of noncollocating noun phrases, verb concordance, and other linguistic anomalies for effective participation in a variety of communicative activities essential in school contexts is an issue of great concern. The question for researchers working in schools in the United States with young second language learners who must use English in order to succeed in school is this: To what degree is the nativelike acquisition of English (assuming that such a level of acquisition is attainable) essential for carrying out the indispensable tasks of school learning? It is well and good that persons of different language backgrounds can use English to buy and sell cheese using flawed language, but is it possible for children to learn *and* succeed academically in schools with English that is not nativelike?

As we argued in Chapter 1, in summarizing the challenges surrounding the testing and reclassification of English language learners, a cursory examination of the efforts carried out to date by individual states and state consortia to assess English language proficiency and to measure EL students' subject matter knowledge makes clear that our current understanding of the best methods for assessing L2 acquisition and growth continues to be limited. We have much to learn not only about assessing language growth and development uniformly but also about the ways in which language limitations interact with the measurement of content area knowledge in standardized assessments.

Recent research on ELLs' performance on large-scale assessments (Parker et al., 2009), moreover, reports that reading and writing scores on examinations of language proficiency (in this case, ACCESS)–and *not* listening and speaking scores–are the most significant predictors of scores on large-scale content assessments of reading, writing, and mathematics. What this implies is that ELLs who do well on standardized tests do so because they can read and write well in English. Either they have been able to learn the content tested by the assessment *because* they read and write this language well or they have been able to *display* knowledge of content that they have learned either through an L1 and/or English. If they read well in English, they must have had the opportunity to read extensively, to engage with a broad variety of complex materials to comprehend and evaluate ideas, and to appreciate nuances in modes and styles of expression. When students do well on content assessments, what we know is that they can read skillfully enough to select correct answers on standardized tests and write well enough to produce the kinds of essays required by such assessments. Their performance on high-stakes assessments, however, does not guarantee that they have acquired nativelike proficiencies in a variety of registers (i.e., language varieties characteristic of specific situations of use, for example, spoken language used in conversations, interviews, sermons, and public speeches and written language used in personal letters, e-mail messages, academic papers, or newspaper articles) produced in real-time. In spite of their scores on academic content measures (and it is the *content* that is academic), such students may still produce flawed English in other contexts and for other purposes. Scarcella (2003), for example, gives an example of a UC Irvine student named Duy who writes an e-mail message containing many "infelicities" to one of his professors. Scarcella (p. 3, citing Rumberger & Scarcella, 2000, p. 1), argues that the student has not yet acquired academic English, a variety of English that she contends "entails the multiple complex features of English required for long-term success in public schools, completion of higher education, and employment with opportunity for professional advancement and financial rewards." She adds that "it involves mastery of a writing system and its particular academic conventions as well as proficiency in reading, speaking, and listening." There are problems with this particular conceptualization because it creates confusion between the language proficiency needed to achieve academically and language that displays nativelike control of specific structures and conventions. We maintain that they are clearly not the same. In the case of the example offered by Scarcella (2003), it is important to emphasize that in order to be admitted to any of the University of California campuses, including UC Irvine, students must complete a set of 15 college-prep courses and take two SAT subject tests in two different subject areas (for example, science and English) AND either the ACT plus Writing or the SAT Reasoning Test. Moreover, in 2003 at UC Irvine, successful applicants had an average high school grade point average (GPA) of 3.86. The middle 50% of the admitted class had an SAT Verbal score between 570 and 660 and a Mathematics score between 590 and 690.

What this indicates is that, in spite of the flawed informal language of his written English e-mail, Duy must have developed a set of essential receptive proficiencies in written and oral English that allowed him to learn from instruction given in English, to complete required written assignments, and thus to pass the 15 requisite college preparation courses for college entrance.

He must have also acquired the high-level literacy skills that allowed him learn from texts and to function successfully on standardized tests.

From a common sense perspective, then, and drawing from the experiences of students like Duy, it appears that in order to learn academic content from instruction that is offered in English and to do well on large-scale content assessments, children must be able to do the following:

1. Develop receptive and productive competence in spoken English

   - Comprehend the English spoken by their teachers (directions, explanations, presentations)
   - Comprehend the English spoken by their peers in order to draw information from group discussions and activities
   - Produce oral language to participate in group discussions, obtain additional information, and ask for clarification
   - Produce oral language to request clarification, expansion, and so on from the teacher
   - Produce oral language to display information or understanding as requested

2. Develop high-level literacy abilities in English

   - Develop high-level reading comprehension skills in order to read to learn from texts
   - Read extensively in order to develop a broad vocabulary, a knowledge of textual conventions, and the discourse practices of written English in different disciplines
   - Produce written texts using appropriate textual and formal conventions

Accuracy in production would be most important in the writing of formal academic papers, which require written edited English. Such production typically involves what can be referred to as "language after thought," that is, language that is produced when there is ample time to think, to revise and to rework ideas, and, as a final step, to edit the language appropriately.

Principle 4, then, argues for erring on the side of caution in the case of measuring English language proficiency. Because we know that how we define proficiency and what we measure on standardized tests has a profound impact on children's access to instruction in subject matter areas and on their opportunity to learn, we must make certain that these doubts and questions about language assessment become part of the discourse on language minority education and that we communicate concerns about relying on a much-challenged native-speaker norm in language proficiency assessments to policy makers, test preparers, other researchers, and practitioners.

FINAL THOUGHTS:
DESIGN EXPERIMENTS AND ENGLISH LANGUAGE LEARNERS

In a paper published in 1997 Ann L. Brown reflected on devising design experiments and on the importance of research in classroom settings for working toward a theoretical model of learning and instruction rooted in a firm empirical base. She argued that psychologists should be primary consumers of design experiments "that show what it is that children are ready to learn easily and what is resistant to exquisitely designed instruction" (p. 400). In the case of second language learning there continue to be many arguments about whether acquiring an L2 is similar or different from acquiring an L1 and whether and how learning a language in school is similar to or different from learning other academic subjects taught in academic settings. Tomlinson (2007a) echoes Brown's (1994) position about the need for school practices to be closely aligned with theories of (language) learning and development and argues for more "action research," and not what he terms "academic projects which measure in laboratory conditions only what is measurable or what is already known" (p. 283). Criticizing the field of applied linguistics, he contends:

> My view is that much of what is dogmatically done in first and other language learning has never been validated by empirical research (e.g., unprepared reading aloud around the class; mechanical drilling, listening and repeating; following a presentation-practice-production approach). If there are indications from research and experience that something different might facilitate language acquisition and development, then it is worth trying it for real and finding out how valuable it is. After all there is not that much to lose. (p. 282)

We too argue for increased attention by teachers and researchers to creating and structuring contexts in which we can learn more about the process of second language acquisition. Our experience in carrying out the *One-on-One English* design experiment, because it took place in an after-school context, was in many ways much less complex than carrying out research in intact classrooms. We believe, however, that engineering particular forms of learning in natural environments is essential to our understanding of the process of second language acquisition over time in children. We must carry out formative and design experiments in a multitude of second language class-rooms in order to reduce the gap between teaching practice and learning. We particularly need to understand whether 30:1 ratios make sense for "teaching" language to children, whether direct instruction of linguistic elements helps youngsters internalize the linguistic system, and whether, as Tomlinson (2008) argues, current teaching materials "make a significant contribution to the failure of many learners of English as a second, foreign, or other language to even acquire basic competence in English and to the failure of most of them to develop the ability to use it successfully" (p. 3).

For us, involvement in design research offered us the opportunity to try out informed hunches about children's interactions with ordinary speakers of English and to closely document changes over time in children's ability to use English in face-to-face communication for a variety of purposes. Our research was aimed at increasing our understanding of the process of L2 acquisition in young children when they had frequent and regular access to English. We did not aim to produce replicable or broad-scale educational solutions. We clearly understood that, while volunteers are an important resource, educational contexts cannot depend on volunteers. During the 5 years that we worked in a single school setting, we had the opportunity of learning a great deal about the potential facilitating function of the speech of ordinary speakers of English, about the ways in which children learn to inter-act in a developing language, and about ways in which they begin to use the language to engage in topics and activities that interest them. Our next steps are to make use of what we learned to contribute positively to the acquisition, development, and education of young immigrant children.

Transcription Conventions

xx	inaudible
,	pause distinguishing breath group
?	rising intonation
!	exclamation
[	overlapping speech, line is indented to where speech started
-	interrupted turn
(( ))	nonverbal communication (in italic)
( )	English translation (in italic)
bold	turn or segment of interest

Complete Summary of Children's Turn Types

For this analysis, children's turns were coded in five different categories:

1. Single-word turns: These turns consisted of a single word in English.
2. Phrase turns: These turns contained a single English phrase, defined as more than one word in English, but not containing both a subject and predicate in English. There may have been other talk in Spanish within the turn.
3. Sentence turns: These turns contained an English sentence, defined as containing a subject and predicate both in English.
4. Phrase and sentence turns: These turns contained an English phrase and an English sentence.
5. Multisentence turns: These turns contained two or more English sentences.

	Spring 2005	Fall 2005	Spring 2006
Marisol	49 turns	11 turns	26 turns
Single-word turns	18%	9%	8%
Phrase turns	29%	9%	4%
Sentence turns	14%	27%	35%
Phrase + sentence turns	2%	0	4%
Multisentence turns	0	55%	58%
Selena	20 turns	27 turns	33 turns
Single-word turns	5%	0	3%
Phrase turns	20%	15%	12%
Sentence turns	55%	60%	18%
Phrase + sentence turns	5%	6%	4%
Multisentence turns	15%	15%	58%

	SPRING 2006	FALL 2006	SPRING 2007	FALL 2007	SPRING 2008
Ernesto	31 turns	10 turns	14 turns	6 turns	9 turns
Single-word turns	6%	0	0	0	0
Phrase turns	19%	40%	0	17%	0
Sentence turns	39%	40%*	29%	17%	33%
Phrase + sentence turns	3%	0	7 %	0	0
Multisentence turns	23%	0	64%	67%	67%
Fabiola	30 turns	20 turns	27 turns	32 turns	33 turns
Single-word turns	50%	25%	11%	16%	9%
Phrase turns	10%	20%	56%	31%	3%
Sentence turns	7%	5%	15%	25%	61%
Phrase + sentence turns	0	0	11%	6%	12%
Multisentence turns	0	0	4%	16%	15%

	FEB. 2006	SPRING 2006	FALL 2006	SPRING 2007	FALL 2007	SPRING 2008
Elsa	26 turns	37 turns	15 turns	33 turns	16 turns	31 turns
Single-word turns	0	5%	13%	3%	0	0
Phrase turns	27%	27%	13%	15%	6%	13%
Sentence turns	27%	54%	33%	58%	13%	45%
Phrase + sentence turns	0	0	13%	3%	6%	0
Multisentence turns	0	11%	27%	21%	75%	32%
Aracely	APRIL 2006 15 turns	6 turns	11 turns	14 turns	10 turns	11 turns
Single-word turns	7%	0	0	0	0	0
Phrase turns	7%	0	9%	0	0	9%
Sentence turns	80%	17%	55%	7%	40%	73%
Phrase + sentence turns	0	0	0	0	0	0
Multisentence turns	0	83%	27%	93%	60%	18%

Note. Percentage totals do not add up to 100% because other turns existed that were not coded, including turns exclusively in Spanish and unintelligible turns.

*All Ernesto's sentence turns in this assessment consisted of the repeated formula "I don't know."

Comparison of English Language Proficiency Standards in CELDT, WIDA, and ELDA (Levels 3–5)

CELDT–Scoring Rationale for Speaking: 4 Picture Narrative	WIDA–Performance Definitions for the Levels of English language proficiency	ELDA–K-2 Performance Level Descriptors for Speaking
LEVEL 3		
Story is coherent and includes explanation of major events, but does not provide much elaboration (e.g., explanations of details and context). Vocabulary resources are generally adequate to perform the task. The student sometimes cannot find the right word. Response is generally adequate grammatically. Errors rarely interfere with communication. Student may have an accent and/or make some errors in pronunciation, but pronunciation is generally accurate and usually does not interfere with communication.	General and some specific language of the content areas Expanded sentences in oral interaction or written paragraphs Oral or written language with phonological, syntactic, or semantic errors that may impede the communication but retain much of its meaning when presented with oral or written, narrative or expository descriptions with occasional visual and graphic support	Students . . . are no longer wholly dependent on practiced, memorized, or formulaic language. They restructure learned language to communicate on a range of subjects. Their speech is still marked by errors in modality, tense, agreement, pronoun use, and inflections. These errors seldom interfere with communication in simple sentences, but do interfere in complex constructions. Intermediate level students are limited in vocabulary, especially academic vocabulary. They can retell, describe, narrate, question, and give instructions, although they lack fluidity and fluency when not using practiced or formulaic language. They often use language to connect, tell, and sometimes to expand on a known topic.

207

CELDT–Scoring Rationale for Speaking: 4 Picture Narrative	*WIDA–Performance Definitions for the levels of English language proficiency*	*ELDA–K–2 Performance Level Descriptors for Speaking*

LEVEL 4

Story is coherent and effective, including explanation of major events, with appropriate elaboration (e.g., explanations of details and context). Contains more complex sentence structure.

Vocabulary resources are well developed. The student can almost always find the appropriate word. Uses precise word choice.

Response displays few grammatical errors and contains varied grammatical and syntactical structures. Any errors are minor (e.g., difficulty with articles or prepositions) and do not interfere with communication.

Student may have an accent, but both pronunciation and intonation are generally accurate and do not interfere with communication.

Specific and some technical language of the content areas

A variety of sentence lengths of varying linguistic complexity in oral discourse or multiple, related paragraphs

Oral or written language with minimal phonological, syntactic, or semantic errors that do not impede the overall meaning of the communication when presented with oral or written connected discourse with occasional visual and graphic support

Students . . . are able to restructure the language they know to meet the creative demands of most social and academic situations. They can supply mostly coherent, unified, and appropriately sequenced responses to an interlocutor. They use some devices to connect ideas logically and they use a range of grammatical structures. They make some errors in modality, tense, agreement, pronoun use, and inflections. Students have sufficient vocabulary to communicate in non-academic situations and most academic ones. They can engage in extended discussions. They can often use language to connect, tell and expand on a topic; and can begin to use it to reason. They are fluent but may still hesitate in spontaneous communicative situations.

CELDT–Scoring Rationale for Speaking: 4 Picture Narrative	WIDA–Performance Definitions for the levels of English language proficiency	ELDA–K–2 Performance Level Descriptors for Speaking
LEVEL 5		
	The technical language of the content areas

A variety of sentence lengths of varying linguistic complexity in extended oral or written discourse, in-cluding stories, essays, or reports

Oral or written language approaching comparability to that of English proficient peers when presented with grade-level material. | Students . . . can supply coherent, unified, and appropriately sequenced responses to an interlocutor. They use a variety of devices to connect ideas logically. They understand and can use a range of complex and simple grammatical structures, as appropriate for topic and type of discourse. Their grammar and vocabulary is comparable to that of a minimally proficient native English speaker– grammar errors very seldom impede communication and their range of school-social and academic vocabulary allows a precision of speech comparable to a native English speaker. They can effectively engage in non-interactive speech. They can use language effectively to connect, tell, expand, and reason. They show flexibility, creativity, and spontaneity in speech in a variety of contexts. |

Bibliography of Children's Books

Carle, E. (1969). *The very hungry caterpillar.* Cleveland: World Publishing company.

Christelow, E. (1989). *Five little monkeys jumping on the bed.* New York: Scholastic.

Freeman, D. (1968). *Corduroy.* New York: Scholastic.

Galdone, P. (1970). *The three little pigs.* New York: Clarion Books.

Galdone, P. (1972). *The three bears.* New York: Clarion Books.

Galdone, P. (1973). *The little red hen.* New York: Clarion Books.

Galdone, P. (1975). *The gingerbread boy.* New York: Clarion Books.

Houghton, E. (1990). *Walter's magic wand.* London: Orchard Books.

McLeod, E. W. (1975). *The bear's bicycle.* New York: Little Brown Books for Young Readers.

Williams, V. B. (1982). *A chair for my mother.* New York: Greenwillow Books.

Notes

Introduction

1. The term *hypersegregated, linguistically isolated schools* is used here to refer to schools in which English language learners are 90% or more of the enrolled students.

2. The census defines *linguistically isolated* households as those in which everyone over the age of 14 speaks English less than "very well." We use the term *linguistic isolation* as synonymous to *linguistic segregation*.

Chapter 1

1. *Fossilization* is a term used in a variety of ways by both practitioners and researchers to refer to persistent non-nativelike features of learners' language production. Such features are thought to be resistant to instruction and exposure and are thought to be a fundamental characteristic of the implicit systems of all L2 learners. As Han and Odlin (2006) point out, originally, the term was used by Selinker (1972) to refer to linguistic items, rules, and subsystems that learners tend to keep in their interlanguage in spite of instruction. There are no satisfactory explanations of why this process occurs to a greater or lesser degree in different individuals. In spite of its original definition, the term is used by both researchers and practitioners to refer to errors (perhaps the bad habits of the old behaviorist perspective) that learners will make unless they are systematically instructed in the structure of the language and their errors are corrected. The reader is directed to Han and Odlin (2006) for a full discussion of the use of fossilization as both *explanans* and *explanandum*.

2. For a variety of reasons but principally because of the belief that accuracy is somehow directly related to students becoming aware of the distance between their production and that of native speakers (comprehensible output, noticing), much attention has been given to corrective feedback. As Ellis (2005b) points out, "The theoretical motivation for this interest lies in the claim that L2 learning (unlike L1 learning) requires negative evidence as well as positive evidence (i.e., learners need to be shown what is NOT correct as well as provided with examples of what IS correct" (p. 19). Unfortunately, as Ellis also points out, research on the effectiveness of corrective

213

feedback is mixed both because it is used inconsistently and carried out ambiguously by teachers. Many researchers (e.g., Doughty & Varela, 1998; Leeman, 2003) suggest that for error correction to be effective students must clearly notice what is being corrected.

3. Given some researchers' interest in input and interaction and the negotiation of meaning (e.g., Gass, 1997; Long, 1981, 1983, 1996), there has been an increased interest in the use of group work with L2 learners. Jacobs (1998) claims that among the advantages of group work are: decreasing anxiety and increasing motivation coupled with increasing the quantity of learner speech, speech acts, enjoyment, independence, social integration, and learning. In spite of its appeal and its coherence with other collaborative approaches currently being used in the teaching and learning of other subjects, a number of researchers (Prabhu, 1987; Wong Fillmore, 1992) have pointed out that there are dangers in using group work in a context in which all students are L2 learners. They claim that in order to acquire language EL students need to be exposed to nativelike models of language and such models are not available in classrooms in which students are all at the beginning or even intermediate stages of acquiring the language. The fear is that if implicit systems are constructed by learners based on the language data (input) that surrounds them, they will build them based on what Wong Fillmore referred to as "junky" data or possibly highly flawed language.

4. For a discussion of this point, the reader is directed to Tomlinson (2008). This critical review includes discussions of general coursebooks, children's materials, and materials used in teaching English for Academic Purposes (EAP) around the world and concludes that existing materials create an illusion of language learning, confuse language learning with skills development, and provide learners with "too much decontextualized experience of language exemplification and not nearly enough experience of language in fully contextualized use" (p. 8).

5. For a complete discussion of academic language, the reader is referred to Alvarez (2008).

Chapter 2

1. The statistics we give for "Golden Hills Elementary" and its community in this introductory section were obtained from the following data sources: *Current Population Survey* of the U.S. Census Bureau (http://www.census.gov/), the *Bay Area Census* (http://www.bayareacensus.ca.gov), and California Department of Education's Dataquest (http://data1.cde.ca.gov/dataquest/).

2. Although a major finding of the National Reading Panel (2000) was that there is "strong evidence substantiating the impact of systematic phonics instruction on learning to read" (pp. 2–132, cited in Cummins, 2007), the NRP also reported that systematic phonics instruction was unrelated to reading comprehension for low-achieving and normally achieving students beyond first grade.

3. It should be noted that in 1996 the members of the California Instructional

Resources Evaluation Panel recommended that *Open Court* not be placed on the California's textbook adoption list (Holland, 1996, cited in Moustafa & Land, 2002). However, the panel's recommendations were overruled by the California Board of Education and *Open Court* was placed on the California textbook adoption list and eventually became the largest reading textbook adoption (McGraw-Hill, 2000, p. 11).

4. *Open Court* has been both praised and criticized by educators. Proponents of the curriculum believe that its emphasis on phonics and reading comprehension strategies taught through very explicit instruction benefits children. Opponents of the curriculum criticize the explicit (scripted) instruction and argue that it does not meet the needs of linguistically diverse and economically disadvantaged students (Moustafa & Land, 2002; Peck & Serrano, 2002; Stritikus, 2006).

5. Using a model of test usefulness, Bachman and Palmer (1966) propose six essential qualities for language tests: reliability, construct validity, authenticity, interactiveness, impact, and practicality.

6. The California English Language Development Test (CELDT) is administered at Golden Hills once a year at the beginning of the school year. The test is administered and scored by a variety of the staff at the school. Although the CELDT was helpful in aiding teachers in recommending students for the program, we found that the CELDT scores were not diagnostic enough and tended to aggregate large differences in language. For example, both Ernesto and Fabiola received a score of 1 on the CELDT but clearly (as evidenced by their initial assessment data in Chapter 5) had different language learning needs that were not indicated by their CELDT scores.

7. The Census Bureau defines a *linguistically isolated household* as one in which no one 14 years old and over speaks only English or speaks a non-English language and speaks English "very well." We speak of linguistically isolated schools as those in which English language learners are schooled almost entirely with other English language learners.

Chapter 3

1. Volunteers engaged in several different activities as they worked with books and young English learners. They engaged in *picture walks,* which involved leafing through books and talking about the objects found in the illustrations and in *story talks,* which involved using pictures to tell a story. The focus of story talks was on the narrative itself. In story talks, illustrations and pictures were used to model the telling of a story as opposed to teaching vocabulary, naming objects, and predicting the possible content of the book, which is often the purpose of picture-walk activities.

Story-talk book activities had several purposes:

1. Providing young ELLs access to English
2. Increasing young ELLs' ability to participate in English interactions with adult volunteers
3. Developing ELLs' overall interest in books and in learning to read

Our strong focus on book activities as well as on story structure and narrative was also due to the fact that the CELDT, the California language assessment instrument used to reclassify all English language learners, directly tests ELLs' ability to narrate stories in English using a sequence of line drawings. We hypothesized that working with young ELLs on story narratives could contribute to their successful performance on state language assessments over time. In the case of beginners, the point of a story-talk activity was to use illustrations to expand children's receptive vocabulary, to develop their ability to follow narratives illustrated with pictures, to begin to develop their English comprehension abilities, and to persuade them that *One-on-One English* would be pleasant.

2. During the first years of the program, materials were stored on campus and volunteers planned their sessions and selected books and games that they believed would work with their student before they arrived at the school. During the final 2 years of the program, materials were stored at Golden Hills Elementary and volunteers selected them from a rolling cart that was brought to the classroom. Often the children were very involved in selecting the materials they wanted to work with.

3. We are using the term *interpersonal language* as used in the Standards for Foreign Language Learning (National Standards in Foreign Language Education Project, 1996). The standards contrast three different communication modes. The *interpersonal mode* involves speaking and listening in face-to-face communication and reading and writing between individuals who come into personal contact. The *interpretive mode* involves receptive communication of oral or written messages, and the *presentational mode* involves spoken or written communication for an audience.

Chapter 4

1. Total Physical Response (TPR) is a method developed by James Asher (1969) that involves the teacher's issuing commands (e.g., sit down, stand up) to early language learners who respond with physical movement. TPR is used for a variety of purposes including developing listening comprehension and receptive vocabulary. It also used by some instructors to develop productive competence when, after extensive modeling, the student is encouraged to issue similar commands to the teacher who also responds with physical movement (pointing, standing, jumping).

2. We are indebted to Elaine Horwitz (2009) for this conceptualization which encompasses feelings that learners have about their presentation of self through the language being acquired. She considers "authentic self-presentation" to be a key element of language competence and argues that many language learners feel uncomfortable in a new language because they cannot present themselves "authentically" and express their individuality.

3. While an extensive analysis of the impact of children's looks and personalities on volunteers is beyond the scope of this work, we mention these details because there is a body of research on the effect of phenotype and physical features on school

attainment among Mexican Americans (e.g., Arce, 1987; Fergus, 2009; Munguia & Telles, 1996; Rolethford et al., 1983; Telles & Munguia, 1990, 1992). This literature suggests that the lightest skin tone and the most European-looking youngsters are more successful academically than their darker-skinned counterparts. In describing children's skin color in this chapter, we agree with the teacher quoted by Olmedo (1997), who said that "to ignore something as obvious as skin color, is to suggest something wrong with that difference" (p. 254). The notion of colorblindness (i.e., the view that it is racist to notice color) and the challenges of talking about race in school settings have been noted by a number of researchers (e.g., Castro Atwater, 2008; Olmedo, 1997; Schniedewind, 2005; Solomon et al., 2005). At the same time, it is our position that children's appearances do matter. According to a meta-analysis conducted by Jackson, Hunter, and Hodge (1995), a large number of studies have been conducted on the relationship between physical attractiveness and perceived intellectual competence. In our case, we observed that more attractive children were easier to match with volunteers (including Latino volunteers) than were children who were less good looking, and we were aware that preference for lighter skin is also present in Latin America, which has been well documented by Knight (1990).

Chapter 5

1. Students who were participating in the program for their third year were given the text that they had not retold the previous year. In the fall the examiner modeled retelling the other text rather than the one the child would be narrating, as these students were more advanced now. For example, in 2006–07, Ernesto had retold *The Three Little Pigs*. Therefore, in 2007–08 the examiner modeled narrating *The Three Little Pigs* and then gave Ernesto *The Three Bears* to narrate.

2. In this chapter we have punctuated transcripts as sentences and used quotation marks for reported speech for readability and to make evident the changes in students' narratives as texts.

3. We have excluded the conjunction *and* from this analysis because it is difficult to determine when it is used to conjoin a compound sentence and when it is used to string together a series of independent sentences or phrases.

4. A comparison of the proficiency standards of the three assessments by level–intermediate (3), early advanced (4), and advanced (5)–is included in Appendix C.

Chapter 6

1. For an extensive review of research supporting the Simple View of Reading (SVR) with both native speakers and second language learners, readers are referred to Durgunoglu (2009).

2. According to Cummins (2008), the attempt to distinguish Basic Interpersonal Communicative Skills (BICS) from Cognitive Academic Language Proficiency

(CALP) was a response to notions of a "global language proficiency." He argues that the conflation of conversational and academic dimensions of language proficiency created academic difficulties for ELLs, including their inappropriate placement in special education or premature exit from bilingual or ESL programs. In an analysis of referrals of linguistic minority students for psychological, reading, or speech and hearing assessment, Cummins (1984) found that teachers described many children as able to function well in interpersonal communication. Teachers then assumed that students' academic difficulties were the cause of learning problems rather than recognizing that students still needed to learn other registers of English used in academic settings. From the teacher referral forms, Cummins concludes that, "for most children English interpersonal communicative skills appear to develop quite rapidly during the first year or so." (p. 33). Because the only data provided of students' fluency with interpersonal English were teachers' comments on referral forms, it is not clear how these interpersonal communication skills were defined or assessed by teachers.

3. For a more complete discussion of this point, readers are referred to Valdés, MacSwan, & Alvarez (2009).

4. SIOP and SDAIE refer to instructional models aimed at addressing the academic needs of ELLs. SIOP (Sheltered Instruction Observation Protocol) consists of eight interrelated components (lesson preparation, building background, comprehensible input, strategies, interaction, practice/application, lesson delivery, review/assessment) that allow teachers to deliver instruction that meets the academic and linguistic needs of ELLs. The SIOP model is most frequently implemented in content-based or thematic classes. SDAIE (Specially Designed Academic Instruction In English) is a teaching approach for teaching academic content (social studies, science) to students who are English learners. SDAIE strategies emphasize the concept of comprehensible input and accomplish this through the use of various strategies (e.g., realia, visuals, graphic organizers, and planned opportunities for interaction) to make the content accessible. Implementation of these approaches varies widely.

References

Abedi, J. (2004). The No Child Left Behind Act and English language learners: Assessment and accountability issues. *Educational Researcher, 33,* 4–14.

Abedi, J. (2007). *English language proficiency assessment in the nation: Current status and future practice.* Davis, CA: University of California.

Abedi, J. (2008). Classification system for English language learners: Issues and recommendations. *Educational Measurement: Issues and Practice, 27*(3), 17–31.

Achiba, M. (2003). *Learning to request in a second language: A study of child interlanguage pragmatics.* Clevedon, England: Multiilingual Matters.

Alvarez, L. (2008). *Examining conceptions of academic language.* Unpublished qualifying paper, Stanford University, California.

American Council on the Teaching of Foreign Languages (ACTFL), (1996). *Standards for foreign language learning; Preparing for the 21st century.* Yonkers, NY: National Standards in Education Project.

Arce, C. H., Munguia, E., & Frisbie, W. P. (1987). Phenotype and life chances among Chicanos. *Hispanic Journal of the Behavioral Sciences, 9,* 19–32.

Asher, J. J. (1969, January). The total physical response to second language learning. *The Modern Language Journal, 53*(1), 3–17.

Atkinson, D., Nishino, T., Churchill, E., & Okada, H. (2007). Alignment and interaction in a sociocognitive approach to second language acquisition. *Modern Language Journal, 91(2),* 169–188.

August, D., & Hakuta, K. (Eds.). (1997). *Improving schooling for language-minority children: A research agenda.* Washington, DC: National Academy Press.

Bachman, L. F. (1998). Appendix: Language testing–SLA research interfaces. In L. F. Bachman & A. D. Cohen (Eds.), *Interfaces between second language acquisition and language testing research* (pp. 177–195). Cambridge: Cambridge University Press.

Bachman, L. F., & Palmer, A. S. (1996). *Language testing in practice: Designing and developing useful language tests.* Oxford: Oxford University Press.

Baily, A. L., & Butler, F. A. (2007). A conceptual framework of academic English language for broad application to education. In A. Bailey (Ed.), *The language demands of school: Putting English to the test.* New Haven, CT: Yale University Press.

Baker, E. L. (2007). 2007 presidential address–the end(s) of testing. *Educational Researcher, 36*(6), 309–317.

Barab, S., & Squire, K. (2004). Design-based research: Putting a stake in the ground. *Journal of the Learning Sciences, 13(1),* 1–14.

Bardovi-Harlig, K., & Dörnyei, Z. (2006). Introduction to the special issue on themes in SLA research. In K. Bardovi-Harlig & Z. Dornyei (Eds.), *Themes in SLA Research, AILA Review* [Special issue], *19*, 1–2.

Bendixsen, S., & Guchteneire, P. D. (2004). Best practices in immigration services planning. Retrieved February 1, 2008, from http://www.unesco.org/most/migration/article_bpimm.htm

Berman, R. (2004). Between emergence and mastery: The long developmental route of language acquisition. In R. Berman (Ed.), *Language development across childhood and adolescence* (pp. 9–34). Amsterdam: John Benjamins.

Berman, R., & Slobin, D. (1994). *Relating events in a narrative: A crosslinguistic developmental study.* Hillsdale, NJ: Erlbaum.

Beyer, T., & Kam, C. H. (2009). Some cues are stronger than others: The (non)interpretation of 3rd person present *s* as a tense marker by 6- and 7-year-olds. *First Language, 29*(2), 208–227.

Bialystok, E. (2001). *Bilingualism in development: Language, literacy, and cognition.* Cambridge: Cambridge University Press.

Bialystok, E., & Hakuta, K. (1994). *In other words: The psychology and science of second language acquisition.* New York: Basic Books.

Bley-Vroman, R. (1989). What is the logical problem of foreign language learning? In S. Gass & J. Shacter (Eds.), *Linguistic perspectives on second language acquisition* (pp. 41–68). Cambridge: Cambridge University Press.

Block, D. (2003). *The social turn in second language acquisition.* Edinburgh: Edinburgh University Press.

Brindley, G. (1998). Describing language development: Rating scales and SLA. In L. F. Bachman & A. D. Cohen (Eds.), *Interfaces between second language acquisition and language testing research* (pp. 112–140). Cambridge: Cambridge University.

Brown, A. L. (1992). Design experiments: Theoretical and methodological challenges in creating complex interventions in classroom settings. *Journal of the Learning Sciences, 2*(2), 141–178.

Brown, A. L. (1994). The advancement of learning. *Educational Researcher, 23*(8), 4–12.

Brown, A. L. (1997). Transforming schools into communities of thinking and learning about serious matters. *American Psychologist, 52,* 399–413.

Brown, R. (1973). *A first language: They early stages.* London: George Allen & Unwin Ltd.

California Department of Education. (2008)."Williams" case. Retrieved April 24, 2010, from http://www.cde.ca.gov/eo/ce/wc

California Secretary of State. (1998). *Proposition 227: English language in public schools.* Retrieved April 24, 2010, from http://primary98.sos.ca.gov/VoterGuide/Propositions/227text.htm

California State Board of Education. (2007). *Reading/language arts framework for California public schools.* Sacramento: California Department of Education.

Canagarajah, A. S. (1993). Critical ethnography of a Sri Lankan classroom: Ambiguities in student opposition. *TESOL Quarterly, 27*(4), 601–626.

Canagarajah, A. S. (1999). *Resisting linguistic imperialism in English teaching.* Oxford: Oxford University Press.

Canagarajah, S. (2005). Critical pedagogy in L2 learning and teaching. In E. Hinkel (Ed.), *Handbook of research in second language teaching and learning* (pp. 931–949). Mahwah, NJ: Erlbaum.

Capps, R., Fix, M. E., Murray, J., Ost, J., Passel, J. S., & Herwantoro, S. (2005). *The new demography of America's schools: Immigration and the No Child Left Behind Act.* Washington, DC: Urban Institute.

Castaneda v. Pickard, 648 F.2d 989 (5th Cir. 1981)

Castro Atwater, S. A. (2008). Waking up to difference: Teachers, colorblindness and the effects on students of color. *Journal of Instructional Psychology, 35*(3), 246–253.

Cekaite, A. (2008) Developing conversational skills in a second language: Language learning affordances in a multiparty classroom setting. In J. Philp, R. Oliver, & A. Mackey (Eds.), *Second language acquisition and the younger learner: Child's play?* (pp. 105–129). Amsterdam: John Benjamins.

Chomsky, N. (1957). *Syntactic structures.* Berlin: Mouton.

Chomsky, N. (1959). Review of "Verbal behavior" by B. F. Skinner. *Language, 35,* 26–58.

Chomsky, N. (1965). *Aspects of the theory of syntax.* Cambridge: MIT Press.

Chomsky, N. (1980). *Rules and representations.* New York: Columbia University Press.

Chomsky, N. (1981). Principles and parameter in syntactic theory. In N. Hornstein & D. Lightfoot (Eds.), *Explanation in linguistics: The logical problem of language acquisition* (pp. 32–75). London: Longman.

Civil Rights Act of 1964, P.L. 88-353, 78 Stat. 241 (1964).

Clark, E. V. (2003). *First langue acquisition.* New York: Cambridge University Press.

Clark, H. H. (1996). *Using language.* New York: Cambridge University Press.

Clahsen, H. (1985). Profiling second language development: A procedure for assessing L2 proficiency. In K. Hyltenstam & M. Pienemann (Eds.), *Modeling and assessing second language acquisition* (pp. 283–331). Clevedon, England: Multilingual Matters.

Consentino de Cohen, C., & Clewell, B. C. (2007). *Putting English language learners on the educational map.* Washington, DC: Urban Institute.

Cook, V. (1999). Going beyond the native speaker in language teaching. *TESOL Quarterly, 33*(2), 185–209.

Cook, V. (2002). *Portraits of the L2 user.* Clevedon, England: Multilingual Matters.

Cook-Gumperz, J., & Kyratzis, A. (2001). Child discourse. In D. Schiffrin, D. Tannen, & H. Hamilton (Eds.), *The handbook of discourse analysis* (pp. 590–611). Oxford: Blackwell.

Corder, S. P. (1967). The significance of learners' errors. *International Review of Applied Linguistics, 5,* 161–170.

Corder, S. P. (1981). *Error analysis and interlanguage.* Oxford: Oxford University Press.

Coulthard, M. (Ed.). (1992). Advances in spoken discourse analysis. London: Routledge.

Crookes, G. (1989). Planning and interlanguage variability. *Studies in Second Language Acquisition, 11,* 367–383.

Crookes, G. (1997). SLA and language pedagogy: A socioeducational perspective. *Studies in Second Language Acquisition, 19,* 93–116.

Cummins, J. (1981). The role of primary language development in promoting educational success for language minority students. In California State Department of Education (Ed.), *Schooling and language minority students: A theoretical framework* (pp. 3–49). Los Angeles: National Dissemination and Assessment Center.

Cummins, J. (1984) *Bilingualism and special education: Issues in assessment and pedagogy.* Clevedon, England: Multilingual Matters.

Cummins, J. (2007). Pedagogies for the poor? Realigning reading instruction for low-income students with scientifically-based reading research. *Educational Researcher, 36*(9), 564–572.

Cummins, J. (2008). BICS and CALP: Empirical and theoretical status of the distinction. In B. Street & N. Hornberger (Eds.), *Encyclopedia of language and education, Vol. 2. Literacy* (2nd ed., pp. 71–83). New York: Springer Science and Business Media LLC.

De Bot, K. (2008). Introduction: Second language development as a dynamic process. *Modern Language Journal, 92*(2), 166–178.

De Houwer, A. 1995. Bilingual language acquisition. In P. Fletcher & B. MacWhinney (Eds.), *The handbook of child language.* Cambridge: Blackwell.

Del Vecchio, A., & Guerrero, M. (1995). *Handbook of English language proficiency tests.* Albuquerque, NM: Evaluation Assistance Center-Western Region.

Deuchar, M., & Quay, S. (2000). *Bilingual acquisition: Theoretical implications of a case study.* New York: Oxford University Press.

Dimroth, C. (2008). Perspectives on second language acquisition at different ages. In J. Philp, R. Oliver & A. Mackey (Eds.), *Second language acquisition and the younger learner: Child's play?* (pp. 53–79). Amsterdam: John Benjamins.

Doughty, C., & Long, M. H. (2003). *The handbook of second language acquisition.* Oxford: Blackwell.

Doughty, C., & Varela, E. (1998). Communicative focus on form. In C. Doughty & J. Williams (Eds.), *Focus on form in classroom second language acquisition* (pp. 114–138). Cambridge, England: Cambridge University Press.

Duff, P. A. (1995). An ethnography of communication in immersion classrooms in Hungary. *TESOL Quarterly, 29*(3), 505–537.

Duff, P. A. (2002). The discursive co-construction of knowledge, identity, and difference: An ethnography of communication in the high school mainstream. *Applied Linguistics, 23*(3), 289–322.

Dulay, H., & Burt, M. (1973). Should we teach children syntax? *Language Learning, 23*(2), 245–258.

Dulay, H., & Burt, M. (1974). Natural sequences in child second language acquisition. *Language Learning, 24*(1), 37–53.

Durán, R. P. (2008). Assessing English-language learners' achievement. *Review of Research in Education, 32,* 292–327.

Durgunoglu, A. Y. (2009, October). *The impact of L1 oral proficiency on L2 (reading) comprehension.* Paper presented at the National Research Council workshop on the Role of Language in School Learning: Implications for Closing the Achievement Gap, Menlo Park, CA.

Edmondson, W. (1981). Spoken discourse: A model for analysis. London: Longman.

Ellis, R. (1997). SLA and language pedagogy: An educational perspective. *Studies in Second Language Acquisition, 19*(1), 69–92.

Ellis, R. (2005a). *Instructed second language acquisition: A literature review.* Wellington, New Zealand: Research Division, Ministry of Education.

Ellis, R. (2005b). Principles of instructed language learning. *System, 33,* 209–224.

The Equal Opportunities Act of 1974 (20 U.S.C. §1703)

Fergus, E. (2009). Understanding Latino students schooling experiences: The relevance of skin color among Mexican and Puerto Rican high school students. *Teachers College Record, 111*(2), 339–375.

Ferguson, C. A. (1975). Toward a characterization of English foreigner talk. *Anthropological Linguistics, 17,* 1–14.

Fillmore, C. J. (1981). Pragmatics and a description of discourse. In P. Cole (Ed.), *Radical pragmatics* (pp. 143–166). New York: Academic Press.

Firth, A., & Wagner, J. (2007). Second/foreign language learning as a social accomplishment: Elaborations on a reconceptualized SLA. *Modern Language Journal* (Focus Issue), *91,* 800–819.

Flynn, S. (1987). *A parameter-setting model of L2 acquistion: Experimental studies in anaphora.* Dordrecht, The Netherlands: Reidel.

Francis, D., & Rivera, M. (2007). Principles underlying English language proficiency tests and academic accountability for ELLs. In J. Abedi (Ed.), *English language proficiency assessment in the nation: Current status and future practice* (pp. 13–32). Davis: University of California.

Frawley, W., & Lantolf, J. P. (1985). Second language discourse: A Vygotskyan perspective. *Applied Linguistics, 6*(1), 19–44.

Fry, R. (2007). *How far behind in math and reading are English language learners?* Washington, DC: Pew Hispanic Center.

Gallimore, R., & Tharp, P. (1988). *Rousing minds to life: Teaching, learning, and schooling in social context.* New York: Cambridge University Press.

Garrod, S., & Pickering, J. J. (2004). Why is conversation so easy? *Trends in cognitive science, 8*(1), 8–11.

Gass, S. M. (1997). *Input, interaction, and the second language learner.* Mahwah, NJ: Erlbaum.

Gass, S. M., & Mackey, A. (2007). Input, interaction, and output in second language acquisition. In B. Van Patten & J. Williams (Eds.), *Theories in second language acquisition: An introduction* (pp. 175–199). Mahwah, NJ: Erlbaum.

Gass, S. M., & Selinker, L. (2001). *Second language acquisition: An introductory course.* Mahwah, NJ: Erlbaum.

Gee, J. P. (1995). First language acquisition as a guide for theories of learning and pedagogy. *Linguistics and education, 6,* 331–354.

Genesee, F., Lindholm-Leary, K., Saunders, W., & Christian, D. (2006). *Educating English language learners: A synthesis of research evidence.* New York: Cambridge University Press.

Gibson, J. J. (1977). The theory of affordances. In R. Shaw & J. Bransford (Eds.), *Perceiving, acting, and knowing: Toward an ecological psychology* (pp. 67–82). Hillsdale, NJ: Erlbaum.

Gifford, B. R., & Valdés, G. (2006). The linguistic isolation of Hispanic students in California's public schools: The challenge of reintegration. In A. Ball (Ed.), *With more deliberate speed: Achieving equity and excellence in education-realizing the full potential of Brown v. Board of Education* (pp. 125–154). Yearbook of the National Society for the Study of Education (v. 105). Malden, MA: Blackwell.

Goffman, E. (1963). *Behavior in public places.* New York: Free Press.

Goffman, E. (1981). Replies and responses. In E. Goffman (Ed.), *Forms of talk* (pp. 5–74). Philadelphia: University of Pennsylvania Press.

Goldenberg, C. (2008). Teaching English language learners: What the research does—and does not—say. *American Educator 32*(2), 8–23, 42–44.

Goodell, E. W., & Sachs, J. (1992). Direct and indirect speech in English-speaking children's retold narratives. *Discourse Processes, 15*(4), 395–422.

Goodwin, C. (1981). *Conversational organization: Interaction between speakers and hearers.* New York: Academic Press.

Goodwin, C., & Duranti, A. (1992). Rethinking context: an introduction. In A. Duranti & C. Goodwin (Eds.), *Rethinking context* (pp. 1–42). Cambridge: Cambridge University Press.

Goodwin, C., & Goodwin, M. H. (1992). Assessments and the construction of context. In A. Duranti & C. Goodwin (Eds.), *Rethinking context* (pp. 147–189). Cambridge: Cambridge University Press.

Gravemeijer, K., & Cobb, P. (2006). Design research from a learning design perspective. In J. van den Akker, K. Gravemeijer, S. McKenney, & N. Nieveen (Eds.). *Educational design research* (pp. 17–51). New York: Routledge.

Greeno, J. G. (1994). Gibson's affordances. *Psychological Review, 101*(2), 336–342.

Gumperz, J. (1977). Sociocultural knowledge in conversational inference. In M. Saville-Troike (Ed.), *Linguistics and anthropology* (pp. 191–211). 28th Annual Round Table Monograph Series on Languages and Linguistics. Washington, DC: Georgetown University Press.

Gumperz, J. (1982). *Discourse strategies.* Cambridge: Cambridge University Press.

Hakimzadeh, S., & Cohn, D. (2007). *English usage among Hispanics in the United States.* Washington, DC: Pew Hispanic Center.

Hakuta, K. (1974). A preliminary report on the development of grammatical morphemes in a Japanese girl learning English as a second language. *Working Papers on Bilingualism, 3,* 18–43.

Hakuta, K. (1976). A case study of a Japanese child learning English as a second language. *Language Learning, 26,* 321–351.

Haladyna, T. M., & Downing, S. M. (2004). Construct-irrelevant variance in high-stakes testing. *Educational Measurement: Issues and Practice, 23*(1), 17–27.

Han, Z., & Odlin, T. (2006). Introduction. In Z. Han & T. Odlin (Eds.), *Studies of fossilization in second language acquisition* (pp. 1–20). Clevedon, England: Multilingual Matters.

Harklau, L. (1994). ESL versus mainstream classes: Contrasting L2 learning environments. *TESOL Quarterly, 28,* 241–272.

Hatch, E. (1978). Applied with caution. *Studies in Second Language Acquisition, 2,* 123–143.

He, A. W., & Young, R. (1998). *Talking and testing: Discourse approaches to the assessment of oral proficiency.* Amsterdam: John Benjamins.

Hellerman, J. (2007). The development of practices for action in classroom dyadic interaction: Focus on task openings. *Modern Language Journal, 91*(1), 83–96.

Hellerman, J. (2008). *Social actions for classroom language learning.* Clevedon, England: Multilingual Matters.

Hoff, E. (2009). *Language development* (4th ed.). Belmont, CA: Wadsworth.

Horwitz, A. R., Uro, G., Price-Baugh, R., Simon, C., Uzzell, R., Lewis, S., et al. (2009). *Succeeding with English language learners: Lesson learned from the Great City Schools.*

Washington, DC: The Council of the Great City Schools.

Horwitz, E. K. (2009). Cultural identity and language anxiety: How self-concept and cultural expectations interact with performance in a second language. In P. Cheng and J. X.Yan (Eds.), *Cultural identity and language anxiety* (pp. 57–69). Guilin, China: Guangxi Normal University Press.

Hoover, W. A., & Gough, P. B. (1990). The simple view of reading. *Reading and Writing, 2*(2), 127–160.

Huntington, S. P. (2004). *Who are we? The challenges to America's national identity.* New York: Simon & Schuster.

Hurtado, N., Marchman, V. A., & Fernald, A.(2007). Spoken word recognition: Latino children learning Spanish as a first language. *Journal of Child Language, 33,* 227–249.

Hyltenstam, K., & Abrahamsson, N. (2003). Maturational constraints on SLA. In C. Doughty & M. Lang (Eds.), *The handbook of second language acquisition* (pp. 539–588). San Francisco: Blackwell.

Jackson, L. A., Hunter, J. E., & Hodge, C. (1995). Physical attractiveness and intellectual competence: A meta-analytic review. *Social Psychology Quarterly, 58*(2), 108–122.

Jacobs, G. (1988). Co-operative goal structure: A way to improve group activities. *ELT Journal, 4*(2), 97–101.

Johnson, M. (2004). *A philosophy of second language acquisition.* New Haven, CT: Yale University Press.

Kelly, L. G. (1976). *Twenty-five centuries of language teaching.* Rowley, MA: Newbury House.

Klein, W. (1998). The contribution of second language acquisition research. *Language Learning, 48*(4), 527–550.

Knight, A. (1990). Racism, revolution, and indigenismo: Mexico 1910–1940. In A. Helg, R. Graham, A. Knight, & T. Skidmore (Eds.), *The idea of race in Latin America–1870–1940* (pp. 71–113). Austin: University of Texas Press.

Kopriva, R. J. (2008). *Improving testing for English language learners.* New York: Routledge.

Kramsch, C. (Ed.). (2002). *Language acquisition and language socialization: Ecological perspectives.* London: Continuum.

Krashen, S. (1982). *Principles and practice in second language acquisition.* Oxford: Pergamon.

Krashen, S. (1985). *The input hypothesis: Issues and implications.* New York: Longman.

Krashen, S., & Terrell, T. D. (1983). *The natural approach: Language acquisition in the classroom.* Oxford: Oxford University Press.

Lafford, B. A. (2007). Second language acquisition reconceptualized? The impact of Firth and Wagner (1997). *Modern Language Journal* (Focus Issue), *91,* 735–756.

Lantolf, J. P. (Ed.). (2000). *Sociocultural theory and second language learning.* Oxford: Oxford University Press.

Lantolf, J. P. (2006). Sociocultural theory and L2. *Studies in Second Language Acquisition, 28,* 67–109.

Lantolf, J. P., & Appel, G. (1994). Theoretical framework: An introduction to Vygotskian approaches to second language research. In J. P. Lantolf & G. Appel (Eds.), *Vygotskian approaches to second language research* (pp. 1–32). Westport, CT: Ablex Publishing.

Lantolf, J. P., & Frawley, W. (1983). *Second language performance and Vygotskyian psycho-linguistics: Implications for L2 instruction.* Paper presented at the Eleventh Linguistic Association of Canada and the United States (LACUS) Forum, Laval University, Québec.

Lantolf, J. P., & Thorne, S. L. (Eds.). (2006). *Sociocultural theory and the genesis of second language development.* Oxford: Oxford University Press.

Larsen-Freeman, D. (1978). An ESL index of development. *TESOL Quarterly, 12,* 439–448.

Larsen-Freeman, D. (2002). Language acquisition and language use from a chaos/complexity theory perspective. In C. Kramsch (Ed.), *Language acquisition and language socialization: Ecological perspectives* (pp. 33–46). London: Continuum.

Larsen-Freeman, D. (2007). Reflecting on the cognitive-social debate in second language acquisition. *Modern Language Journal,* (Focus Issue), *91,* 773–787.

Larsen-Freeman, D., & Cameron, L. (2008). Research methodology on language development from a complex systems perspective. *Modern Language Journal, 92*(2), 200–213.

Larsen-Freeman, D., & Long, M. H. (1991). *An introduction to second language acquisition research.* London: Longman.

Lau v. Nichols, 414 U.S. 563 (1974).

Lave, J., & Wenger, E. (1991). *Situated learning: Legitimate peripheral participation.* New York: Cambridge University Press.

Lazarin, M. (2006). Improving assessment and accountability for English language learners in the No Child Left Behind Act (NCLR Issue Brief No. 16). Washington DC: National Council of La Raza.

Leeman, J. (2003). Feedback in L2 learning: Responding to errors during practice. In R. M. DeKeyser (Ed.), *Practice in a second language* (pp 111–137). Cambridge, England: Cambridge University Press.

Lemann, N. (1997, November). The reading wars. *Atlantic Monthly.* Retrieved October 30, 2009, from http://www.theatlantic.com/past/docs/issues/97nov/read.htm

Lesaux, N., Koda, K., Siegel, L., & Shanahan, T. (2006). Development of literacy. In D. August & T. Shanahan (Eds.), *Developing literacy in second-language learners: Report of the National Literacy Panel on language-minority children and youth* (pp. 75–122). Mahwah, NJ: Erlbaum.

Lewis, D. K. (1969). *Convention: A philosophical study.* Cambridge, MA: Harvard University Press.

Lightbown, P. (1984). The relationship between theory and method in second language acquisition research. In A. Davies, C. Criper, & A. Howatt (Eds.), *Interlanguage* (pp. 241–252). Edinburgh: Edinburgh University Press.

Lightbown, P. M. (1985). Great expectations: Second-language acquisition research and classroom teaching. *Applied Linguistics, 6*(2), 173–189.

Lightbown, P. M. (2000). Anniversary article: Classroom SLA research and second language teaching. *Applied Linguistics, 21*(4), 431–462.

Linquanti, R., & George, C. (2007). Establishing and utilizing an NCLB Title III accountability system: California's approach and findings to date. In J. Abedi (Ed.), *English language proficiency assessment in the nation.* Davis: University of California.

Long, M. H. (1981). Input, interaction, and second-language acquisition. In H. Winitz (Ed.), Annals of the New York Academy of Sciences, Vol. 379. *Native language and foreign language acquisition* (pp. 259–278). New York: New York Academy of Sciences.

Long, M. H. (1983). Native speaker/non-native speaker conversation and the negotiation of comprehensible input. *Applied Linguistics, 4*(2), 126–141.

Long, M. H. (1996). The role of the linguistic environment in second language acquisition. In W. C. Ritchie & T. K. Bahtia (Eds.), *Handbook of second language acquisition,* (pp. 413–468). San Diego, CA: Academia Press.

McGraw-Hill Companies. (2000). *This is the company . . . : Annual report 2000.* New York: Author.

McLaughlin, B. (1978). *Second-language acquisition in childhood.* Hillsdale, NJ: Erlbaum.

McLaughlin, B. (1987). *Theories of second language acquisition.* London: Edward Arnold.

Mehan, H. (1979). *Learning lessons.* Cambridge, MA: Harvard University Press.

Meisel, J., Clahsen, H., & Pienemann, M. (1981). On determining developmental stages in natural second language acquisition. *Studies in Second Language Acquisition, 3*(1), 109–135.

Mitchell, C. B., & Vidal, K. E. (2001). Weighing in the ways of the flow: 20th-century language instruction. *Modern Language Journal, 85*(1), 26–38.

Mitchell, R., & Lee, C. N. (2008). Learning a second language in the family. In J. Philp, R. Oliver, & A. Mackey (Eds.), *Second language acquisition and the younger learner: Child's play?* (pp. 255–277). Amsterdam: John Benjamins.

Mori, J. (2007). Border crossings? Exploring the intersection of second language acquisition, conversation analysis, and foreign language pedagogy. *Modern Language Journal* (Focus Issue), *91,* 849–862.

Moustafa, M., & Land, R. E. (2002). The reading achievement of economically-disadvantaged children in urban schools using "Open Court" vs. comparably disadvantaged children in urban schools using non-scripted reading programs. *Yearbook of the Urban Learning, Teaching, and Research Special Interest Group of the American Educational Research Association,* pp. 44–53.

Munguia, E., & Telles, E. D. (1996). Phenotype and schooling among Mexican-Americans. *Sociology of Education, 69,* 276–289.

Myles, F. (2003). The early development of L2 narratives: A longitudinal study. *Marges Linguistiques, 5,* 40–55.

Nation, I. S. P. (2001). *Learning vocabulary in another language.* Cambridge: Cambridge University Press.

National Reading Panel. (2000). *Teaching children to read: An evidence-based assessment of the scientific research literature on reading and its implications for reading instruction.* Washington, DC: National Institute of Child Health and Human Development.

National Research Council, Mathematics Learning Study Committee. (2001). *Adding it up: Helping children learn mathematics.* J. Kilpatrick, J. Swafford, & B. Findell (Eds.). Washington, DC: National Academy Press.

National Standards in Foreign Language Education Project. (1996). *Standards for foreign language learning; Preparing for the 21st century.* Yonkers, NY: Author.

Nemser, W. (1971). Approximate systems of foreign language learners. *International Review of Applied Linguistics in Language Teaching, 9*(2), 115–124.

Ninio, A., & Snow, C. (1996). *Pragmatic development: Essays in developmental science.* Boulder, CO: Westview Press.

Ninio, A., Snow, C., Pan, B. A., & Rollins, P. R. (1994). Classifying communicative acts in children's interactions. *Journal of Communicative Disorders, 27*, 157–187.

No Child Left Behind Act of 2001, 20 U.S.C. § 6319 (2008).

Norris, J. M., & Ortega, L. (2000). Effectiveness of L2 instruction: A research synthesis and quantitative meta-analysis. *Language Learning, 50*(3), 417–528.

North, B. (1998). Scaling descriptors for language proficiency scales. *Language Testing, 15*(2), 217–264.

Norton, B. (1995). Social identity, investment, and language learning. *TESOL Quarterly, 29*(1), 9–31.

Norton, B. (1997). Language, identity, and the ownership of English. *TESOL Quarterly, 30*(2), 409–429.

Norton, B. (2000). *Identity and language learning: Gender, ethnicity, and educational change.* New York: Longman.

Ochs, E. (1988). *Culture and language development: Language acquisition and language socialization in a Samoan village.* Cambridge: Cambridge University Press.

Ochs, E. (1991). Socialization through language and interaction: A theoretical introduction. *Issues in Applied Linguistics, 2*(2), 143–147.

Ochs, E. (2002). Becoming a speaker of culture. In C. Kramsch (Ed.), *Language acquisition and language socialization: Ecological perspectives* (pp. 99–120). New York: Continuum.

Ogle, D. M. (1986). K-W-L: A teaching model that develops active reading of expository text. *The Reading Teacher, 39*, 564–570.

Oliver, R. (1998). Negotiation of meaning in child interactions. *Modern Language Journal, 82*, 372–386.

Oliver, R. (2000, February). Age differences in negotiation and feedback in classroom and pairwork. *Language Learning, 50*, 119–151.

Olmedo, I. (1997). Challenging old assumptions: Preparing for inner-city schools. *Teaching and Teacher Education, 13*(3), 245–258.

O'Malley, J. M., Chamot, A. U., & Kupper, L. (1987). Learning strategies in second language position. *Applied Linguistics, 10(4),* 418–435.

Ortega, L., & Iberri-Shea, G. (2005). Longitudinal research in second language acquisition: Recent trends and future directions. *Annual Review of Applied Linguistics, 25*, 26–45.

Paradis, J. (2007). Second language acquisition in childhood. In E. Hoff & M. Shatz (Eds.), *Blackwell handbook of language development* (pp. 387–405). Malden, MA: Blackwell.

Parker, C., Louie, J., & O'Dwyer, L. (2009). *New measures of English language proficiency and their relationship to performance on large-scale content assessments* (Issues and Answers Report, REL 2009-No. 066). Washington, DC: U.S. Department of Education, Institute of Educational Sciences, National Center for Education Evaluation and Regional Assistance, Regional Educational Laboratory Northeast and Islands.

Parrish, T., Perez, M., Merickel, A., & Linquanti, R. (2006). *Effects of the implementation of Proposition 227 on the education of English Learners, K–12: Findings from a five-year evaluation.* Palo Alto, CA: AIR and WestEd.

Peck, S., & Serrano, A. (2002, April). *Open Court and English language learners:Questions and strategies.* Paper presented at the annual meeting of the American Association for Applied Linguistics, Salt Lake City, UT.

Pennycook, A. (1990). Towards a critical applied linguistics for the 1990s. *Issues in Applied Linguistics, 1*(1), 8–28.

Pennycook, A. (1999). *English and the discourses of colonialism.* New York: Routledge.

Pennycook, A. (2001). *Critical applied linguistics: A critical introduction.* Hillsdale, NJ: Erlbaum.

Peterson, C., & McCabe, A. (1983). *Developmental psycholinguistics: Three ways of looking at a child's narrative.* New York: Plenum Press.

Peterson, C., & McCabe, A. (1991). Linking children's connective use and narrative macrostructure. In A. McCabe & C. Peterson (Eds.), *Developing narrative structure* (pp. 29–53). Hillsdale, NJ: Erlbaum.

Peterson, C., & McCabe, A. (1997). Extending Labov and Waletzky. *Journal of Narrative and Life History, 7*(1–4), 251–258.

Philp, J., & Duchesne, S. (2008). When the gate opens: The interaction between social and linguistic goals in child language development. In J. Philp, R. Oliver, & A. Mackey (Eds.), *Second language acquisition and the younger learner: Child's play?* (pp. 83–103). Amsterdam: John Benjamins.

Philp, J., Oliver, R., & Mackey, A. (Eds.). (2008). *Second language acquisition and the younger learner: Child's play?* Amsterdam: John Benjamins.

Pica, T. (1994). Research on negotiation: What does it reveal about second-language learning conditions, processes and outcomes? *Language Learning, 44,* 492–527.

Pickering, M. J., & Garrod, S. (2004). Toward a mechanistic psychology of dialogue. *Behavioral and Brain Sciences, 27,* 169–226.

Plyler v. Doe. 457 U.S. 202 (1982).

Prabhu, N. S. (1987). *Second language pedagogy.* New York: Oxford University Press.

Reeves, T. (2006). Design research from a technology perspective. In J. Van den Akker, K. Gravemeijer, S. McKenney, & N. Nieveen (Eds.), *Educational design research* (pp. 52–66). London: Routledge.

Reinking, D., & Bradley, B. A. (2008). *Formative and design experiments: Approaches to language and literacy research.* New York: Teachers College Press.

Ritchie, W. C., & Bhatia, T. K. (1996). *Handbook of second language acquisition.* San Diego, CA: Academic Press.

Rivera, C., Stansfield, C. W., Scialdone, L., & Sharkey, M. (2000). *An analysis of state policies for the inclusion and accommodation of English language learners in state assessment programs during 1998–1999.* Arlington, VA: George Washington University, Center for Equity and Excellence in Education.

Rolethford, J. J., Stern, M. P., Caskill, S. P., & Hazuda, H. P. (1983). Social class, admixture, and skin color variation in Mexican Americans and Anglo-Americans living in San Antonio Texas. *American Journal of Physical Anthropology, 61,* 97–102.

Rost, M. (1990). *Listening in language learning.* London: Routledge.

Rumberger, R. W., & Scarcella, R. (2000). *Academic English linguistic minority research institute newsletter* (Vol. 1). University of California, Santa Barbara: Linguistic Minority Research Institute.

Sacks, H. (1995). *Lectures in conversation.* Malden, MA: Blackwell.

Saunders, W. M., Foorman, B. R., & Carson, C. D. (2006). Is a separate block of time for oral English language development in programs for English learners needed? *The Elementary School Journal, 107(2),* 181–198.

Scarcella, R. (2003). *Academic English: A conceptual framework* (Technical Report No. 2003-1). Santa Barbara, CA: Linguistic Minority Research Institute.

Schegloff, E. (2007). *Sequence organization in interaction: A primer in conversation analysis* (Vol. 1). Cambridge: Cambridge University Press.

Schieffelin, B. B., & Ochs, E. (1986). *Language socialization across cultures.* New York: Cambridge University Press.

Schniedewind, N. (2005). "There ain't no white people here!": The transforming impact of teachers racial consciousness on students and schools. *Equity and Excellence in Education, 38,* 280–289.

Schwartz, B. (2003). Child L2-acquisition: Paving the way. In B. Beachley, A. Brown, & F. Conlin (Eds.), *Proceedings of the 27th annual Boston University Conference on Language Development* (pp. 26–50). Somerville, MA: Cascadilla Press.

Scollon, R. (2002). Cross-cultural learning and other catastrophes. In C. Kramsch (Ed.), *Language acquisition and language socialization: Ecological perspectives* (pp. 121–139). London: Continuum.

Selinker, L. (1972). Interlanguage. *International Review of Applied Linguistics in Language Teaching, 10(3),* 209–231.

Sharwood Smith, M. (1994). *Second language learning: Theoretical foundations.* London: Longman.

Short, D. J., & Fitzsimmons, S. (2007). *Double the work: Challenges and solutions to acquiring language and academic literacy for adolescent English language learners.* New York: Alliance for Excellent Education.

Sinclair, J. M., & Coulthard, R. M. (1975). *Towards an analysis of discourse.* Oxford: Oxford University Press.

Solano-Flores, G., & Trumbull, E. (2003). Examining language in context: The need for new research and practice paradigms in the testing of English-language learners. *Educational Researcher, 32,* 3–13.

Solomon, J., & Rhodes, N. (1995). *Conceptualizing academic language* (Research Report No. 15). Berkeley, CA: National Center for Research on Education, Diversity, and Excellence.

Solomon, R. P., Portelli, J. P., Daniel, B.-J., & Campbell, A. (2005). The discourse of denial: How white teacher candidates construct race, racism and "white privilege." *Race, Ethnicity, and Education, 8(2),* 147–169.

Solorzano, R. (2008). High-stakes testing: Issues, implications, and remedies for English language learners. *Review of Educational Research, 78(2),* 260–329.

Snow, C. (1987). Beyond conversation: Second language learners acquisition of description and explanation. In J. P. Lantolf & A. Labarca (Eds.), *Research and second language learning: Focus on the classroom* (pp. 3–16). Norwood, NJ: Ablex.

Snow, C., & Blum-Kulka, S. (2002). From home to school: School-age children talking to adults. In S. Blum-Kulka & C. Snow (Eds.), *Talking to adults: The contributions of multiparty discourse to language acquisition* (pp. 327–341). Mahwah, NJ: Erlbaum.

Snow, C., & Ferguson, C. A. (Eds.). (1977). *Talking to children: Language input & acquisition.* Cambridge: Cambridge University Press.

Stenhouse, L. (1975). *An introduction to curriculum research and development.* Portsmouth, NH: Heinemann.

Stritikus, T. T. (2006). Making meaning matter: A look at instructional practice in additive and subtractive contexts. *Bilingual Research Journal, 30*(1), 219–227.

Swain, M. (1985). Communicative competence: Some roles of comprehensible input and comprehensible output in its development. In S. Gass & C. Madden (Eds.), *Input in second language acquisition.* Rowley, MA: Newbury House.

Swain, M. (1993). The output hypothesis: Just speaking and writing aren't enough. *Canadian Modern Language Review, 50*(1), 158–164.

Swain, M. (1995). Three functions of output in second language learning. In G. Cook & B. Seidlhofer (Eds.), *Principle and practice in applied linguistics: Studies in honour of H. G. Widdowson* (pp. 125–144). Oxford: Oxford University Press.

Swain, M. (2000). The output hypothesis and beyond: Mediating acquisition through collaborative dialogue. In J. P. Lantolf (Ed.), *Sociocultural theory and second language learning* (pp. 97–114). Oxford: Oxford University Press.

Swain, M. (2005). The output hypothesis: Theory and research. In E. Hinkel (Ed.), *Handbook of research in second language teaching and learning* (pp. 471–483). Mahwah, NJ: Erlbaum.

Tannen, D. (1989). *Talking voices: Repetition, dialogue, and imagery in conversational discourse.* Cambridge: Cambridge University Press.

Taylor, T. J., & Cameron, D. (1987). *Analysing conversation.* Oxford: Pergamon Press.

Telles, E. D., & Munguia, E. (1990). Phenotypic discrimination and income differences among Mexican-Americans. *Social Science Quarterly, 71,* 682–696.

Telles, E. D., & Munguia, E. (1992). The continuing significance of phenotype among Mexican-Americans. *Social Science Quarterly,* 120–122.

TESOL. (2006). ESL standards for pre-K–12 students, online edition. Retrieved December 9, 2009, from http://www.tesol.org/s_tesol/seccss.asp?CID=113&DID=1583

Tharp, R. G., & Gallimore, R. (1988). *Rousing minds to life.* Cambridge: Cambridge University Press.

Thompson, K. (2009). *The role of research-based ideas about language acquisition in California's curriculum materials for English language development.* Unpublished qualifying paper, Stanford University, California.

Tomasello, M. (2003). *Constructing a language: A usage-based theory of language acquisition.* Cambridge, MA: Harvard University Press.

Tomlinson, B. (2007a). Conclusions. In B. Tomlinson (Ed.), *Language acquisition and development: Studies of learners of first and other languages* (pp. 282–283). London: Continuum.

Tomlinson, B. (2007b). Introduction: Some similarities and differences between L1 and L2 acquisition and development. In B. Tomlinson (Ed.), *Language acquisition and development: Studies of learners of first and other languages* (pp. 1–12). London: Continuum.

Tomlinson, B. (Ed.). (2008). *English language learning materials: A critical review.* London: Continuum.

Tong, F., Lara-Alecio, R., Irby, B., Mathes, P., & Kwok, O. (2008). Accelerating early academic oral English development in transitional bilingual and structured English immersion programs. *American Educational Research Journal, 45*(4), 1011–1044.

Toohey, K. (1999). The author responds to comments on Kellen Toohey's "Breaking them up, taking them away": ESL students in Grade 1'. *TESOL Quarterly, 33*(1), 132–136.

Toohey, K. (2000). *Learning English at school: Identity, social relations, and classroom practice.* Bristol, UK: Multilingual Matters.

Unsworth, S. (2005). *Child L2, Adult L2, Child L1: Differences and similarities: A study on the acquisition of direct object scrambling in Dutch.* Unpublished dissertation, Utrecht University, Utrecht, The Netherlands.

U.S. Department of Education. (2002). Reading First. In *No Child Left Behind* (Part B, Subpart 1). Retrieved April 24, 2010, from http://www.ed.gov/policy/elsec/leg/esea02/pg4.html

Valdés, G. (1996). *Con respeto: Bridging the distances between culturally diverse families and schools: An ethnographic portrait.* New York: Teachers College Press.

Valdés, G. (2001). *Learning and not learning English: Latino students in American schools.* New York: Teachers College Press.

Valdés, G. (2003). *Expanding definitions of giftedness: The case of young interpreters from immigrant communities.* Mahwah, NJ: Erlbaum.

Valdés, G. (2004). Between support and marginalisation: The development of academic language in linguistic minority children. *International Journal of Bilingualism and Bilingual Education, 7*(2–3), 102–132.

Valdés, G., MacSwan, J., & Alvarez, L. (2009, October). *Deficits and differences: Perspectives on language and education.* Paper presented at the National Research Council workshop on the Role of Language in School Learning: Implications for Closing the Achievement Gap, Menlo Park, CA. Available at http://www.nationalacademies.org/cfe/Role_of_Language_Workshop_Agenda_October_15-16_2009.html

Valdez-Pierce, L., & O'Malley, J. M. (1992). *Performance and portfolio assessment for language minority students.* Washington, DC: National Clearinghouse for Bilingual Education.

Van den Akker, J., Gravemeijer, K., McKenney, S., & Nieveen, N. (2006). Introducing educational design research. In J. Van den Akker, K. Gravemeijer, S. McKenny, & N. Nieveen (Eds.), *Educational design research* (pp. 3–7). London: Routledge.

Van den Branden, K. (2008). Negotiation of meaning in the classroom: Does it enhance reading comprehension? In J. Philp, R. Oliver, & A. Mackey (Eds.), *Second language acquisition and the younger learner: Child's play?* (pp. 149–169). Amsterdam: John Benjamins.

Van Lier, L. (2000). From input to affordance. In J. P. Lantolf (Ed.), *Sociocultural theory and second language learning* (pp. 245– 259). Oxford: Oxford University Press.

Van Lier, L. (2002). An ecological-semiotic perspective on language and linguisitics. In C. Kramsch (Ed.), *Language acquisition and language socialization: Ecological perspectives* (pp. 140–164). London: Continuum.

Van Lier, L. (2004). *The ecology and semiotics of language learning: A sociocultural perspective.* Dordrecht, The Netherlands: Kluwer Academic.

Van Patten, B. (1996). *Input processing and grammar instruction: Theory and research.* Norwood, NJ: Ablex.

Van Patten, B. (2003). *From input to output: A teacher's guide to second language acquisition.* Boston: McGraw-Hill.

Walker, D. (2006). Toward productive design studies. In J. Van den Akker, K. Grave-meijer, S. McKenney, & N. Nieveen (Eds.), *Educational design research* (pp. 8–13). London: Routledge.

Watson-Gegeo, K. A. (2004). Mind, language, and epistemology: Toward a language socialization paradigm for SLA. *Modern Language Journal, 88*(3), 331–350.

Wells, C. G. (Ed.). (1981). *Learning through interaction: The study of language development.* Cambridge: Cambridge University Press.

Wells, C. G. (1985). *Language development in the pre-school years.* Cambridge: Cambridge University Press.

Wendel, J. (1997). *Planning and second language production.* Unpublished doctoral dissertation. Temple University–Japan, Tokyo.

White, L. (1989). *Universal grammar and second language acquisition.* Amsterdam: John Benjamins.

White, J. (2008). Speeding up acquisition of his and her: Explicit L1/L2 contrasts help. In J. Philp, R. Oliver, & A. Mackey (Eds.), *Second language acquisition and the younger learner: Child's play?* (pp. 193–228). Amsterdam: John Benjamins.

Wong Fillmore, L. (1976). *The second time around: Cognitive and social strategies in second language acquisition.* Unpublished doctoral dissertation, Stanford University, Palo Alto, California.

Wong Fillmore, L. (1982). Language minority students and school participation: What kind of English is needed? *Journal of Education, 164*(2), 143–156.

Wong Fillmore, L. (1985a, July). *Second language learning in children: A proposed model.* Paper presented at the Issues in English Language Development for Minority Language Education conference, Arlington, VA.

Wong Fillmore, L. (1985b). When does teacher talk work as input. In S. Gass & C. Madden (Eds.), *Input in second language acquisition* (pp. 17–50). Rowley, MA: Newbury.

Wong Fillmore, L. (1991). When learning a second language means losing the first. *Early Childhood Research Quarterly, 63*(3), 323–347.

Wong Fillmore, L. (1992) Learning a language from learners. In C. Kramsch & S. McConnel-Ginnet (Eds.), *Text and context: Cross-disciplinary perspectives on language study* (pp. 46–66). Lexington, MA: Heath.

Zuengler, J., & Miller, E. R. (2006). Cognitive and sociocultural perspectives: Two parallel SLA worlds. *TESOL Quarterly, 40*(1), 35–58.

Index

235

About the Authors

Guadalupe Valdés is the Bonnie Katz Tenenbaum Professor of Education at Stanford University. Her work has focused on the English–Spanish bilingualism of Latinos in the United States and on discovering and describing how two languages are developed, used, and maintained by individuals who become bilingual in immigrant communities. Valdés's investigations of Latino students in elementary, middle school, high school, and college has led to six books and more than 70 articles. Her book *Con Respeto: Bridging the Distance Between Culturally Diverse Families and Schools* examines the lives of K–3 English language learners and their families. The book *Learning and Not Learning English* follows four middle-school students over a 2-year period. *Expanding Definitions of Giftedness: Young Interpreters of Immigrant Background* focuses on high school students who serve as young interpreters for their parents, and her most recent book, *Developing Minority Language Resources: The Case of Spanish in California,* examines Spanish language maintenance and instruction in both secondary and postsecondary institutions. Her book *Bilingualism and Testing: A Special Case of Bias* is seen as a timely classic that explores the growing challenge of increased use of standardized tests. Valdés is a member of the American Academy of Education and a Fellow of the American Educational Research Association (AERA).

Sarah Capitelli is an assistant professor of education at the University of San Francisco in their Teacher Education Department. She received her Ph.D. from Stanford in educational linguistics. Dr. Capitelli taught elementary school for 7 years–2 in Venezuela and 5 in Oakland, California, in a Spanish bilingual classroom. Her research focuses on better understanding and improving conditions for learning and teaching in linguistically segregated schools.

Laura Alvarez is a doctoral candidate in educational linguistics at Stanford University. Alvarez taught fourth and fifth grades in a Spanish bilingual program in Oakland, California, and earned an M.A. in education with an emphasis on teaching from Mills College. Her research focuses on understanding and supporting bilingual children's academic language and literacy development in their first and second languages.